Rome at War with Rome

Rome at War with Rome
Civil War & Rebellion 67-69 A.D.

Bernard W. Henderson

With a Short Extract from Tacitus
by William Bodham Donne

Rome at War with Rome
Civil War & Rebellion 67-69 A.D.
by Bernard W. Henderson
With a Short Extract from Tacitus by William Bodham Donne

FIRST EDITION

First published under the titles
Civil War and Rebellion in the Roman Empire
Tacitus (Extract)

Leonaur is an imprint of Oakpast Ltd

Copyright in this form © 2014 Oakpast Ltd

ISBN: 978-1-78282-311-7 (hardcover)
ISBN: 978-1-78282-312-4 (softcover)

http://www.leonaur.com

Publisher's Notes

The views expressed in this book are not necessarily those of the publisher.

Contents

Preface	9
The Campaign of Otho and the Vitellians	11
The Flavian Invasion of Italy	100
The Rebellion on the Rhine	165
Postscript	231
Galba—Otho (Extract from *Tacitus*)	233
Vitellius (Extract from *Tacitus*)	246

To
My "Greats" Pupils at Exeter College
And in Particular
To Those
My Companions on the Road in Italy

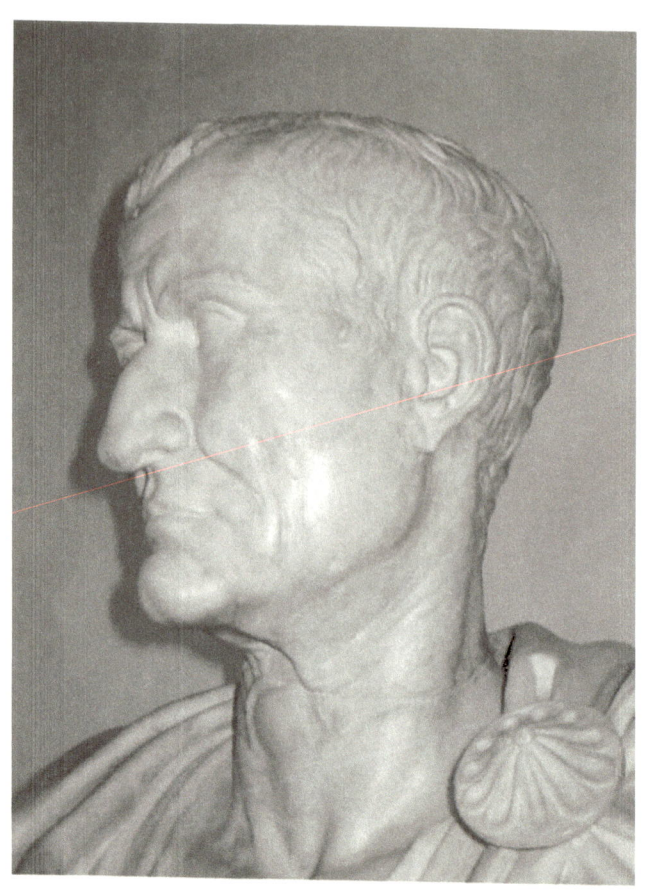

GALBA

Preface

From the days of the elder Pliny to the present there have been many who have written concerning the history of the Civil Wars of A.D. 69 and 70. Of the writers whose works are extant, Tacitus stands easily first. Without his *Histories* we should indeed have but an inferior story of the struggle between the Emperors Otho and Vitellius, and a still poorer story of that between Vitellius and Vespasian. And yet always from the very first the strategic and military aspect of the three campaigns narrated by Tacitus has been neglected. To write the history of those campaigns by the aid of, and as illustrative of, modern strategical principles is the main purpose of this book.

Two recent writers, it is true, have to some extent recognised the interest and value of such a treatment of Tacitus' story. Gerstenecker in 1882 contributed some suggestions on the military history of the war between Otho and Vitellius. These, however, seem to me of peculiarly little value in spite of their considerable length, lacking alike in military knowledge and in insight. Mommsen's short paper, on the other hand, published in 1871, is full of valuable suggestions. It will always be almost impertinent for any student of Ancient History to commend any paper by the German master. This article, however, is very brief, deals scarcely at all with the strategy of the campaigns before the actual contact of the opposing armies upon the field of battle, and is still, I think, in one or two respects unduly captive to Tacitus, whom Mommsen himself has called, once and for all time, "the most unmilitary of historians."

For in very truth the inadequate and short-sighted treatment of the military problems and history of these two years has to be referred back to the Roman historian. The more often I read Tacitus, the more convinced I become that in matters military his information represents little but the common gossip of the camp, the talk of the private soldier or subordinate officer, reproduced at second-hand with all the literary power of a great writer who possessed the most vivid visualising power (if I may so call it). The troops on the bloodstained plain outside the red walls of Cremona battled, as it were, before Tacitus' very eyes, as he sat writing in his study. But the historian was but a pleader at the Roman bar who had taken to history. How should such a rhetorician care to inquire very deeply into the strategical causes which led to that battling in that precise position? He seems to have felt no interest in any such inquiry, and distance of time did not increase for him clearness of vision.

Generals are criticised hastily; impossible plans are ascribed to them; strategies are ignored or misrepresented; events strategically connected are treated as isolated movements; success or apparent failure is the one criterion of judgment. With all this, the troops' endurance and pluck are rightly recognised; brilliance and "dash" are duly appraised. But the result of such an attitude to events is but an unsatisfactory military history, as we in this country have had recent cause to know. Yet it is surely the military history of these campaigns which is of great, perhaps chief, interest. "Nothing," remarks a modern writer of military history, "is so misleading as the camp gossip which is reproduced in many memoirs."[1] Tacitus' "camp gossip" has been too faithfully repeated as the whole sound sense of the matter by historians who have had to rely almost entirely upon his narrative for their facts.

During these last twelve years it has been my good fortune to roam on foot many times in different parts of Italy. If in this book I now attempt, after two recent visits of my own to the actual theatre of war in the Lombard plain, to trace again the history of these campaigns, it is with the hope chiefly of calling attention to a somewhat neglected part of them, namely, the strategical and geographical questions which they involve. For this more prosaic purpose such fineries of language as, for example, adorn Merivale's record of these wars cannot be allowed to me. For me the Vitellian columns of invasion cannot be seen "beetling on the summits of the Alps," nor can Otho be found "bounding from his voluptuous couch at the first sound of the trumpet." An insistence on a different method of treatment of these wars must be, if it so happen, my justification for yet another handling of an old theme.

Bernard W. Henderson.

Oxford, March 1908.

---

1. Maj.-Gen. Sir J. F. Maurice, *The Diary of Sir John Moore*, ii.

CHAPTER 1

The Campaign of Otho and the Vitellians

After a war one ought to write not only the history of what has happened, but also the history of what was intended; the narrative would then be instructive.—Von der Goltz.

§1. THE ORIGINS OF THE CIVIL WAR

Soon after daybreak on the 9th of June *A.D.* 68 the Roman Emperor Nero died by his own hand. He who had been for thirteen years the master of the Roman world ended his life in squalor and in misery, with only three freed slaves and a treacherous centurion present to watch his death. He who was the last descendant of Julius Caesar, the last prince of the Julian line, enjoyed for resting-place on the last evening of his life the gloomy underground cellar of a villa in the suburbs of his capital; for the furniture of his death-chamber a scanty mattress and a ragged quilt; for the final banquet a little lukewarm water and old crusts of bread. Thanks to others' falseness and his own faint-heartedness he had to die. His cruelty and lust had cost him many friends; his passion for art and music had cost him more.

But the chief cause of his ruin was the indifference shown by him towards his troops, towards the art of war, towards the practice of the camps. The nobles, who had found a ruthless persecutor in him; the philosophers, who wrote him down a frenzied tyrant; the Christians, who supposed him to be the Antichrist, lord of a world abandoned by God,—these all rejoiced at his miserable end and defamed his memory. But the lower classes in Rome mourned for him. Unknown hands yearly decked his tomb in the gardens of the Pincian Hill with spring and summer flowers. The countless inhabitants of Italy and the provinces of the Roman Empire had no reason to welcome his overthrow. Not a few of these in the past had enjoyed his care for them, and might in gratitude sorrow for his fall. Neither had the Imperialist any reason to denounce this the last Julian Emperor. Britain had been well-nigh lost, but the triumphant courage of Nero's *legionaries* had saved it to the Empire.

The war upon the eastern frontier with Rome's old and bitter Parthian enemy had at last been ended, not without glory to the Roman arms, and now, after a century of hostility, there was a fair promise that the agreement reached would be an enduring peace with honour. But all such blame and all such praise availed Nero little when his soldiers felt no love for him, and had no reason to admire him or fear him as their general. When the standard of rebellion was raised in distant Spain, his Guards at Rome, piqued and deceived, deserted their prince. Nero, abandoned, treacherously betrayed, slew himself. The whole Empire, if it had good cause for joy at the death of the man, had speedily reason to regret the downfall of the emperor.

For now, to use the words of the Roman historian Tacitus, the secret of the Empire was revealed. "A prince could be appointed elsewhere than in the city of Rome." Hitherto, under Tiberius, Caligula, Claudius, and Nero, the Imperial power had in practice been but the heirloom of the Julian family. Now the last of the family was dead. Yet some emperor there must be. The vast body of the Empire could not "stande without governour."[1]

But there was no heir to the throne. The prince must now in actual fact be "elected," and thus the theory of election which, as a theory, had persisted from the beginning must be realised in practice. Men flattered themselves that such an election was a sign of liberty restored. It was in reality no gain to liberty that the might of armed force now took the place of such a right as inheritance might give. It was no gain to liberty that "two common soldiers of the line took upon themselves the task of transferring the Empire over the Roman people from one prince to another, and transferred it."[2]

At this time, in fact, the army of the Roman world was not at unity with itself. Upon the death of Nero different armies in different quarters of the Empire set up their own popular leaders and generals as claimants to the Imperial power. Why should the legions of Germany,

---

1. Sir H. Savile's translation of Tacitus, *Histories, i.*(1591).
2. Tacitus, *Histories*, i. All references henceforward to Tacitus in the notes which give a number only are references to the *Histories*.

or the proud *praetorians* of Rome, submit to an *imperator* appointed by the troops in Spain? Why should the veteran and victorious army of the East or the hardy garrison of the Danube frontier tamely accept an Emperor at the hands of the rebel soldiery of the Rhine? The miserable death of Nero was ominous of the greater misery to come, of the terrors of a year of savage civil strife. The Empire was the prize for which the armies battled; Italy was the battle-ground. Twice within eight months armies of invasion swept down over the Alps upon the unhappy land. "Ah, would that Italy had never been dowered at Fortunes hands with the luckless gift of beauty!" cried the Florentine poet of the seventeenth century:—

*Ch' or giù dall' Alpi non vedrei torrenti
Scender d'armati, e del tuo sangue tinta
Bever l'onda del Po gallici armenti.*

But now it was the very Empire of the Roman world which called the rivals down to Italy.

Nero had been indifferent to war and its pursuits. Such interests were unworthy of an artist, if not of an emperor. This indifference on his part revenged itself upon the fairest of all beautiful lands. Four Roman emperors perished within twenty months. Two of these, Nero and Otho, fell by their own hand. Two, Galba and Vitellius, were murdered in open daylight by order of their conquerors. The death of each of these selfish and ambitious princes might have seemed a gain to the Roman world, had not each been followed by such a successor. Then at the last Vespasian came, and the land had peace. It was always Italy which paid the chief part of the price of this, the contending of the emperors. Those who have ever seen her dancing sunlight and luxuriant plains, her rushing rivers and her sombre mountains, know that this land alone might seem worth all the striving.

Servius Sulpicius Galba[3] had already been in arms against his emperor for some two months when the Roman Senate elected him "*princeps*" on the day of Nero's death. He was a man of high birth, descended on his mother's side from Lucius Mummius, the destroyer of Corinth in 146 B.C. After a long and honourable civil and military career in other parts of the Empire, Galba had been sent by Nero to govern the province of Hispania Tarraconensis (North East Spain) eight years before, and there as governor he had stayed ever since. There, too, increasing years and familiarity with his duties had pres-

---

3. His *praenomen* Lucius he changed to that of Servius in *A.D.* 68.

ently changed him from a vigorous and efficient governor to one careless and indolent. No one, he said, had to render an account of his idle hours. But an alarming rebellion in the neighbouring land of Gaul broke out in the spring of *A.D.* 68, and compelled him to take action either with or against the rebels. Impelled by the offers of the rebel leader Vindex and by his own personal ambition, he chose the former course and renounced his allegiance to Nero. The Gallic rebellion indeed was promptly crushed by the Roman Army in the district of Upper Germany under its famous general Verginius Rufus.

But the infection of disloyalty was in the air, and even Verginius' victorious troops were eager to march to Rome and set up their general there as emperor. But Verginius was well content with his achievement. He had saved the integrity of the Roman Empire and now would preserve his own. It was still possible to find in the Roman Empire a general of repute who was untainted by any ambition save by that of serving his country. He declined the offered gift of Empire, and his troops had sullenly to acquiesce. Galba therefore, despite his great miscalculation, reaped the fruits of Verginius' refusal, and had his short-lived joy of them. He was now an old man of seventy-three years of age, but the crisis called out his better military qualities.

On receiving from Rome the tidings of Nero's death and of his own election as *princeps* he marched for Rome at the head of a newly-raised legion, the Seventh Galbiana,[4] and found his progress unopposed. Towards the middle of October in the year *A.D.* 68 he entered the city, and though his entry had been marred by scenes of needless bloodshed and panic, no rival yet disputed with him his possession of the Imperial power. For some three months after his entry Galba remained Emperor of Rome. But then the end came. It took but these three months for him to lose the popularity which, by remaining unknown, he had gained.

His ministers and dependents justly earned dislike by their venality and greed, and this dislike was extended to the old emperor, who made no attempt to check their rapacity. His own severity, amounting in cases to cruelty, his age, his ugliness, above all his fatal parsimony, cost him the support of all classes in the city, who were quick to contrast him in all these respects with the Nero whom he had supplanted.

---

4. This legion later was known as the Seventh Gemina, but this title seems to have been given it first by Vespasian, when he disbanded the First legion (so Heraeus, note to Tac. i.). Galba evidently sent it almost at once to Pannonia, as it is found here in January *A.D.* 69.

He was, it is true, a brave disciplinarian, and scorned to secure by purchase the doubtful fidelity of his wavering Guards. The exhausted state of the Roman Treasury would indeed have amply justified the greatest thrift and the most careful financial administration on the part of any ruler save one who, like Galba, could only buy the goodwill of the soldiery by donatives, the affection of the unruly populace by extravagance. Tacitus' biting epigram has characterised Galba for all time: "*Omnium consensu capax imperii nisi imperasset.*" (Tac. i.) The disaffection of the troops in Germany and the treachery of one of his disappointed adherents in Rome showed how shifting and unstable was the foundation of honesty upon which Galba had striven to build his rule. It was not for the enjoyment of such an emperor that Nero had been overthrown.

The trouble began in "Germany." This was the name given by the Romans of this time to the districts lying on the left bank of the River Rhine from Lake Constance to the sea. Augustus had renounced the attempt to add to the Empire territory over the river, and the German savages between the Rhine and the Elbe remained independent of Roman government henceforward. Those tribes who lay immediately opposite the Roman settlements and garrisons on the left bank were to a certain degree civilised by their acquaintance with their Roman neighbours and Romanised kinsmen, and Roman traders ventured in their pursuit of wealth to penetrate districts which were to the Roman legionary forbidden land.

But the venturesome traders took their lives in their hands, as they had done among the independent Gallic tribes in the days of Julius Caesar, and the farther east they travelled among the black forests and mountains of the land which is modern Germany, the more barbaric and terrible they found the German tribes. Migrations of whole peoples were not uncommon, and each tribe lived by plundering its neighbours when the whim seized it. Restless savagery and lust for bloodshed, precarious peace and internecine war, such were the pursuits and characteristics of the hordes who roamed the lands east of the Rhine. The more restless cast greedy eyes on the fields lying west of the river; the more peaceable were driven by the irresistible pressure of wild tribesmen from the unknown forests of the interior to strive to put the barrier of the river between themselves and their assailants.

The Roman Empire was therefore compelled to "police" its side of the Rhine by a strong standing army. For this purpose the left bank was marked out into two districts, each of which was garrisoned by four legions with auxiliaries to help them, and was under the military control of a governor, the Legatus Augusti *pro praetore*. "Upper Germany" stretched from Lake Constance to a point midway between Coblenz and Bonn (now Brohl, between Andernach and Remagen); "Lower Germany" reached from this point to the sea. For civil administration "Germany" belonged to the province of Gallia Belgica down to the days of Domitian; for financial, at least half a century longer.[5]

But the governor of Belgica had no regular troops at his command, so pacified by now seemed the Gauls; and the two governors of Upper and Lower Germany, commanding, as they did, powerful armies on the frontiers, were the men on whose sagacity depended the security of the Empire, on whose fidelity that of the emperor at Rome.

Galba shortly after his accession had recalled the governor of Upper Germany, Verginius Rufus, and executed the governor of Lower Germany, Fonteius Capito. To take their places he had appointed to Upper Germany an old and infirm man, Hordeonius Flaccus, who proved utterly unable to control turbulence or mutiny among his troops. To Lower Germany he sent Aulus Vitellius.

Vitellius was then fifty-five years of age. His career up to that time had been a curious mixture of good and evil. As a boy he had been in attendance upon the morose old Emperor Tiberius in his retreat on the island of Capri, and men were therefore but too ready to speak ill of him. In Rome he had won the young Caligula's favour by his skill in chariot-driving, and the goodwill of the next emperor, Claudius, by his love of dicing. But when sent out as governor of Africa by Nero he too, like other Roman nobles of the time, left his worst qualities behind him in Rome, and displayed integrity and justice in his administration, so that at the last crisis of his life only Africa showed any zeal on his behalf. He had returned from Africa in *A.D.* 61, and lived the next seven years, it seems, in obscure retirement at Rome. Either his integrity as governor or his gluttony, which was notorious, reduced him to such straits of poverty that when Galba commanded him to proceed as governor to Lower Germany in the autumn of *A.D.* 68 he left his family behind him living in a hired garret, and pawned his mother's earrings to obtain the money necessary for his travelling expenses. By such means he was able to reach his province on the 1st of December of this year.

Both new governors found their troops sullen and disloyal to Gal-

---
5. See chapter. 3, §3.

ba. The attempt of the army of Upper Germany to proclaim Verginius emperor had recently been baffled first by his refusal, and, soon after, by his recall to Rome. But they loved Galba none the better for that. Galba had recently been lavishing favour on the Gauls, rebels to the Empire, whom they, true soldiers of the Empire, had lately crushed. Galba was but the nominee of the troops in Spain, troops whom they, the proud and warlike frontier army of Germany, could have annihilated with ease.

Neither governor was a disciplinarian; neither was attached to Galba by any ties of affection or loyalty. The troops' discontent was not long in coming to a head. The legions of Upper Germany refused the military oath of allegiance to Galba on the 1st of January A.D. 69, and in default for the moment of a rival emperor they proclaimed as rulers of the State the Senate and People of Rome. But Republicanism had never any real influence in the Roman army after the days of Sulla a century and a half ago. The legions of Upper Germany had not long to wait before they found a new emperor. Next day their comrades in Lower Germany, who the day before had taken the oath of allegiance to Galba with very bad grace, renounced it, and proclaimed their governor, Vitellius, emperor at Cologne.

The army of Upper Germany at once accepted him, and followed the example on January 3. Vitellius for his part was far too slothful and too flattered to resist the dangerous honour. Two men, each of them in command of a legion, both of great influence with the armies, found it an easy task to persuade him. Fabius Valens, of Anagni, *legate* of the First legion in Lower Germany, was an able general who had won Nero's favour by doubtful means and his troops' admiration by soldierly qualities. Aulus Caecina Alienus of Vicenza, also *legionary legate* in Upper Germany, was a younger man and the darling of the troops. Handsome, tall, and energetic, he was also to show true military qualities of daring and resource. He had at first, when *quaestor* of the province of Baetica in Spain, been a partisan of Galba, until his friendship was changed to enmity when Galba ordered his prosecution for embezzlement. These two men, Valens in the Lower Province, Caecina in the Upper, worked hard to secure the proclamation of Vitellius by the troops. By the 3rd of January their object was won. The army of Germany was united in its declaration. Vitellius was named emperor, and open defiance hurled in Galba's face.

When in a few days news of this reached Rome the old emperor affected to make light of it. But it finally determined him to take a step which he had for some time past been meditating, and to associate with himself a younger man as colleague in the Empire. There was both good precedent for the plan and also every hope of strengthening his own position thereby, had he chosen his colleague wisely. Unhappily for himself, Galba made a foolish choice, and paid for it in a week with his life.

The man whom he presented to the troops and to the Senate as his comrade henceforward in the burdens of Empire came of an honourable but unlucky family. Lucius Calpurnius Piso was by now thirty years of age. Two of his elder brothers he had already seen slain—the one by Claudius, the other by Nero. He himself had lived long in exile, and was equally without experience of civil administration or military service. Staid, sedate, melancholy, he was a man on whose honour the old emperor could rely for sober counsel and loyal support. But he was not a man to gain the devotion of the Guards or fascinate the populace. And even on the very day of his adoption by the emperor, when the greedy *praetorians* might not unreasonably have received the donative customary on any such occasion, Galba's old-fashioned thrift conceded nothing.

His maxim, that it was his wont to choose his soldiers and not to purchase them, was worthy of an ancient Roman, but won small sympathy from the Praetorians of his day. Piso's adoption by Galba on the 10th of January *A.D.* 69 was received sullenly by the troops in Rome—men soon so resolute to fight and quick to follow a general whom they knew and loved, but impatient of control and resentful of what they deemed neglect. Civil war was already threatening, and military discipline is the first virtue to fly at its approach.

The discontent of the Guards was all the more dangerous because it quickly found a leader, in whose heart anger at Galba's choice of Piso burned all the more deeply because he himself had expected to be chosen. And indeed Marcus Salvius Otho, of Ferento in South Etruria, had some reason to indulge in his hopes, now disappointed.

Otho is one of those perplexing figures in history whom it is very easy to condemn and very hard to dislike. His wayward brilliance and calm courage, his strong affections and the gentleness and mercy which he showed when emperor even to his enemies, were qualities which endear him to the memory of following ages as they won for him the praise and the love of the Romans of his own day. Yet his youth had been stained by vice, luxury, and immodesty, and he gained his power by base treachery and murder. But the men of his own day judged these faults of character the more leniently as they were the more familiar with them in men who had none of Otho's charm to compensate. As Nero had won men's approval, so did Otho also, and when the careless Roman mob nicknamed him Nero, Otho gladly accepted the name at their hands.

Now in these early days of January Otho had counted on Galba's choice falling on himself. He had done good service to the emperor in Spain. For Nero had determined to take Otho's beautiful wife Poppaea for his own, and to secure this end had banished the husband to honourable yet real exile as Governor of Lusitania, the modern Portugal, in *A.D.* 58. Here he had of necessity stayed ten years, surprising all who had known his dissolute life in Rome by his suavity and uprightness, when once removed from the accursed atmosphere of the Court at Rome. But he never forgave Nero for Poppaea's loss, and it was one of his earliest acts as emperor to set up again the statues of her which the mob had overthrown. Hence when Galba had meditated treason, Otho had urged him on. At his side he had come to Rome. Presently in his place he had hoped to reign. Now he suddenly found a younger, untried, and unpopular man preferred before him.[6]

It was an age when few men in high places acted on any principles save those of personal ambition; when safety was sought in treachery; when treason was the speediest refuge in distress. Five days' plotting followed. Then on the morning of January 15, Otho left the side of the old Emperor Galba as he stood sacrificing—"importuning the Gods now of another man's Empire"—and, muttering some lying excuse, hurried to the *praetorians'* camp, which lay by the city wall a short distance away.

A handful of troops acclaimed him emperor. Galba and Piso, lured down to the forum from the height of the *Palatine*, were abandoned by an indifferent mob and treacherous soldiers to their fate, and Otho reigned sole Emperor of Rome. Fourteen days before, the army of Germany had proclaimed Vitellius Emperor. The rivals must meet in open war. All embassies passing between the two were useless, for neither would yield place to the other. Galba had been treacherously slain. But open war should decide between Otho and Vitellius.

§2. The Troops Engaged

Civil war between Otho and Vitellius, the first of the three great

---

6. For the Nero-Otho-Poppaea story and its different versions see my *Life and Principate of the Emperor Nero*.

wars of these years *A.D.* 69 and 70, was thus imminent in the month of January in the former year. The various parts of the whole Roman Empire would have to choose sides. Some of the provinces, however, were "unarmed," that is, possessed no regular troops in them, and their goodwill or hostility therefore counted for little in a struggle which only the sword could decide. For at this time the Roman Army, apart from the garrison of Rome, was for the most part distributed along the frontiers of the Roman Empire, and the provinces within those frontiers enjoyed security without the presence of troops. Even of the frontier provinces some were garrisoned only by local auxiliary troops, and their contribution to the military strength of either side could be but trifling, while their sympathies were determined by the wishes of a neighbouring province of which Roman *legionaries* formed the garrison.

The Roman Army at this time consisted of thirty legions, and a force of "auxiliaries" which probably equalled in strength that of the legions.[7] The *legionaries*, all of whom were Roman citizens, may have numbered upward of a hundred and fifty thousand men. All of them were men who had made the practice of arms their profession; all of them were heavy-armed; most of them were disciplined and efficient. Each legion bore a number, and almost always a distinctive title; and in some of the legions regimental pride and loyalty were strong inducements to valour. The legionary cavalry, however, were few in number, and the bulk of the horse, as well as considerable numbers of infantry, mostly light-armed, were supplied by the auxiliaries.

These were organised corps, known as *alae* (of cavalry) and *cohortes* (both infantry and cavalry, or infantry only), usually marked by a number and a special name. The name was sometimes derived from the man who first enrolled the corps, sometimes from the nationality of the troops who composed it, sometimes from the particular equipment which distinguished it from other troops. These special corps were either five hundred or a thousand strong. The auxiliaries for the most part were at this time not Roman citizens, but earned the citizenship by twenty-five or more years' service, and were granted it by the emperor on their discharge. *Legionaries* served twenty years with the colours, but after that term of service many continued in the army,

---

7. This is generally assumed, and is a conclusion based on Tacitus (*Annals*, iv. 5, and *Histories*, v. 1); but though the numbers and names of a vast number of auxiliary *alae* and *cohortes* are now known, it is quite impossible to supply any more precise data of their total strength.

being formed into special *cohortes veteranorum*.

The Roman military system was thus a long-service system. And although a legion or auxiliary corps was always liable for service in any part of the known world, there had been developing since the beginnings of the Empire a tendency to keep the same troops in the same province for years together, and to recruit the legions on the spot. The legions were established in more or less permanent camps, and while these "*castra stativa*" served as headquarters for the troops, in course of time civil settlements of veterans, with their wives and families, and of traders, began to cluster round the military lines. Thus the children of the legionaries grew up in close touch with the legions, and the children of the auxiliaries in like manner would be able and inclined to take service in the legions, for which service they were duly qualified as soon as their fathers had received the Roman citizenship on their discharge. The problem of recruiting became an easy one, and the Roman Army was in truth a voluntary army, although the old civic liability on every citizen to be called out to war was never formally abolished. Always every citizen must be ready and able to fight for his country if need arose.

But since the days of Marius the Roman Army was never the "Nation in arms," except in theory. In compensation for this, the experience and courage of the *legionaries* were alike notable, and the numbers of the army, though small, were adequate for all the work, defensive and offensive, which it was from time to time called on to perform. Military service on the whole was popular. The troops were well cared for during service, and a system of pensions provided comfort for them in their old age. The permanent camps upon the frontiers were centres of Romanisation and civilisation just where such were most needed, namely, on the outskirts of Empire, where Rome came into contact with still uncivilised and savage tribes. The camps guarded the frontiers, proved the beginnings of towns later to be famous, and were places of refuge when the unquiet natives threatened war. And the steady growth in the number of Roman citizens during the first two centuries of the Empire, with all that this implied in the feeling of pride, responsibility, and dignity, on part of the individual, was due chiefly to the Roman military system as established by the first and greatest of the emperors, Augustus.

Upon this system, now comfortably practised for half a century, and upon this Roman army distributed for the most part in cantonments along the frontiers of the Empire, there broke the storm of civil war. Then was shown the one great blemish of the system; for it could not but stimulate the growth of local sympathy in the various frontier armies at the expense of their loyalty to the Empire as a whole and to the emperor at Rome. This danger was less ominous so long as the emperor was known through the Roman world either to be, like Tiberius, a soldier himself, of tried military capacity, or to be one who, like Claudius, would always put himself at the head of his troops—at least at the end of a difficult or dangerous campaign. The danger was also less ominous if the governors of the frontier provinces were changed from time to time and not allowed protracted periods of command.

Nero had been the first emperor to disregard both principles together. He had in consequence been deserted by the troops, and perished. The danger of local feeling, of local rivalries, in the frontier armies, became at once pronounced, and the length and bitterness of the civil wars of *A.D.* 69-70 were directly the result. And hence, when finally Vespasian won the victory, the interest taken both by him and by all his successors in the army and its welfare is very marked. Whether the emperor were a man of war, like Domitian or the great Trajan, or a cultured gentleman and man of peace, like Hadrian or Antoninus Pius, or a veritable philosopher, like Marcus Aurelius, made no difference. He was bound to know his troops and to be known by them.

The civil wars enforced this lesson of the Roman military system. They also emphasised another danger of the system which becomes clear in the great native rebellion on the Rhine towards their close, and will then be explained. But at the outset, when the Roman legionaries were called on to choose sides between Otho and Vitellius, there seemed no reason why they should hesitate to take up arms for the one or the other, according as their private interests or affections or passions should command. For eighteen months selfishness was lord paramount of most men in the Roman Empire.

The Roman Army was agreed on but two things: firstly, that it would not restore the Republican form of government; secondly, that so splendid an opportunity for fighting and for plunder as had now arisen was not to be let go. In the course of the struggle the troops from time to time displayed courage to the point of heroism, and loyal affection for at least one of their generals to the degree of the very passion of love itself. Yet the main interests of the campaigns are strategical and military. They are no battle for Country or for Liberty when war is glorious, and to refrain from arms is contemptible.

The Eastern provinces and their armies, Italy and the garrison of Rome, and the regular troops of the "Danube" frontier, were for the most part in sympathy with Otho; the Western half of the Empire was with Vitellius. But some of the adherents on both sides were too far removed from the scene of conflict to take an active part in it.

The army of the Eastern frontier (including Egypt) consisted of eight legions. Three of these—the Fourth Scythica, Sixth Ferrata, and Twelfth Fulminata—were stationed in Syria. The Governor of Syria at this time was Caius Licinius Mucianus, an able soldier and statesman, who had been appointed to this duty by Nero in *A.D.* 67. Three more legions were still engaged in quelling the fierce rebellion of the Jews, which was to be ended by the fall of Jerusalem on September 2, *A.D.* 70.[8] These legions were the Fifth Macedonica, the Tenth Fretensis, and the Fifteenth Apollinaris. Their general was Titus Flavius Vespasianus, at this time a man of fifty-nine years of age. Vespasian was of humble origin, from a small hamlet near Rieti in the highlands of the Abruzzi in Central Italy, but of long and honourable service and of proved military ability.

In the first conquest of Britain under Claudius he had subdued the Isle of Wight after many battles, and since then, after peaceful duty as Governor of Africa, had been chosen by Nero to command in the Jewish war. A keen and active soldier, blunt, outspoken, hardy, thrifty, and temperate, a man possessing alike common sense and dry humour, Vespasian was reserved by the Fates to heal the wounds of the Roman Empire after the sore months of civil war were ended. But in January *A.D.* 69 he was still busily engaged with the war in Judaea, and not ready to make his bid for Empire. He had sent the elder of his two sons Titus and Domitian to carry his homage to Galba from the seat of war. But the news of Galba's death reached Titus when he arrived at Corinth on his voyage to Italy. Titus therefore returned from Greece to Syria, and both Vespasian and Mucianus with their respective armies swore fidelity to Otho.

Finally, in Egypt there were two legions, the Third Cyrenaica and the Twenty-Second Deiotariana. This restless, rich, and turbulent country was at this time happily controlled by a governor of striking ability, Tiberius Julius Alexander. He was a Jew by birth who had renounced Judaism, and after serving with Corbulo in the Armenian

---

8. For this Jewish war, see my *Life and Principate of Nero*, chap. x. §5.

war had been made Prefect of Egypt by Nero in *A.D.* 63, and continued in that office under Galba. A long edict by him is still preserved, checking the extortion of officials and the greedy activity of professional informers. Under his direction Egypt and its army were well disposed to Otho. Subsequently he acted as chief of staff to Titus in the Jewish war, with zeal and ability.

The eight legions in the East took no part in the civil war between Otho and Vitellius, but their open sympathy with the former quickly bore fruit after the triumph of his rival. For the time being, however, "the East was undisturbed."

The Roman province of Africa had lately been greatly disturbed by the foolish ambition of the legate of the one legion, the Third Augusta, which at this time occupied the military district of Numidia (which for administration counted as part of Africa). This man, Lucius Clodius Macer, had revolted against Nero and posed falsely as a Republican enthusiast, when in reality he was seeking his own selfish ends. Galba had secured his death without difficulty, and thereupon the province was only too happy to be quiet, "being content with any kind of a prince after its experience of a petty master." Following the lead of its chief town Carthage, it professed mild interest in Otho's cause. But its legion took no part in the war.

If Otho was thus unable to use nine friendly legions in the East and South, Vitellius in like manner, though to a less degree, could not employ all the troops who wished well to his cause in the West.

In Britain there were now left three of the famous four legions which had "conquered" the island under Claudius and kept it for the Empire at the time of the furious rising of the natives led by Queen Boudicca (Boadicea) against Nero. These legions were the Second Augusta, Ninth Hispana, and Twentieth Valeria Victrix. Their old comrades of the Fourteenth Gemina had lately been transferred to Dalmatia.

The Governor of Britain at the time of Galba's accession was Marcus Trebellius Maximus. But he incurred the displeasure of his troops, and the men of the Twentieth legion took upon themselves to turn him out of the country without more ado. In his absence the legates of the three legions administered the province, sharing the duties between them, until Vitellius after his victory sent out a new governor in the person of Marcus Vettius Bolanus. Separated by the sea from the rest of the Empire, and with trouble threatening from the tribesmen of Yorkshire and the north, the army of Britain displayed no lively interest in the opening stages of the civil wars.

Spain was garrisoned by the two legions, the Sixth Victrix and the Tenth Gemina. Galba had been followed as governor of the district Tarraconensis by the historian Cluvius Rufus; and Otho, familiar with the land, and a fellow-courtier with Cluvius under Nero, had hoped to gain the support of the Spanish Army and strengthen his position in Spain by favours bestowed on the province. New settlers were sent by him to the two colonies of Hispalis (Seville), in the province of Baetica in South Spain, and Augusta Emerita (Merida) in Lusitania (Portugal), and the Roman citizenship was probably bestowed by him on the Lusones, a Celtiberian tribe round the sources of the Tagus. Certain "towns of the Mauri" also, lying in the district of Mauretania, the other side of the Straits of Gibraltar, such as Tingi (Tangiers), were added by him to Baetica for administrative and revenue purposes. But neither the Spanish provinces nor the Spanish army nor Cluvius Rufus gave Otho any support.

It may well be that the soldiers resented his murder of their former governor Galba. Indeed, when the procurator of Mauretania, one Lucceius Albinus, threatened Spain in Otho's interests, Rufus guarded the Straits and persuaded Albinus' army to murder their procurator. This, however, was the only service which the Spanish Army rendered to Vitellius; and later they abandoned his cause when his doom was coming close.

Of the thirty legions of the Roman army, fourteen, therefore, were not concerned with the war between Otho and Vitellius. The remaining sixteen were divided in allegiance. Seven legions in Germany and one in Gaul, on the one hand, formed Vitellius' army of invasion. On the other hand, seven stalwart legions in the "Danube provinces" and one at Rome declared for Otho, who besides commanded the support of the garrison of Rome, the most famous regiments of "Guards." Four of the seven legions of the German army were stationed in the Lower Province, three in the Upper; all seven being on the left bank of the Rhine and in the immediate neighbourhood of the river. Nearest the sea the "Old Camp," Castra Vetera, served as the usual headquarters for two legions, the Fifth Alaudae and the Fifteenth Primigenia. The First legion was probably encamped at Bonn, near the southern frontier of the province, and between these two camps the Sixteenth legion lay at Novaesium. In Upper Germany Mainz supplied a double camp for the two legions, the Fourth Macedonica and Twenty-Second Primigenia, while the Twenty-First Rapax was stationed at Vindonissa, east of the great northward bend of the Rhine.[9]

The four Gallic provinces—Belgica on the north, Lugdunensis in the centre, Aquitania on the southwest, and Narbonensis on the south-east—were sufficiently guarded against the barbarians by the powerful garrison in the two Germanies on the Rhine, and only the city of Lugdunum itself at the meeting-place of the Rhone and Saône was guarded by troops. Here in the most important city of the whole land were stationed the First Italica legion; an auxiliary cavalry regiment, the *ala* Tauriana, so called from the name of Statilius Taurus, who first enlisted it; and the eighteenth *cohort* of the Guards. The town and garrison of Lugdunum embraced eagerly the cause of Vitellius. Twenty miles down the Rhone, nestling, like its enemy, under precipitous heights, lay the hated city of Vienne, and never did bitterness felt by one little Greek city-state for a neighbour exceed that anger which Lugdunum cherished against Vienne, both towns though they were of the Empire. This hostility was doubtless partly due to tribal feeling, partly perhaps to the very Greek element persisting in the valley of the Rhone.

And it is curious to reflect that just as Lugdunum was the new proud centre for the great political institution of Caesar-worship, so it was at Vienne that Christianity, the foe of, and at last the victor over, the Imperial cult, had its chief beginnings in the West. During the recent revolt of Vindex and his Gauls, Vienne had been enthusiastic for the national cause; Lugdunum had triumphed over her when the Roman legions of Germany crushed the national rising.[10] Yet Galba, Emperor of Rome, had shown favour to Vienne; and Otho had actually named as consul one of her citizens. Lugdunum would never forgive this injustice, nor forget the slight put upon her loyalty. Old ally of the Germany, she welcomed the day when Vitellius' troops marched downstream she hoped, upon her enemies as well as on his own.

The military camp of Vindonissa was but a few miles from the eastern border of Roman Germany. The point where the Rhine flowed out of Lake Constance marked the beginning of that district, and the river formed its frontier from the lake to the sea. A few miles north of that camp there rose in the recesses of the Black Forest a far mightier

---

9. It must be remembered that some of the evidence for these places as headquarters for these legions belongs to the year 70. But in the absence of contrary evidence we may suppose it to be true of the year before. Throughout I use the more familiar name of the place, whether ancient or modern.

10. For Lugdunum *v*, Vienne in the revolt of Vindex see my *Life of Nero*, chap. xi. §5.

and more wonderful river, the course of which from its source to its outflow into the Black Sea traced for many years the northern limit of the Roman advance into the heart of Europe. Along its southern bank the Romans made four districts. Raetia, the most westerly, stretched from the frontier of Upper Germany at Lake Constance, and south of this from the land of the Helvetii and the Lake of Geneva, to the valley of the lower Inn and the point where this muddy, rushing river joins its waters to the cool, clear, beautiful stream of the Danube at Passau.

From this point Noricum reached well-nigh as far as Vienna, to be succeeded by the province of Pannonia, whose northern and eastern boundaries alike were formed by the Danube. The issue of the River Save from the west into this river at Belgrade was the beginning of the province of Moesia, which stretched all the many hundred miles from this point along the southern bank to the sea.

As the Danube far excels the Rhine in power, so did the native tribes north of the river surpass those beyond the Rhine in restlessness and terror. If the "Army of the Danube" in the middle of the century was slightly inferior in numbers to the troops who guarded the line of the Rhine, this was due to the fact that the greater danger which threatened the Roman peace from the trans-Danubian peoples seemed less imminent during the first half of the first century, and came to be realised more and more vividly only towards its close. None the less there were already seven legions appointed to form this army. In Raetia and Noricum no *legionaries* were stationed. Just as in earlier days the master of an army in Cisalpine Gaul between the Alps and the Rubicon had held the key to Italy in his grasp, so now when Italy reached as one country to the Alpine chain the governor of the district of Raetia, which commanded all the northern passes over the mountains, would have had Italy and the Emperor of Rome too directly and immediately at his mercy, had he been placed in control of a legionary army.

Raetia, therefore, was but a minor command under control of a procurator, and his only troops were such native levies as he could raise in the case of any sudden peril. If a serious danger threatened the Raetian frontier, the governor of Upper Germany must see to it. In the same way, Noricum was administered by a procurator only, who depended for his protection ultimately on the legions in the province of Pannonia on his eastern border. The great frontier commands were those of Pannonia and Moesia.

In Pannonia, in January A.D. 69, were two legions—the Seventh

Galbiana and Thirteenth Gemina; in Moesia three—the Third Gallica, which had newly come to the province from Syria, the Seventh Claudia, and the Eighth Augusta; and as a great reserve force to the army of the Danube, two legions kept the province of Dalmatia—the Eleventh Claudia, and the most famous of the legions of the war in Britain, the Fourteenth Gemina. This province of Dalmatia extended all down the eastern shore of the Adriatic Sea, from the promontory of Istria on the north to the Macedonian frontier by Lissus on the south. Thus its army acted as a great rearguard alike to the troops in Pannonia on the north and to those in Moesia on the east. And its two legions are justly counted as part of the Army of the Danube.

These legions of Dalmatia, Pannonia, and Moesia duly swore allegiance to Otho in the early part of the year *A.D.* 69. They were too widely separated from one another to be likely eagerly to act in concert on behalf of some nominee of their own. Moreover, Otho was the emperor accepted by the Senate and People of Rome, ruling from the city of Rome, which was the very "head of the Empire and glory of all the provinces," and there was no reason why they should love the rival set up by the rebellious army of Germany. The appreciation of Otho, however, was of a slightly passive nature, save in the case of the legion from Britain, the Fourteenth, which was enthusiastic on his behalf. (Tac. ii.).

Moreover, the Governor of Moesia, Marcus Aponius, and his troops had suddenly in the spring of this year a task imposed upon them which left them small leisure for pondering over Otho's virtues. Already, in the winter, the Roxolani, a tribe belonging to the wild Sarmatian hordes of Eastern Europe, had raided across the frontier and cut to pieces two *cohorts* of auxiliaries. And now in the early spring they repeated their attack, encouraged by the rumours of civil war among their foes which had rapidly spread to them. Nine thousand horsemen clad in chain armour or leathern jerkins crossed the Danube to plunder. Then the Third legion, with auxiliaries to help them, did good work for Rome.

On a February day, when the deep snows of winter were melting and rain was falling, when the rude tracks were well-nigh impassable, and horses could scarcely keep their feet, the Roman infantry fell unexpectedly upon the straggling and unsuspecting foe, and had them at their mercy. They were unable to ride away; they were hurled from their horses or pierced by the Roman javelin; they lay prostrate in the watery snow, and were unable to struggle to their feet for the weight of their armour; their pikes, their long swords, needing two hands to wield, were useless; shields they had none, nor any courage to defend themselves on foot against the exultant legionary and his native ally. They put their trust in their horses, and they were destroyed with an utter destruction by the short stabbing-blade of the Roman. Only a handful of the raiders escaped to lurk in the marshes, there miserably to die of cold or wounds.

Otho gladly seized the chance given him by the annihilation of the Sarmatians to reward the Governor of Moesia and the legates of all three legions, though only one of the three had won the victory. But it was no time for making distinctions and exciting jealousies. It was for him to gain the goodwill of all the officers. And the Danube Army might reasonably now be proud of, and loyal to, an emperor on whose brief annals they had been the first to inscribe deeds worthy of remembrance. With this intent, Otho celebrated their prowess and published it abroad in Rome. And the seven legions of the Army of the Danube were true to him to the day of his death.

There remained the garrison of Rome itself, which was devoted to his cause, and such other troops as were to be found in Italy. In Rome itself at this time a large body of troops was gathered together. Foremost among these were the soldiers who formed the regular garrison of the city—nine *cohorts* of Praetorian Guards, and seven *cohorts* of Urban Guards. The strength of a *cohort* was one thousand men. The *Praetorians*, the only troops whom Italy contributed regularly to the Imperial forces, were the very flower of the Roman Army.

All had volunteered for the service, which lasted for them only sixteen years, and was rewarded by higher pay than that which the legionary received. They were commanded by two *prefects*, men specially chosen by the emperor out of the staff of his own Civil Service, and this *prefecture* formed the crown of the Service. The seven Urban *cohorts* were men well trained and fought well, but they were held in less repute than the "Guards" proper. In these sixteen *cohorts* Otho had a force of sixteen thousand men, the most famous regiments in the army, and all enthusiastic for a prince to whom they had given the power.

Besides these, there was then at Rome the First Adjutrix legion, newly levied by Nero from the sailors of the fleet, and recently given its legionary "eagle," the ensign and emblem of due enrolment, by Galba. But on their entry into Rome Galba's troops had hewn down many of these *legionaries*, who had poured out of the city somewhat turbulently to greet the new emperor and clamour for their "eagle." Hence he had been frightened, and had given orders to slay. The sole tradition, therefore, of the new regiment was one of hatred for the dead prince, and it could be trusted to serve his slayer well. Moreover, its spurs were yet to win, and the men were not unmindful of this when a few months later they stood face to face in their first battle with a veteran regiment of the German Army.

Besides the Guards and this legion there also chanced to be in Rome detachments of troops properly belonging to the armies of Britain, Germany, and the Danube. For just before his death Nero had summoned these "*vexilla*" and "*numeri*" to Italy when he was making preparations for an expedition against the Alans in the Caucasus. The revolt of Vindex had caused him to call these forces hurriedly to Rome, where they remained, it seems, after his death and during the short Principate of Galba.

Finally, there was one *cohort*, the Seventeenth, in garrison at Ostia[11]; and upon the River Po, whither the storm-clouds of invasion were sweeping, one auxiliary squadron of horse, nine hundred and sixty strong, the *ala Siliana*, was stationed. Nero had called it to Italy from Egypt on the news of Vindex's revolt, and sent it north to guard the line of the river.[12]

These then were the troops which might be counted on by both sides as able to take part in the coming civil war:—

1) On the Vitellian side:

Legio I.	in Lower Germany,			at Bonn
Legio V. Alaudae	„	„		at Castra Vetera
Legio XV. Primigenia	„	„		„
Legio XVI.	„	„		at Novaesium
Legio IV. Macedonica,	in Upper Germany,			at Mainz
Legio XXII. Primigenia	„	„		„
Legio XXI. Rapax	„	„		at Vindonissa

---

11. The Cohortes XVII. and XVIII. are counted on from the Urban Cohorts (Coh. X.-XVI.), just as these are counted on from the Praetorian (Coh. L-IX.). Under Tiberius, Cohors XVII. is in garrison at Lugdunum "*ad monetam*" (Tac. *Ann*, iii.; C.I.L. xiii. 1499; Tac. *Hist*, i.). But as in *A. D.* 69 it is found at Ostia, it is probable that Nero recalled it from Lugdunum and sent it there, placing Cohors XVIII. at Lugdunum instead. For Leg. I. Adjutrix and the garrison of Rome, cf. Tac. i; ii. The Caspian expeditionary troops, cf. my *Life of Nero*, and references in note.

12. The *ala Siliana*, so called from C Silius, *legate* of Upper Germany under Tiberius. Tac. *Ann*, i. 31; *Hist*, i.

Legio I. Italica	in Gaul	at Lugdunum
Ala Tauriana	„	„
Cohors XVIII.	„	„

and an indeterminate but large number of auxiliaries, horse and foot, besides such irregulars, native levies, etc., as could be enlisted.

(2) On the Othonian side:

Legio VII. Galbiana, in Pannonia
Legio XIII. Gemina   „
Legio III. Gallica, in Moesia
Legio VII. Claudia   „
Legio VIII. Augusta   „
Legio XI. Claudia, in Dalmatia
Legio XIV. Gemina   „
Legio I. Adjutrix   in Rome
Cohortes I.-IX (Praetorian) „
Cohortes X.-XVI. (Urban) „
Cohors XVII. at Ostia
Ala Siliana in Upper Italy

and an indeterminate but large number of auxiliaries, horse and foot, besides such irregulars, native levies, etc., or gladiators from the schools at Rome, as could be enlisted.

The struggle, therefore, seemed likely to be one between the troops in Germany and Gaul on the one side, and those of Italy and the Danube provinces on the other. In this reckoning each of the rivals could employ eight legions. Vitellius' army numbered over a hundred thousand men of all arms. When he moved on Italy, his two advance columns consisted, the one of forty thousand, the other of thirty thousand men, when they left the Rhine, and the column which marched through Gaul continually gathered in fresh troops from the country. Vitellius himself followed later with the rest of his available strength, and he too received reinforcements on the march, as by this time the army in Britain found itself able to contribute to his forces. Only a few men were left behind under Hordeonius Flaccus to garrison the bank of the Rhine against the peril from the natives over the river, who happily for the time remained quiet.[13]

---

13. Tac. ii. The numbers of the columns of Caecina and Valens are given precisely by Tacitus; but Vitellius himself is described as to follow "*tota mole belli*," i. If we insisted on this very vague and worthless phrase, we might increase Vitellius' available numbers to 150,000 men. But the lower total seems to me the more probable.

To resist this attack, Otho had two armies to put into the field. At Rome his army cannot have largely exceeded twenty-five thousand men in number, though the majority of these were excellent soldiers. But in the Danube provinces his troops, when and if concentrated into a single striking force, would scarcely be inferior to the German army in number. The emperor could reckon them as at least upwards of seventy thousand men of all arms.

In actual numbers, as also in the probable quality of the soldiers, Otho was thus not inferior to Vitellius. But one great difference in his situation became clear at once. The Army of Germany was more easily concentrated, more easily set in motion under one command. His own troops consisted of two widely separated armies—the smaller Army of Italy, the larger Army of the Danube. But this last army also was far from being concentrated. The obvious base for its military operations, and therefore its place of muster, was Aquileia, the town looking due southwards over the Adriatic. Aquileia is today a petty village in the marshes, some fifty-five miles north-east of Venice. But in Roman days, when Venice did not exist, it was the most important military stronghold on the Italian north-eastern frontier, and the great military roads from the "Danube provinces," Dalmatia, Pannonia, and Moesia, first converged upon it.

The chief military centre of Pannonia, the town of Poetovio, lay a hundred and fifty miles to the east of it; the chief town of Moesia, Naissus, some four hundred miles beyond Poetovio, and from Scodra, chief town of Dalmatia, to Aquileia direct was also four hundred miles. There is no evidence of the actual position of the legions of the three provinces in January *A.D.* 69. But it was evident that to muster the whole, or even a considerable part of, the Army of the Danube at Aquileia would require much organisation, and take probably a longer time than was needed for the mobilisation of the German army within striking distance of Italy. Although Otho sent orders at once to the nearest legions, those of Pannonia and Dalmatia, to march on Italy, yet the enemy possessed the great initial advantage of a concentrated over a dispersed army.

The very force of circumstances therefore dictated the initial strategy of the coming campaign. The strategic initiative rested with the Vitellians. It was not only because Otho was actual Emperor of Rome and Vitellius challenged his right to rule, that the Army of Germany had to attack. Before a soldier left camp, the strategy of offence and invasion was clearly marked out for the Vitellians by the position of the opposed armies and their numbers. When Otho's scattered armies were united, it might well be that they would prove more than equal to Vitellius' troops. But at the outset there existed great gaps between the dispersed fragments of the Othonians. While they were mustering, Vitellius must strike. Possibly even he might have the opportunity to penetrate between the foe's divided forces. This "strategy of penetration" gives the chance of dividing up and defeating the enemy in detail. It has risks and obvious perils of its own, and all its success depends upon careful timing. But at the outset it was clear to all concerned that circumstances and numbers dictated to the Vitellians the strategy of offence and the invasion of Italy. They possessed the strategical initiative.

§3. The Strategical Aspect of the Opening Campaign

The Army of Invasion had two ultimate bases of operation. These may be taken to be Cologne for the force in Lower Germany, and Vindonissa for that in Upper Germany. The objective of both forces was the enemy's army, which must be destroyed. That army was not likely to be met north of the Alps, nor indeed north of the Po, for reasons partly of time, partly of strategy, which were obvious to both sides.[14] The theatre of war was likely to be the great plain of this river, that plain which has been the scene of more fighting in the course of history than even have the Low Countries. The immediate geographical objective, therefore, of the Army of Invasion was the section of the Po between Placentia on the west and Hostilia on the east.

At the former place was the crossing of the river by the great highway which led south-east, skirting the Apennines, to Ariminum and so to Rome; and this road would have to be pursued by a force crossing any of the Alpine passes on the west and north-west of Italy, And at Hostilia was the second chief crossing of the river by the road which ran from Verona on the north to join the great highway at Bologna, (Bononia), fifty miles to the south; and by this road an army marching by any of the northern passes down on Italy would have to come.

It was therefore necessary for the Army of Germany to cross the Alps as speedily as possible. The natural difficulties of the passage of the mountains in early spring by a large force, as well as the problem of supplies, made it expedient for the Vitellians to divide their army. Moreover, it was important to secure Gaul, as this country lay on the

---

14. I postpone the explanation of these to the paragraphs dealing with the strategical position of the Othonians.

flank and in rear of the advance, and further to increase the numbers of the invading army by Gallic reinforcements swept in during the forward movement. But if the whole army marched through Gaul and over one of the western passes, the delay caused by the long detour might well imperil the success of the whole campaign. Therefore it was decided that the Army of Germany should remain divided, and that two columns of invasion should march at once. The Vindonissa column was to proceed direct from Upper Germany to Italy; the Cologne column, as it may be called, was to march through Gaul, and strike thence eastwards over one of the western passes of the Alps. The distance to be marched by the Cologne column was nearly three times as great as that of the other. It would arrive later at the objective, and there join the Vindonissa army, should the latter need help.

The Army of Defence had also two ultimate bases of operation—Rome for the Army of Italy, and Aquileia for the Army of the Danube. Both of these were similarly many miles away from the river Po, and, besides this, the concentration of the whole or, at least, part of the Army of the Danube at Aquileia must first be effected. A diagram may serve to illustrate the strategical position at the beginning of the campaign.[15]

Although the distance from Rome to the objective was longer than that from Vindonissa, the time taken by an army marching from Rome would be much shorter, as the natural difficulties which hindered the pace of the Vindonissa column were far greater, and, as it proved, these troops indulged in some petty fighting with the tribes north of the Alps before they set out resolutely on the road.

A. Strategical Opportunities of the Othonians.—

Until the Danube army arrived in North Italy to co-operate with them, Otho's troops in that country were so greatly inferior in numbers to the approaching invaders that their only possible strategy at first was a defensive one. It is true that such a strategy, unless it were unexpectedly crowned by a decisive victory on the field of battle, could never be expected to end the war.

> The records of warfare contain no instance, when two armies were of much the same quality, of the smaller army bringing the campaign to a decisive issue by defensive tactics. Wellington

---

15. The diagram is drawn roughly to scale according to the distances which the troops marched by the ways they actually pursued, and these are the distances given in round numbers.

and Lee both fought many defensive battles with inferior forces. But neither of them under such conditions ever achieved the destruction of the enemy. They fought such battles to gain time, and their hopes soared no higher.—*Stonewall Jackson*, by Lieut.-Col. Henderson, vol. ii.

Defence was forced upon the Army of Italy until their comrades should arrive, but only for so long. For defence pure and simple sometimes wins battles, but wars scarcely ever.

It was therefore, above all, important to retard the advance of the Vitellians into Italy by every possible means. All Othonian efforts in Italy had to be directed at first to secure this end, and to give time for the Army of the Danube to arrive. The questions, therefore, which arose were two. Firstly, what precise line of defence should be chosen? Secondly, what means of delaying the enemy's march could be employed?

(1) Two possible lines of defence suggest themselves at once to a general who wishes to defend North Italy, namely, the Alps and the Po.

But for Otho the blocking of the Alpine passes was impossible. In the first place, had he even wished to block them, time, distance, and numbers forbade this. Actually he had in North Italy in January *A.D.* 69 but one small regiment of horse, the *ala* Siliana, and this quickly turned traitor to his cause. The troops in Rome could scarcely reach the Alpine passes on the north and northwest before the troops of Upper Germany had seized them. And it would be madness for them to block the western passes, whither they might have arrived in time, when the foe advancing from the north would already be down in the plain of the Po. But even if the Vitellians delayed their approach, and thus gave Otho time to block the passes (and he could not count upon this for a moment), the emperor was quite uncertain which route or routes his foe would choose. The Army of Italy, scarcely twenty-five thousand strong, would have been distributed along the chain of mountains in isolated, widely separated fragments. A reverse suffered in any single pass would snap at once the chain of resistance. The whole scheme of defence would have been destroyed, and the entire army would have been in danger of piecemeal annihilation.

In the next place, the proper method of defending a mountain ridge is not the blocking of the passes, when several such passes over the ridge exist. To place a division sitting on top of each pass in entrenchments, however strong, is but to court disaster. No mountain barrier, whether Himalaya or Pyrenees, Jura or Alps, ought to be defended in this way, or ever has been for long successfully defended in this way. Picquets and outposts, varying in strength, must be placed in the actual passes. But the main Army of Defence must be kept on the more level ground behind the ridge, concentrated and as near to the issues of the passes as the nature of the ground allows.

From such a position it can deal a vigorous blow at its foes when these, forcing back the outposts, struggle by one or more passes with difficulty over the mountains, and emerge more or less exhausted upon the lower ground beyond. It is then that they must be attacked, before they have recovered from the stress of the passage of the heights, when a dangerous country lies immediately in their rear, and when, if they have chosen to cross by more passes than one, the detachments of their troops are perhaps separated by the difficult foothills of the mountain ridge. Then the Army of Defence, perfectly informed by its outposts of the advance of the enemy, with its communications from the flanks to the centre running easily over the more level country which the army occupies, can move to the attack with vigour unimpaired and confidence high, and by a tactical offensive give its strategical defensive the victory. Such was the strategy by which, for instance, the Argives ought to have defended their northern rampart of mountains against King Agis of Sparta in 418 B.C. Such is the strategy by which Italy today would defend her Alpine barrier against a foe to north or west of it.

Unhappily, Otho had neither men enough nor time enough to choose this, which otherwise would have been the right, method of defending Italy. He was compelled to abandon all thought of holding the line of the Alps. He could not prevent the enemy's columns, marching by widely different routes, from concentrating in the plain of the Po unhindered. In modern history, in the Napoleonic wars and in the fighting for the liberation of Italy, "the battles lost or won at the foot of the Alpine passes, and in the vineyards of the great northern plain, Rivoli, Marengo, Magenta, Solferino,"[16] decided then too the fate of Tuscany, Rome, and the South. As Otho could not guard the foot of the passes, he must fall back upon the second natural line of defence—upon the river which flows through the great northern plain and its vineyards.

This line could be more easily defended. To the west lay the great fortress of Placentia, south of the river, placed upon the military road where it crossed the Po, and guarding the passage of the river. Placentia, (Piacenza), if garrisoned strongly and resolutely held would be an invaluable "pivot of manoeuvre" for Otho's defending army, which, with its left flank secured by the fortress, could deploy eastwards along the river in safety.[17] In the same way the crossing of the river to the east must be secured and defended, and at the same time the communications with the Danube Army at Aquileia must be kept open and safe from the enemy. A strong garrison at Verona or at Mantua would best achieve this double object. It was vital to Otho to take precautions against the risk that the enemy would come down upon Italy by the Brenner Pass and seek to thrust in between his own army and that at Aquileia, severing the communications between these. At least the

---

16. Trevelyan, *Garibaldi's Defence of the Roman Republic*.
17. "A 'pivot of manoeuvre' is a force, fortress, or natural obstacle which secures a flank" (Henderson, *Science of War*).

Mantua-Hostilia line must at all costs be stoutly defended.

The Army of Italy, therefore, should be spread along the line of the river from Placentia to Hostilia, with special concentration of strength at both ends of the line. And as at the western end the fortress in itself offered a means of strong defiance, the bulk of the defending forces must be directed to the eastern part of the line of defence.

This line the Vitellians would doubtless assault with vigour. But it was unlikely that they would try to break it in the middle, at least at first, or that, if they tried, they would succeed in the attempt. The river here is wide and deep, with shifting sandbanks and dangerous eddies, and its current, swollen in spring, is impetuous. It was far more probable that they would attack one of the two ends. A successful forcing of the eastern end would indeed be ominous of disaster for Otho. His army here must see to it that this did not happen. But the point of attack nearest to the most probable place of concentration for the Vitellians in North Italy was certainly Placentia. If then the enemy combined to assault this fortress, if they even forced the passage of the river here, then at once the advantage which Otho possessed in his double base of operations would come into play. For as the Vitellians advanced down the great road from Placentia, the Othonians defending the river could retire before them unhurt, and fall back upon their second base Aquileia. This would compel the enemy to choose one of two courses of action. They might either neglect this force or pursue after it. If they dared to neglect it, and to press on regardless down the great highway for Rome, by so doing they would expose their own line of communications defenceless to the force at Aquileia.

This then, strengthened by the arrival of the Danube army, would sally forth to cut the line. Now it is one of Napoleon's sayings that the secret of war lies in the communications. It is true that under exceptional circumstances an army can afford to cut itself loose from its line of communications with the base—when, that is, it is prepared to live entirely upon the country through which it is marching. But for the most part in all warfare, ancient as well as modern, an army needs to keep its communications open with some friendly base in the rear of its advance for the safe convoy of supplies and reinforcements, and if it is invading a hostile land it is likely to be extremely sensitive as to the perfect safety of its line or lines of communication with the rear.

By neglecting this principle Alexander at Issus was trapped in a hopeless position, unless he won a great tactical victory. Napoleon at Madrid hurriedly abandoned all his year's schemes for the conquest of Portugal because a small British force moved boldly out in the far north of Spain to threaten his line of communications with France.

Therefore a Vitellian invading force advancing down the road to Rome was not likely to allow the enemy to cut the one line by which reinforcements could come to it, the one line by which its own retreat, in case of disaster, was secured. Threatened by an advance from Aquileia, the Vitellians would surely turn to face the advancing foe. They would then find themselves in a position which is the most hazardous position for an army compelled to fight a decisive tactical engagement. This is the position technically known as that of an army with its "front to a flank." A diagram may make this clear:—

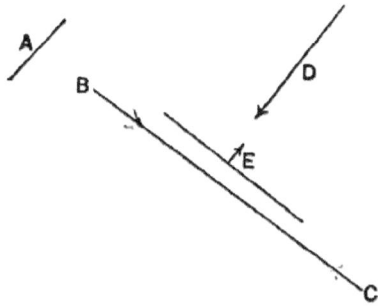

A = Vitellian base, over the river beyond Placentia.
BC = Direction of Vitellian march for Ariminum.
CB = Line of Vitellian communications with their base.
D = Direction of Othonian attack on CB from Aquileia.
E = Vitellian front to meet the attack.

The Vitellians in this position have been formed to a front on their left flank. When a force is thus drawn up, the enemy's main attack is always directed upon the flank which is nearest to the base. For if the force can be defeated on this flank its line of communications is thereby cut, and the whole force is separated from the hope of succour. Whereas if it is worsted on the flank farthest removed from the base, the line of communications is still open to the defeated army, and retreat, if difficult, is at least possible for them. As a general, if not his army, must always take into account his position in the event of defeat as well as in that of victory (unless he is staking all on a single throw, and wishes for no choice save that between victory and annihilation), the Vitellian commander could not contemplate with equanimity an advance which might compel him at any moment to form front to a flank in face of the enemy, if he was unwilling to surrender altogether his line of communications to their mercy.

If then the Vitellians forced the passage of the river at Placentia, it was more probable that they would not straightway pursue their march southeast along the road. They would rather follow upon the heels of the retiring Othonians towards Aquileia. This would suit Otho well. He would be retreating in the direction of the advancing Army of the Danube, and the aim of his defence of the river—concentration with this—would be achieved. Doubtless it was better not to abandon the whole of North Italy to the invader, for political if not for military reasons. The invader should not be allowed to cross the river without fighting, at least to prevent murmurs and discouragement in Rome and among the emperor's troops. But if, by fighting, the foe forced the passage at Placentia, even so the tactical would not be a strategical defeat for Otho.

(2) The first means of delaying the Vitellian advance was, therefore, the occupation in force of a line of defence on the River Po from Placentia to Hostilia. Twenty thousand or twenty-five thousand men could surely maintain their position here for some time, helped, as they would be, by the river. It is true that this could be but a temporary measure of passive defence.

> The defence of rivers ... has hardly ever been successful for any length of time. Neither the Danube nor the Rhine has stopped armies.

A river, like a mountain range, is an "insurmountable impediment which is invariably surmounted."[18] The Po could not be permanently held, any more than was the Tugela, in the face of repeated and vigorous attempts to force the passage, especially when, as in both these cases, thanks to inferior numbers or irresolution, no counter-stroke over the river could be dealt the assailants by the defending army. But as a means of delay rather than as a permanent obstacle the river was of the greatest value to the Army of Italy.

The second means of delay was the fleet. The command of the sea was absolutely Otho's. An invasion of North Italy from Germany, it might seem, affords the least possible chances that the command of the

---

18. Von der Goltz, *The Nation in Arms,* Cf. Hamley, *Operations of War*, part v.

sea should have any influence at all upon the conduct of operations. No more unpromising field for the application of the pet modern theory, it might be urged, could possibly be found. Yet none the less, as in the days of the second Punic war, although for different reasons, so in the civil war of *A.D.* 69, the invader of Italy had cause to regret the fact that the control of the sea rested with the defender.

The reason for this in *A.D.* 69 was that the flank of an army which proposed to cross one of the western passes over the Alps was vulnerable from the sea. If Otho could spare the troops, a force could speedily be conveyed on shipboard to Fréjus, and there landed. With the fleet as its base it could march up country to threaten the right flank of a column crossing the Alps by the Mont Genèvre or Mont Cenis Pass. If the enemy turned upon it with superior numbers, it could retreat to the coast as securely, for example, as the British Army of the Peninsula in 1808-1809 fell back on the fleet at Corunna when pursued by the thronging battalions of the French. And every soldier thereby detached from the invading army, every hour's delay to the final concentration of the Vitellians in North Italy, was so much pure gain to the emperor.

This, indeed, would be but a minor operation, intended to cause a diversion, and by no means the chief drama to be played in the theatre of war. But, as its object would be entirely consistent with, and favourable to, the development of Otho's main strategical plan for the beginning of the campaign, it would be entirely justifiable. The expeditionary force to be sent with the fleet must not, indeed, be so large that the main army on the Po would be too weak, owing to its absence, to fulfil the task of defence assigned to it. Nor, again, must it be so small that its intended menace could be contemptuously neglected by the enemy. Some expeditionary force must be sent, if the fleet were to be of any service at all. Thus when Napoleon's line of communications with France in his invasion of Italy in 1796 ran along the coast through Savona, the British fleet, although it "completely dominated the Mediterranean littoral," was quite unable to threaten these communications, since it had no force on board with which to strike a blow at them. The use of an army for such operations, conveyed by and based upon a fleet, however inferior in numbers this army may be to the enemy, is a vital element in the strategy of the command of the sea, although this principle seems hard to realise from the days of Pericles down to our own generation.

If then Otho could spare a few thousand men from the Army of

Italy to be carried on ship and disembarked at Fréjus or some other port on the coast of Provence—the "Province"—this might be a second useful means of delaying the advance and concentration of the enemy till such time as the Army of the Danube arrived at Mantua.

Then at last would come the time for offence, and Otho's united army could be sent against the enemy to hurl them back through a land long since exhausted by their stay in it; back against the grim barrier of the mountains which cut them off from safety—back with weakened strength and diminished numbers, to perish, starved and fighting, penned up against the Alpine wall. "Happy the soldier to whom fate assigns the part of assailant." Or perhaps Otho need not wait for the arrival of the entire Danube Army when once these were hard at hand. "The essential in war is not the massing of troops but their co-operation." (Von der Goltz)

"Envelopment, not mere weight of numbers, is the true secret of decisive success," (Henderson, *Science of War*). Some more daring plan of attack might suggest itself which promised speedier victory than the frontal attack by a united army. Could not the stubborn fighting, the many weary miles of marching which lay between the river and the mountains, the last desperate stand of despairing men,—could not all this be avoided by some masterpiece of manoeuvre and surprise?

But all such plans must for the present be delayed until the Danube army should arrive. Meanwhile one step was enough. Strategy cannot look to the horizon lest she stumble in the ditch at her feet." No plan of operations can with any safety include more than the first collision with the enemy's main force," (Von der Goltz). So for the time the Army of Italy should make resolute defence along the line of the Po, and the command of the sea should be used to assist it to delay the Vitellians' advance.

This strategy surely promised well. It had, however, two defects in chief. It failed to prevent ultimately the enemy's concentration in the plain of the Po, though delay might be caused by the fleet. And the strategy of defence, however temporary, might at any time impair the confidence and morale of the men of the army on the river, and especially so at a time of civil war, when all the troops were excited and impatient. For the game of war as played in the field is anything but the War-game of the drill hall. Would the Guards, the flower of the Roman army, consent to stand for some weeks on the defensive against a hated foe? If they obeyed such orders, would their military fire and zeal not be impaired? Such questions had to be considered by the emperor.

Yet he knew that his men were devoted to his cause. The strategy of defence on the river was the wisest for him, and Otho might well feel that he could rely upon his men for any manoeuvre—even that most dispiriting one of waiting to be attacked. Further than the Po he would not retreat. Not though the Apennines in spring are deep with snow, and their mountain tracks hazardous and well-nigh impassable,[19] would he fall back under cover of their shelter, and seek to lure the foe on to venture into their recesses or perhaps be ensnared between them and the sea. Retreat to the river was far enough. Beyond the river the one maxim laid down by our English general for an invaded country held good for Otho and his men: "No foot of ground ceded that was not marked with the blood of the enemy," (*Diary of Sir John Moore*).

B. Strategical Opportunities of the Vitellians.—

The Vitellians, on the other hand, enjoyed the advantage of being the attacking party, but very few advantages besides. The courage and confidence characteristic of good troops who move to the attack, and apt to be lacking in those kept on the defence, might certainly be theirs. Yet perhaps this would hardly do more for them than compensate for their original inferiority as troops of the line to the Guards. Clausewitz's familiar assertion that the defensive form of warfare is in its nature stronger than the offensive, causes very great searchings of heart to the strategists among his countrymen today. But if ever a strategical position were wanted to justify the assertion, that of the spring of *A.D.* 69 might seem to be the one desired. For then the Vitellian chances of prosperous attack seemed somewhat meagre compared with the Othonian of happy defence. The most obvious, perhaps the only possible, strategy for the invaders was a rapid descent over the mountains to the plain of the Po, and a frontal assault upon the position garrisoned by the Army of Italy.

Time was of the most vital importance to the Vitellians. They must hasten to move upon Italy in time to anticipate a possible blocking of the Alpine passes. They must hasten to fall upon the Army of Italy before the Army of the Danube had time to come to its aid. Only if they could crush the former force before the arrival of the latter in strength would they have the undoubted superiority henceforward in the strategy of the war, should the war continue. The movement

---
19. In April 1907 snow lay 10 to 20 feet deep in places on the Abetone Pass between Modena and Pistoia.

upon Italy in two columns by different passes was necessary. The column which, travelling by the nearer route, first arrived in Italy must, if strong enough, attack the enemy at once; if too weak, or beaten in its onset, it must wait for the coming of the second column to reinforce it. And the race between the reinforcements of both sides would in truth be an anxious one. Speed, concentration, and frontal attack seemed the sole means to the Vitellians of achieving success. And the strength of the defenders' position combined with the means open to them of delaying the assailants' approach might neutralise the advantage of numerical superiority enjoyed by the latter.

An alternative strategy to this of concentration and frontal attack might be considered. The "strategy of penetration" justly wields much fascination, and for modern war has all the support of Napoleon's favourite practice behind it. If the Vitellians could thrust boldly between the two fractions of Otho's gathering army, could they not defeat them in detail? The Brenner Pass in the north offered the easiest access to Italy of all the Alpine passes, and led straight down to the very centre of the hostile position. Could the Vitellian generals use the advantage of superior numbers which they enjoyed at the outset, and drive in a great wedge of their own men, penetrating the defenders' lines midway between Placentia and Aquileia? This alternative strategy deserved consideration by the Vitellians at the beginning of the campaign. But the reasons which caused Caecina to reject it were adequate. (See §4.)

Such were the strategical opportunities of both sides at the outset of the struggle. No campaign ever yet followed precisely the course marked out for it by the strategist. The weavers at the loom of war might think to have but a common and familiar pattern for their work. But the designer who cuts out the cards for them may have indulged a free fancy in the pattern which he gives them.

§4. The March of the Vitellians

Confident in his greater numbers, Vitellius issued orders for the immediate invasion of Italy. He divided his forces into three parts. Two of these were advance columns of invasion; the third was the reserve, to follow later in support.

The advance columns were ordered to penetrate into the valley of the Po by different Alpine passes, (for reasons see above). The first of these, the "Cologne Column" from Lower Germany, under Fabius Valens, was to march through Gaul and cross the Alps by the

Mont Genèvre Pass on the west of the mountains. This column was composed of the Fifth legion with its "eagle," and of detachments ("*vexilla*") of the First, Fifteenth, and Sixteenth legions, together with auxiliary squadrons ("*alae*"), and *cohorts* from "Germany." Its strength was reckoned as forty thousand troops. The second of the advance columns, the "Vindonissa Column," from Upper Germany, was commanded by Aulus Caecina Alienus. It consisted of the Twenty-First legion, detachments of the Fourth and Twenty-Second, and German auxiliaries, and amounted to thirty thousand men. This column was bidden enter Italy on the north-west by the Great St. Bernard Pass. The reserve, consisting of such other forces as could be raised in Germany and elsewhere, was to march under the personal command of Vitellius himself, advancing with such greater deliberation as befitted their general's ripe years, great importance, and unwieldy frame. And, in fact, the campaign was decided six weeks before he himself arrived upon the scene of the decisive battle.

A. The March of Valens[20]—
From its place of concentration on the Lower Rhine, in the neighbourhood of Cologne, Valens' column marched up that river as far as the modern Andernach, a little short of the point where, at Coblenz, the Moselle enters the Rhine. It was probably at Andernach that Valens left the main river and struck over the hills through the territory of the Treveri to the capital of that tribe, now Trèves, in the valley of the Moselle. Thence Valens led his troops to Metz, higher up the valley, and from Metz to Toul, the capital of the Leuci. At Toul the column left the Moselle, and crossed rolling country to the chief city of the tribe of the Lingones, now Langres, hard by the source of the Marne. Here it was joined by eight Batavian *cohorts*. These were properly associated as auxiliaries with the Fourteenth legion.

This legion had belonged to the Army of Britain, but had recently been transferred to Dalmatia. The eight *cohorts*, however, had refused on the march to follow it to its new province, and were sulkily making their way back to Britain when, at Langres, the news of Vitellius' rising reached them. Here then they waited events, until Valens on his arrival added them to his force. They proved but sorry allies. At once they quarrelled violently with his *legionaries*, and, in fact, gave the general endless trouble—not indeed because they had the least sympathy with the Othonian cause (as their actions subsequently showed), but

---

20. The "Battle of Bedriacum," April 15. Visit of Vitellius to the battleground, May 24.

through their native ferocity and impatience of discipline.[21]

The Aedui, into whose territory the army next entered, hastened to buy the goodwill of the soldiers by satisfying their hunger, as they conciliated Valens by satisfying his demands for money and arms. This tribe occupied the high land between the Rivers Saône and Loire, but the army passed through their borders only, following the road which runs from Langres through Dijon to Châlon-sur-Saône, and did not visit their chief city, on the site of the modern Autun, which lay away on the right flank. From Châlon they marched down the valley of the River Saône to its meeting with the Rhone at Lugdunum. Here the townsfolk welcomed them with open arms. Their grudge against Galba for his favour shown to their bitter rivals of Vienne was deep, and Otho had done nothing to appease it. The legions of Germany were their old comrades in arms against the rebel Gauls, and the citizens dreamed fondly that the day of their vengeance upon their enemies lower down the river had dawned at last. And, indeed, it had done so, had not the men of Vienne won safety by tears, entreaties, and gifts to gain the soldiers' pity, and by enormous bribes, it was said, to the general.

At Lugdunum Valens strengthened his force by the addition of the greater part of the garrison of that city, the First legion Italica and the *ala* Tauriana, and left only the Eighteenth *cohort* to guard the place. Then the army marched away downstream, passed peaceably through the streets of Vienne, between the river and the overhanging heights, and followed the left bank of the Rhone through the Allobroges' territory southwards by way of Valence as far as its tributary the Drôme. Thence the column pursued its slow and terrifying way up this stream, extorting money, by menaces and fire, from the little places through which it passed, and, when there was no money, appeasing its disappointment by gratifying its lust.

One hope only of speedy relief from the army's presence was left to the landowners and magistrates on the army's route. Valens' cupidity would sell even this relief for a price. Such profitable trafficking had long been known to Roman generals, and Valens, too, reaped his harvest of gain as he led his troops on their infamous march to Italy. In such wise the army marched by the modern little towns of Die and Luc-en-Diois on the Drôme to Briançon and, crossing the Alps by the Mont Genèvre Pass, came down the Doria Riparia valley by Susa to the Po at Augusta Taurinorum (Turin).

---

21. They subsequently did good service in Britain with Agricola: Tac *Agric*.

But the mountains were not the only difficulty which Valens had to surmount. At some point during the march from Vienne to the Po, and probably before the army had crossed the Alps, he had become conscious that the activity of the enemy's fleet on the coast at Fréjus threatened the security of his right flank, (see §5). Anxious to strengthen the Vitellian forces on the coast, he therefore detached a few of the unruly Batavian *cohorts* from his main army and sent them away to the rescue. Also they were turbulent boasters, and he was glad of the chance to be rid of them. But strategical needs above all dictated the general's orders. His other troops, however, discovered their departure, and resented it. Ignorant of the imperative strategical necessity of guarding their flank and their sole line of communications, they thought only of the strength of their own force, and clamoured that "so powerful a limb should not be torn from the body." They would, they declared, all proceed to the Province, or they would all march to Italy together, (see strategical aspect §3 above).

When Valens attempted to quell the growing disturbance, open mutiny broke out. The general fled in terror, and while he, clad in a slave's garb, lurked concealed in a subaltern's tent, the happy troops ransacked his quarters, searching vainly for the gold of Vienne. When the excitement died down, and anger gave place to repentance and shame, Valens pitifully presented himself again to his men. General and soldiers wept together in the joy of reconciliation, and a few rioters were punished by reprimand. And this is a Roman Army! Truly may the Roman historian remark that in times of civil war the soldiers' license exceeds that of the general.

So Valens led his repentant troops over the Alps to the Po, and down this river to Ticinum. Here at the beginning of April his army was engaged in fortifying a camp when the news reached them that their comrades of the Second Army were in a sore plight lower down the river, at Cremona. Already Caecina and his Vindonissa column had met the enemy and had been defeated. The news called for instant action. Valens broke up his camp and marched at full speed to join his colleague at Cremona. He arrived here in the second week of the month.

B. The March of Caecina.

The headquarters of Caecina and the Second Army were at Vindonissa. This camp was situated on the tongue of land which lies between the Rivers Reuss and Aare. A few miles to the north, the Aare flows into the Rhine between Schaffhausen to the east and Säckingen to the west. In the neighbourhood of the camp and to south and southwest of it lay the tribe of Helvetii, once the early and stalwart foes of Julius Caesar, but now a civilised folk, who supplied auxiliaries to the Roman Army, and had gained in culture what they had lost in pluck. Opportunities for plunder afforded by civil war were even more welcome to Caecina than they were to the more indolent Valens. The tribe and its belongings offered an easy prey to his disciplined troops, and a pretext for attack upon them was the more easily found as they were ignorant of Galba's death and refused to accept Vitellius.

It was Caecina's clear duty to his emperor to press on into Italy with all possible speed. Instead of this he let loose his army upon the unlucky natives, and sent bidding his friends, the procurator of Raetia and his auxiliary troops, to harry them from east and south while he himself descended upon them from the north. The task was as easy as it was profitable, and the miseries of the tribe were great. Their country was laid waste far and wide; their resistance was spiritless and availed them nothing. The hot medicinal springs of Baden on the River Limmat, some sixteen miles to the north-west of the town and lake of Zurich, from which lake the river flows, were already known at this time, and the place, under the title of Aquae Helvetiorum, had become a popular watering-place, frequented by the tribe. Caecina sacked and destroyed it. The Raetian auxiliaries swept down from Lake Constance upon the victims. The refugees from the general slaughter flung away their arms and fled to the hills of the Bötzberg (which form the extreme north-east end of the Jura range, and lie a few miles west of Windisch). They were driven out by a *cohort* of Thracian auxiliaries, and thousands more were butchered in the pursuit.

Caecina next marched upon the capital city of the tribe, Aventicum. This, the modern Avenches, lies hard by the lake of Morat, five miles to the east of the lake of Neuchâtel. Aventicum surrendered. The general allowed the townsfolk to appeal for mercy to Vitellius. They won pardon with difficulty, thanks to a sudden change of feeling towards them on part of Vitellius' army, which, of course, took upon itself to decide the matter. If the Roman legionary of the time could once be induced to weep, then there was hope of mercy at his hands. Streams of tears saved the remnant of the Helvetii from the extremes of Imperial vengeance. Later, Vespasian the emperor bestowed the *Jus Latinum* on the place in recompense for its sufferings at the hands of his enemies, and under the proud title of Colonia Pia Flavia Constans

Emerita Helvetiorum the town might perhaps forget its earlier woes.

While Caecina stayed dallying at Aventicum, news reached him from Italy which called for prompt action on his part. At the outbreak of the war, as has been said, Otho's only troops actually in the valley of the Po were one squadron of auxiliary horse, the *ala* Siliana. But this same *ala* had chanced to be quartered in Africa eight years before, at the time when Vitellius administered the affairs of that province. Its officers therefore succeeded in persuading the men to throw in their lot with their old governor, and the more easily as the numbers and valour of the Army of Germany inspired the regiment with much awe.

It therefore at this point revolted from Otho, and brought over with it to the Vitellian side the four strongest towns of the Transpadane district in North-west Italy, which lay north of the Po. If these four towns, Mediolanum (Milan), Novaria (Novara), Vercellae (Vercelli), and Eporedia (Ivrea), once fell into the hands of the enemy, the Othonians had no choice but to limit their attempts at defence to the line of the river itself. This was the news which reached Caecina at Aventicum. The whole of North-west Italy, with its garrison towns commanding the issues of the Great St. Bernard Pass, was offered to him.

By this pass he had been ordered to enter Italy. But the one little regiment of horse could not hold the tract for long in face of the enemy moving up from the south. Caecina therefore, without more delay, hurried strong reinforcements over the Alps to its help. These consisted of Gallic, Lusitanian, and British auxiliary *cohorts*, detachments ("*vexilla*") of German troops, and another squadron of cavalry, the *ala* Petriana. For the moment, these troops on arrival might well hold in check any attempt by the enemy to cross the Po in force. And then Caecina had to set himself anxiously to consider what his main plan of campaign should now be.

To carry out Vitellius' orders, it was right for him to follow with the rest of his army over the Great St. Bernard, in the wake of his advance guard, as speedily as possible. But the idea of an alternative and more daring strategy was first at least to be considered.

This was the "strategy of penetration." If Caecina could cross the Alps farther to the east he could perhaps thrust his force between the two parts of the Othonian defending army upon the Po. For this purpose the Brenner Pass, by which the great road from Innsbruck crosses the Alps to Verona, was most suitable. It was by far the easiest, the lowest, and the best known of all the Alpine passes. If Caecina came down upon Verona by this route he might hope to cut completely the communications of the Danube army at Aquileia with the Army of Italy upon the river, by penetrating between them. If Valens, then, approached from the west, and if the mobilisation of the Danube legions at Aquileia proceeded slowly, surely the Army of Italy would be caught in the middle and annihilated with ease.

The plan was a tempting one, but very daring. There was always the chance that the penetrating army would find the tables turned and itself be surrounded. If the movements of the Danube Army should be quicker than those of Valens' column, Caecina at Verona or Mantua might find himself very uncomfortably placed, especially if he found any large part of the Army of Italy blocking the way on the Adige at Verona. Valens, too, had already started on his march through Gaul. Even if Caecina sent him an urgent message to hurry, he would not improbably disregard it entirely.

But geographical obstacles proved finally fatal to the plan. The road from Innsbruck to Verona over the Brenner was indeed an easy one. The top of the pass is under 4500 feet in height. But it was by no means such an easy matter to get from the north of Switzerland, where Caecina then was, to the valley of the Inn over the "Raetian heights." For this purpose he would have to march by Lake Constance to the valley of the Ill River at Feldkirch and then cross the mountains to Innsbruck by the Arlberg Pass. This pass is nearly 6000 feet in height. In April 1906 it was deep in snow for several miles on either side of the top, and could be crossed only on snow-shoes. In February *A.D.* 69 it was not likely to have been less difficult of passage by an army. (See note following) That Caecina did consider the plan is shown by the action of the procurator of Noricum, Petronius Urbicus, who was ranged upon the enemy's side. Some fifty miles east of Innsbruck down the Inn River lay the frontier of his province. The procurator, who, like his fellow-procurator of Raetia, had only auxiliary troops at his disposal, promptly destroyed all the bridges over the river, trusting to that fiercely-rushing stream to save him from attack if Caecina came that way.

★★★★★★

Note:—That *"Raeticis jugis"* means the Arlberg Pass is surely beyond doubt. The suggested alternative is that of the Stelvio (or Umbrail) Pass, which leads from Nauders in the Engadine to Bormio and Tirano, and so to Como or to the Val Camonica and Iseo. To reach this pass on the Tyrolese side Caecina's route would have lain by Ragatz, and the Flüela and Ofen Passes first. The heights of the passes are as follows: Arlberg, about 5900 feet; Stelvio, 9000; Flüela, 7835; Ofen, 7070. It seems at least uncertain whether tracks existed over these last three passes in Roman days. However this may be, Caecina could hardly have contemplated coming this way in February. The difficulties of the Arlberg would be as nothing to those of the Stelvio; the latter pass would have been no service to him against the Othonian position. Even had he diverged east from Tirano he would have come down on Iseo, Brescia, and Cremona. These places were much more easily reached from Neuchâtel by the Great St. Bernard. And the Stelvio could not possibly have excited the attention of the procurator of Noricum. Hence my choice of the Arlberg-Brenner combination. I owe thanks to Mr. R. L. Poole for calling my attention to the proposed alternative.

Of course the Great St. Bernard—height 8110 feet—was hard enough to cross, as Napoleon found it in May 1800. But the Stelvio would be much worse. And the Roman column would not march with artillery.

★★★★★★

As a matter of fact, if Caecina had crossed the Arlberg it was not Noricum, with its petty force and unimportant governor, which would have been in his thoughts, but rather the Brenner Pass and Italy; and the procurator had in any case alarmed himself needlessly. Had Caecina come that way, Petronius Urbicus should indeed have made vigorous demonstrations on the flank of the enemy's column at Innsbruck, with intent to delay its passage over the Brenner. Instead of this he was preparing to stand stoutly on the defensive. It is a well-known fact of military history that "all local commanders are firmly convinced always that it is upon them that the brunt of the fighting is destined to fall," (Sir Ian Hamilton, *A Staff-Officer's Scrap-Book,* vol. i."

Petronius Urbicus saw that the pass over the "Raetian heights" led the enemy to the Inn, and concluded that Caecina, if he came that way, meant to attack him. For Petronius, in an anxious position and with a small handful of troops, there was much excuse. But there is little excuse for the strategical blindness of the Roman historian Tacitus, who complacently reproduces the tale that Caecina hesitated whether to attack Noricum or Italy, and finally preferred Italy as being more important.

Such a question could need no deliberation at all. Italy was from first to last Caecina's objective. The very important problem for his decision was that of the pass by which he should deliver his attack on Italy. Petronius Urbicus might easily fail to recognise this. Tacitus has no right to be so blind. (See Note E, "Tacitus as Military Historian.")

Caecina therefore gave up the plan of strategical penetration of the enemy's position. Apart from the military risks which it involved, the delay which the snows of winter would have caused compelled him to abandon it. Probably it was with reluctance that he rejected it; for a few weeks later he strove, on the Po, to pursue this same device of piercing the enemy's lines, though on the later occasion his attempt was one of tactical rather than strategical penetration. (See §7.)

He therefore now resumed his march for Italy by the direct route, carrying out the original orders which Vitellius had given him. From Aventicum he followed in the steps of his advance guard to the head of Lake Geneva, and up the Rhone valley to Martigny. Thence by the Great St. Bernard Pass he crossed the "Pennine Alps" to Aosta, and proceeded down the valley of the Dora Baltea to Eporedia. By the second week in March, a month before Valens' column entered Italy, Caecina had crossed the Alps, and was in touch with the enemy's outposts in the valley of the Po.

§5. The Othonian Measures of Defence

Meanwhile the Emperor Otho was busy arranging for the defence of Italy against the invader. His preliminary measures of defence were two in number. In the first place, he sent part of his force of Guards on board the fleet to Narbonese Gaul, to threaten the flank of Valens' invading column, and at least delay, if they could not interrupt, its march. Secondly, a strong advance guard, under the two generals Annius Gallus and Vestricius Spurinna, was ordered to leave Rome at once for the north. This force consisted of five Praetorian *cohorts*, the First Adjutrix legion, two thousand gladiators, and some detachments of cavalry. It was their duty to secure the line of the Po. As soon as the treachery of the *ala* Siliana was known, it was clearly impossible to hope to hold the country west and north of Placentia, or to attempt to prevent the muster of the Vitellians north of the river. Spurinna therefore, with part of the troops, threw himself into Placentia to block the passage of the river at that fortress, and therewith the great road to the south. Gallus, for his part, moved with the rest of the advance guard to secure the communications with the Danube Army then collecting at Aquileia. This he would best do by crossing the river at Hostilia and moving forward to a position in the neighbourhood of Mantua, which covered that crossing and the road to the east.[22]

To Otho himself at Rome there was still left a considerable number of excellent troops in fighting trim and eager for the fray. He left the city, at the head of these, for the theatre of war in North Italy on March 14. He was accompanied by a large general staff, including the most renowned general of the day, Suetonius Paulinus. In his train came many unhappy senators, reluctantly and of gentle compulsion. These were left behind at Mutina when the army moved forward to the front. Their panics and distresses, their discomforts and perils, their shifts and evasions, form a somewhat humorous relief to what henceforward is but a grim and sombre story.

These military dispositions were sound. The best defensive position was thereby occupied. Means for delaying the muster of the enemy were employed. And, above all, the communications of the army on the Po with that of the Danube provinces were secured. The superstitious and silly folk in the capital criticised gloomily the emperor's speedy departure from Rome. It was the month of the dancings of the sacred priesthood, the *Salii*, and the *Ancilia*, the twelve famous shields, could not be restored to their resting-place in Mars' *Sacrarium* until the month was ended. Surely, they urged, Otho ought to wait in Rome for the sixteen days, until such time as the *Salii* had finished their dancings and the sacred shields were restored to their shrine. The very gods seemed to desire this. Fearsome omens were recorded, and Mars' plain was flooded deep by one of those terrible inundations which the Tiber from time to time inflicts on the city up to this day.[23] No muster or review of the Imperial Army could be held on the Campus Martius, and the Via Flaminia, the great high-road to the north, which, after leaving the city gate, ran parallel to and not far from the river, was blocked for some distance.

But such scruples and hindrances could not delay Otho. The emperor was a soldier, and was well aware of the supreme importance

---

22. Tacitus does not tell us anything of Gallus' movements when he separates from Spurinna. But as when Gallus next appears he is marching from the east on Placentia, the statement in the text is the probable inference, especially as some of the Danube Army is then with him. Cf. Tac 11.

23. The Campos Martius, lying on the river bonk, is peculiarly liable to these floods. The tablets recording the height of the river at such times, *e.g.*, in the Piazza of the Pantheon, are familiar to visitors to Rome. In some cases they are as high or higher than the reader's head.

of time in operations of war. Caecina, he knew, had already crossed the Alps. Delay had proved fatal to Nero; it should not imperil him. By the earliest date which his final preparations allowed, the 14th of March, he led his troops out from Rome. The jumping priests must jump for a fortnight without him. They will jump all the more merrily next year if he comes back in triumph. "*Deorum injurias dis curae.*" Otho will trust rather to the devotion of his soldiers than to divine patronage. Armed with *cuirass* of iron the emperor marched on foot in front of the standards, rough in dress and look, and careless of comfort. This was not the Otho whom men had known in former days. It was a soldier emperor marching to defend his empery.

Yet, excellent though these measures of defence were, the course of events, as they developed, discovered three flaws in them. The force sent on shipboard acted too feebly; the Army of the Danube gathered together too slowly; and Cremona fell into the hands of the foe.

(1) The Action of the Fleets—Otho entrusted the command of the naval expedition to three men. Their incapacity was equalled only by their insignificance. Otho lacked entirely that admirable faculty of being able to choose men, which his predecessor Nero had possessed in marked measure. It was this lack which ruined him. Of the three commanders of the fleet, one was put in irons by his troops; the second was unable to control them; the third to control himself. There was no discipline, and the fleet sailed up the north-west coast of Italy like a pirate fleet, ravaging and murdering. One of the victims was the mother of Agricola; and the Roman historian, who found in this general the hero of his youth, writes bitterly of the ferocity shown by the Othonian troops who were sent on this expedition:—

> It seemed they entred not into Italie, their owne native countrey and soile: as if it had bene forraine coasts and cities of enemies, they burned, wasted, and spoiled, with so much the more outrage and harme because no such invasion was feared, and therefore nothing provided against it: the fields lay full of commodities; the houses wide open; the masters meeting them with their wives and children, through the security of peace, were overtaken with the misery of warre.[24]

---

24. This and the following quotation are from Sir H. Savile's translation of the *Histories, A.D.* 1591. This cannot always be trusted for accuracy, but it deserves to be remembered, and that not only by Mertonians, if for no other reason yet at least for its splendid address "To the Reader."

The hill men who came down to the rescue were easily routed and dispersed by the regular troops, who proceeded in their wrath to sack the town of Intimilium, now Ventimiglia, the Riviera town on the frontier between France and Italy.[25]

> The pezants were beggerly, their armour not worth taking up; and beside, being swift of foote and skilfull in the countrey, they could not be taken: but the sacke of the poore innocent towne paied the reckening, and contented the covetous soldier. The odiousnesse of which fact was greatly increased by a notable example which happened there of a Ligurian woman: who having hid her sonne, the soldiers supposing she had hid her money withall, and thereupon by torture examining hir, where she had hid him, shewing hir belly answered that there he was hid: neyther could she by any manner of torment afterwarde, or death at the length, be induced to change that worthy answere.

While the fleet was thus pleasantly occupied, a messenger rode off in hot haste to Valens imploring help. That general saw at once the danger which, if the plunderers were not checked, threatened not only the coast of the Maritime Alps and the Province, but also his own march to Italy. He therefore sent at once a strong force, mainly of cavalry, including the *ala* Treverorum. This last squadron was under command of a man soon to become only too well known to the Romans, but then merely a subordinate officer of auxiliaries in the Army of Germany. But this man, Julius Classicus, was a great noble in his clan, and one of the leaders in the near future of the rebellion on the Rhine, (see chapter 3). Of this force, part was ordered by Valens to strengthen the garrison of Forum Julii (Fréjus) against the risk of attack. The rest joined the local troops collected for purposes of defence, and marched against the enemy. These they seemed to have found in the neighbourhood.

The brief campaign which followed was, though indecisive in results, not without its interest. It served to illustrate the superiority of the Guards as soldiers over the Vitellian auxiliary troops, and supplied another example of the use which may be made of a fleet during a tactical engagement upon the coast, whereby men can be landed from it ashore on the rear of the enemy's battle line, thus recalling the device employed by Pompey in old days at Dyrrhachium. The

---

25. There is no doubt that Intimilium, not Albintimilium, is the right form.

tide of success in the fighting ebbed and flowed, but on the whole the Othonians had the better of it, and Valens had to send off more reinforcements to the scene of war, (see §4). But at the end both sides withdrew their forces at such a distance from one another that neither the cavalry of the one side nor the fleet of the other could cause any sudden alarm. The Vitellians retired to the low promontory of Antibes; the Othonians to Albingaunum, now the many-towered little city of Albenga, which lies in the small swampy plain of the Centa, sixty-five miles east of Antibes.

At Albenga there is one of the few pieces of open shore of any extent along the whole rocky coast of the Riviera, from Savona to Cannes, and the ships could here be beached. But it was unnecessary to retire so far eastwards for the purpose, as the small harbour of Porto Maurizio would have given excellent shelter to the fleet, and have been more in touch with the enemy. The fact was that both sides had by tacit consent ceased from all warlike activity, and the short maritime campaign was ended. Sardinia and Corsica were, it is true, secured for Otho, but peace henceforward reigned on the coast of Provence.

If these tentative and half-hearted operations of the fleet and the force which it carried are to be viewed merely as an isolated episode in the history of the war (and it is in this light that the Roman historian Tacitus regards them), Otho is convicted of a strategical blunder in commanding them to take place. For thereby he weakened his numbers, already inferior to those of the enemy, by detaching a force for the purpose of a minor operation of war when his whole energies should have been concentrated on the main issue, the defence of North Italy Otho's order would, in this case, be but an example the more of that familiar failing in generalship, for which the dispassionate German critic blames our own commanders in the Boer war.[26] To plunder a town or two on the Riviera, to secure Corsica and Sardinia, to worry the local forces of the enemy,—these were petty successes which counted for nothing in the general course of the war.[27] Whereas the loss of strength which these successes inflicted upon Otho's main army counted for a good deal.

---

26. "The mania of the British leaders for detaching troops for minor operations, whereby they weakened themselves prior to a crisis, often had disastrous results, and might easily have led to a catastrophe at Driefontein also" (*German Official History of the Boer War*, ii). At Driefontein we were compelled to throw all our scanty reserves into the line of battle to carry the position in one last effort.

27. Tacitus himself rightly comments on the small importance of Corsica in this connection,.

But this view of the matter is short-sighted, and based rather on the actual results of the campaign on the coast than on the intentions of the emperor when he sent the fleet. Otho did not intend to use the command of the sea merely to secure such secondary objects. The fleet's activity was meant to harass Valens, to weaken his army, to delay its march. The operations of the fleet were therefore intimately connected with the concentration of the Army of the Danube at Aquileia, and were part of the whole well-designed strategical plan. To a certain extent Otho's hopes were realised. Twice Valens had to detach troops from his column and send them to the coast. And the disturbance caused in his army on one of these occasions, which has been narrated,[28] was a greater success for Otho than he could reasonably have anticipated. It would indeed have been a curious freak on the part of the Genius of War had the command of the sea in this year by the foe cost Valens his life, thanks to the mutinous spirit of his troops. In this event Caecina would in all likelihood have been crushed, and Valens' leaderless column have recoiled on Gaul.

Such events were not to happen, nor could Otho have expected them. But that the action of his fleet did not bring him at least a greater measure of success than it did was due, not to the emperor's strategy, but to his officers' misuse of their chances. Had these, after their victory over the Vitellians on the coast, dared to push up country in the direction of Briançon instead of weakly retiring to Albenga, Valens' whole march over the Alps might have been arrested for at least some days, if not weeks. This delay might well have resulted, as events showed, in the entire destruction of Caecinas column at Cremona. For only Valens' arrival saved his colleague. The Othonian force marching on Briançon could probably have retreated in safety to its base the fleet, had Valens, as might then be hoped, turned savagely upon it with his whole army.

Even had it been cut off and perished, it would by its defeat have won victory for its emperor in the main campaign. In this way failure sometimes spells triumph in the lesson-book of war. In this way Sir John Moore, in like manner trusting to the fleet at Corunna for his base, splendidly hurled his little column at Napoleon's line of communications in North Spain and saved the Peninsula. But Otho's officers lacked either the pluck or the insight of such a general. It may be that they distrusted the uncertain character of their initial success; it may be that they dared not run the great risk involved. It is probable

---

28. See §4.

that they were quarrelling among themselves. Whatever the reason, the fleet and the force on board of it missed their chances, and Otho's position of defence was greatly weakened thereby.

(2) The Mobilisation of the Danube Army.—A second and more damaging flaw in Otho's armour of defence was the fact that the Army of the Danube was concentrating at Aquileia far too slowly. The four legions of Pannonia and Dalmatia were the nearest to the scene of the coming struggle. To some extent they realised the importance of speed, and, since they themselves were not yet ready to march as whole units, each sent forward a special detachment (*"vexillum"*) of its men in front of it. These detachments were each two thousand strong. But even of these only one arrived in time to take part in the first battle in the field, that of Locus Castorum on April 6. Behind this solitary detachment were the three similar ones; behind these the bulk of their legions; and farthest from the theatre of war were the Moesian legions, slowly assembling. This slackness on the part of the Danube Army, says the Roman historian, was due to over confidence: "*E fiducia tarditas inerat.*" Yet it was a time when every day that passed before that army came in strength might spell ruin to their cause and to their emperor. There is no excuse for their deliberation in movement or for their confidence.[29]

(3) The Loss of Italy north of the Po, including Cremona.—Finally, the speed of Caecina's advance guard had already cost Otho dear. When Spurinna arrived at Placentia, he found that a *cohors* Pannoniorum of the Army of Defence had already been captured at Cremona, and this strongly-walled city fell into the enemy's hands about the same time. "All the fields and cities between the Po and the Alps were held by the Vitellian forces." The loss of Cremona, though unavoidable, was a serious disaster. This city lies on the north bank of the Po, some twenty-five miles from Piacenza to the west,[30] and forty from Mantua on the east. It had originally been built three centuries before as a Roman outpost north of the river to keep the Gallic tribes in check, and it was still strongly fortified. There does not seem to have been any bridge in A.D. 69 at the city over the river.

Today there is a bridge over the Po of enormous structure and great length, separated from the city gate by a mile of weary road. But Cremona in A.D. 69 possessed no "bridgehead" on the southern

---

29. See Note A, "The Movements of the Danube Legions" at end of chapter.
30. By road *via* Codogno on the left bonk; in a bee-line, 16 miles only.

bank of the Po, which would have put a force holding the town in a position to turn the flank of the garrison of Placentia, and render the holding of that fortress useless. Yet its seizure by Caecina gave the Vitellian general a strong base of operations for movements of offence against the Othonian line of defence, a place of refuge in the event of defeat or the advance of the enemy in force, and a safe resting-place in which he could await the arrival of his colleague, Valens. Its loss, therefore, to Otho was serious. It was only the emperor's strategical brilliance which later all but turned this loss to positive gain, and made the fortress not Caecina's harbour of refuge but a prison-house for him and his army.[31]

In these three respects, therefore, Otho's position at the beginning of the "tactical chapter" in the history of the campaign was not so favourable as it would have been had his generals been abler men. He himself had made no mistake in his measures of defence. But the force on shipboard had not done its duty; the legions of the Danube army were sluggish; and all the north bank of the Po from Alps to Cremona had fallen at once into the enemy's hands. But if, so far. Fortune had been unkind to the emperor, yet his main line of defence south of the river was stoutly held, and Fortune never yet showered all her favours on one side only in any war. And now at last the armies were in touch. Spurinna at Placentia, Gallus at Mantua, held the two ends of the defensive position. They had to expect that the enemy would seek to break through, and that immediately.

§6. The First Encounters

When Spurinna reached Placentia he found the enemy hard at hand. An outpost force of his own troops, numbering eleven hundred men, was cut off by them between the fortress and Ticinum, the present town of Pavia. His patrols also speedily came into touch with their skirmishers and were roughly handled by them. Their Batavian and German auxiliaries, excited by success and by the sight of a great river again after their many weary miles of mountain roads, adepts as they were at the means of crossing such an obstacle, swarmed across the Po higher up stream and bore down on Spurinna's lines. The general, however, was convinced, as was indeed the case, that Caecina himself and his *legionary* army had not yet arrived. It was his obvious policy to make a reconnaissance in force westwards along the river bank to

---

31. See §7, also see Note B, "The Capture of Cremona by the Vitellians" at the end of the chapter.

discover, if he could, the strength and intentions of the enemy.[32]

With this intent he marched out from Placentia over the Po a day's march, and when night fell fortified his position by the river.[33] He had not met with any opposition, and to advance farther along the stream next day was not prudent. He therefore left patrols along the river bank and withdrew to the fortress. His reconnaissance had been fruitless of results, and his troops were well content to be back again in shelter.

Shortly afterwards Caecina himself with his main army arrived outside the fortress. His march through the plain of North Italy had been a rapid one, and he had kept his men well in hand, not allowing them to plunder the towns through which they passed. Caecina, in fact, had "left his cruelty and profligacy on the other side of the Alps." In presence of the enemy, other and more soldierly qualities had to take the place of these. The citizens of those towns were reduced to grumbling at the general's "barbarian costume," disliking the trousers which he wore, and at his wife Salonina's gallant display on horseback in a purple robe. They were happy that they had no other cause for grumbling than a man's novel taste in dress and a woman's usual love of show and finery. Caecina therefore had no reason to dread any rising in his rear when he crossed the Po above Placentia and marched downstream upon the town.

It was indeed imperative for him to seek to take that fortress. If he neglected it and passed it by, it threatened his one line of communications with Valens' column. Of this general's approach there was as yet no sign, and Caecina must keep the road open at least on the north of the river as far as Cremona, a town now held by his troops. It was

---

32. Tacitus asserts that he was compelled to march out against his own wishes by his insubordinate troops, who realised their folly next day. This seems to me a silly story, told later in the camp, where generals' actions are always pulled to pieces.
33. "*In conspectu Padus*". These words greatly trouble the German editors. Heraeus, *e.g.*, proposes "*e conspectu Padus*," on the ground that, as Placentia lay on the river and as Spurinna crossed it, he must have led his men north, and have been "out of sight of the river," therefore, when he halted them. If Oxford were threatened by an enemy who lay in the direction of Reading, the commander of the Oxford garrison would surely conduct his reconnaissance and feel his way along the Thames, choosing for his night's camp a position at Abingdon. *Would* he strike for the Ridge Way at, *e.g.*, Wantage? Classen proposes "*in conspectu hostis*." *Would* Spurinna be likely to choose such a position for his camp? In the first place, it would have been foolish. In the second place, during his reconnaissance he did not come into touch with the enemy at all. The words "*in conspectu Padus*" present no difficulty at all, from a military point of view. The river would be an additional protection to the camp.

doubtless very expedient to win an early success.[34] It was an attractive method of attack upon the foe's line of defence to assault the extreme flank of it and seek to "roll it up" from west to east. But, above all, it was necessary for him to guard his own communications north of the river from the constant menace of interruption by a sally over the bridge from Placentia, if that fortress remained in possession of the enemy's garrison. Caecina was bound to get possession of it at once if possible.

Negotiations were opened between the two sides, but resulted in nothing save mutual revilings. It was indeed "easier to blame than to praise" the characters of Otho and Vitellius. Caecina therefore wasted little time on words, but for two days delivered a vigorous assault on the fortress. This was stubbornly and successfully resisted by the garrison, and the Vitellians sullenly admitted their first reverse. The first wave of attack spent its fury in vain and retreated.[35] Caecina drew off his defeated army and marched for Cremona, into which town he threw himself. His strategical position was one already of some risk. To the west lay his imperilled line of communications and, if necessary, retreat. In front of him, in the centre of the Othonian line of defence, was a small but active and annoying body of gladiators, under Martius Macer, who made stinging raids over the river—a little hornets' nest which it was hard to reach. And on the east a third enemy speedily appeared.

For Gallus at Mantua, on hearing of the assault on Placentia, had moved forward towards the west, to relieve the pressure on the fortress, the importance of which he well knew. While on the road, north of the river, he received news from Spurinna that Caecina had raised the siege and drawn off his troops. Gallus therefore halted his army and promptly fortified his position. He was then at a village hitherto unknown to history, but henceforward to be doubly famous in the annals of war—the village of Bedriacum.

The broad, dusty Italian high-road which runs today through the great plain of the Po westwards from Mantua, after crossing the Oglio, one of the larger tributaries of the main river, some fifteen miles from the city, passes by two small towns named Bozzolo and Piadena on its way to Cremona. Midway between these towns, which are nine kilometres apart, and a quarter of a mile north of the road, there lies a tiny

---

34. This is the one and only motive ascribed to Caecina by Tacitus! It is by far the weakest of the three.
35. Siege of Placentia at length in Tacitus, ii.

hamlet, consisting of a church and a cluster of small houses nestling together under its spire. This hamlet is named Calvatone. It is as peacefully remote from the dust and traffic of the highway as any Cotswold village which just escapes the great Bath road. But here at Calvatone in Roman days two great roads met—that from Hostilia at the crossing of the Po to the south, and that from Mantua, both making for Cremona. The village where they joined was named Bedriacum. As a military post, when war swept over the plain, it was both important and easily defensible. A force entrenched here covered both the line of communications with Aquileia and the east, and also the crossing of the river by the road which led to the great highway to Ariminum and Rome.

A short distance to the north of it there flowed the river Oglio, a broad muddy stream with steep high bank on the southern side, not easy to cross, whose rapid and broad current turns two long rows of water-mills today, not unlike those on the Danube. There might have been one danger to Gallus when he encamped his legions here—the fear lest the foe should come down into Italy by the Brenner Pass and so cut him off from the Danube Army. But by this time it was known that Caecina had not chosen this way, and there were no enemy in the pass.[36]

At Bedriacum, therefore, Gallus halted his troops. And here he was soon afterwards joined by the main Army of Italy under its generals Suetonius Paulinus and Marius Celsus. A most welcome detachment also of two thousand men from the Thirteenth legion of Pannonia marched into camp, seeming an earnest of the rest of the Army of the Danube to come, and with them came six auxiliary *cohorts* and one cavalry squadron belonging to this army. Caecina and his troops were still at Cremona, a few miles down the broad white road, alone. There was no news of Valens' column. And the garrison at Placentia kept grim watch upon his line of retreat.

But the Vitellian general was not down-hearted. Always in war the force which attacks is likely to fight better than that which is attacked. Caecina s army was a strong one—stronger in numbers almost certainly than the full muster of Otho's men at Bedriacum. He resolved at once to take the offensive, lest delay should bring the Danube army upon the scene. Purely frontal attacks, however, were hazardous and costly. He planned to lure the Othonians into a snare and so destroy their army.

---

36. See Note C, "The Site of Bedriacum" at end of chapter.

Some twelve Roman miles east of Cremona, (about 10½ English miles), the Postumian way (which as a great Roman military road was raised up high above the level of the rich, damp, cultivated land on either side of it) ran for a short distance through woods on both sides. On emerging from the trees it passed through vineyards. These Italian vineyards of the north are not the forest of short upright stakes, such as those which line and disfigure the banks of the Rhine and the Moselle, but in North Italy the vine stems are linked from fruit-tree to fruit-tree in long drooping and graceful festoons, while the rich earth in April supplies enough nourishment also to cover the ground under the vines and under the fruit-trees with a green carpet of corn. It is indeed hard to make one's way through the fields by Cremona save where road or track is cut through the vineyards.

Here, just where the road left the cover of the trees, Caecina placed an ambush, at a place called Locus Castorum, ten miles away from the camp at Bedriacum. Some auxiliary infantry were hidden in the woods on either side of the way. The cavalry were ordered to ride forward towards the enemy and provoke them to attack. Then they were to fall back along the road in feigned retreat, drawing the Othonians in pursuit after them through the wood, when the infantry would sally out from the trees and have them at their mercy on either flank.

It was not a very brilliant plan, and Caecina might have foreseen that, in a time of civil war, it would be promptly betrayed to the other side. Moreover, he managed the ordering of his troops clumsily enough. No Roman general, except Julius Caesar, seems ever to have been a master of ambushes and surprises. In this case the biter was bit. Otho's generals, Suetonius and Celsus, were duly told the whole of Caecina's plan, and took their measures accordingly. They marched out from camp, three Praetorian *cohorts* in column on the road: on the right flank the First legion, two auxiliary *cohorts* of foot, and five hundred cavalry; on the left flank the two thousand *legionaries* of the Thirteenth legion, four auxiliary *cohorts* of foot, and five hundred cavalry.

These cavalry formed the extreme wing on either side, and finally one thousand other cavalry formed the rear-guard, keeping open the communications with the camp at Bedriacum, ready, in case of retreat, to open out and let the infantry through, and cover their retirement. In this order the Othonians moved out to meet the foe. Presently the Vitellian cavalry came in sight, charging along the road. At this Suetonius halted his infantry, throwing forward slightly his auxiliary foot on either side of the road; the cavalry under Celsus slowly trotted forward as if to receive the charge of the enemy's horse. These, obedient to orders, promptly began to retire. But then Celsus for his part halted his men. At this unexpected turn of events the Vitellian infantry in the wood seem to have lost patience; for they rose from their ambush, and pouring tumultuously out upon the road came charging down upon Celsus, with their own cavalry, it may be, thrust forward in their van like the foam of a wave.

Nothing could have suited Celsus better. Quietly withdrawing his men, when he came into touch with his infantry, he passed through their ranks, which opened out to allow this, and the pursuing Vitellians suddenly found themselves trapped in the middle of the enemy's foot. The Guards faced them in the front; the auxiliaries threatened them on the flanks; and Celsus with his thousand horse, who had led them into the snare, now emerged again from behind his infantry and threatened to fall upon them on the rear. It was, in fact, very nearly a second Cannae. For it was by this same device that Hannibal long years ago had caught and massacred the Romans.

But Suetonius Paulinus was no Hannibal, and all became confusion. While he was hesitating and troubling himself about ditches and extensions to the flank, as if it were drill upon a field day, not a grim *mêlée* on the field of battle, the Vitellians slipped away from the closing circle into the comfortable shelter of the friendly vineyards. When however they, with greater daring than prudence, reappeared from cover, the Othonians charged at last, and Caecina's men were driven in rout off the field. Nor was their plight in any way redressed by their general; for he had hurriedly sent to Cremona for reinforcements, and these came hastening down the road in small detachments, only to be involved in the general rout and to make confusion worse confounded. The battle on the road became a nightmare of disorder, until Suetonius checked the pursuit and recalled his men. The discomfited Vitellians, grateful for the respite, ignominiously made good their escape to Cremona. They were sated with ambushes for the future. They were the smaller of the two Vitellian armies. Where, they disconsolately asked, were Valens and his larger force? Were they themselves, a "mere handful" in comparison, to bear the whole brunt of the fighting?[37]

---

37. Tacitus's account of the Battle of Locus Castorum is in itself a historical nightmare. The account in the text is an attempt to make sense out of it. But, even so, infantry and cavalry must have been horribly mixed up together. A Roman road is not a Salisbury Plain.

In reviewing the story of this extraordinary battle, the reader must see that both Suetonius and Caecina may be blamed too easily. There were, it is true, bad mistakes made on both sides. Caecina's ambush was a clumsy affair; he could not keep his troops in hand, and when the battle took an unexpected course and went against him, he lost his head completely. To hurry reinforcements in driblets into the firing line when it is yielding is a not uncommon device of inferior generals, and is always worse than useless. But in his general idea of attacking the Othonians at Bedriacum promptly before the Danube Army had arrived to their succour Caecina was absolutely right. The Roman historian blames him for attacking "more hurriedly than wisely," and ascribes his haste to a mere jealous fear lest, if he waited, Valens should acquire all the renown for the war. Tacitus has a genius for misunderstanding the essentials of a military situation. It might so easily have happened that the Danube Army outstripped Valens in its coming. Caecina's was a sound strategical plan spoilt by faulty tactical execution.

In like manner, Suetonius (who displayed no small tactical skill) was over-cautious on the field of battle, and let slip a good opportunity for crushing the enemy. The vigour which he had once shown in the black days of the rebellion in Britain seemed to have deserted him. In battle, something must be risked or nothing will be achieved. But that he was thoroughly justified in calling his men off from the pursuit can hardly be doubted, although men blamed him for this at the time, and his reputation has suffered for this ever since. Had he allowed the pursuit to continue, his critics urged, the Vitellian army must have been annihilated. The result in reality would have been very different. Caecina's force must have outnumbered his own in a proportion of three to two. The fighting had taken place some ten miles from his base camp at Bedriacum. The pursuit, if allowed, would have followed yet another ten miles up to the walls of Cremona. There it would have been stopped abruptly by Caecina's entrenchments; and Suetonius' straggling, exhausted, tired troops would at once have been exposed to a counter-stroke of the rudest and most effective kind. In refusing to permit his men to incur this risk, Otho's general displayed a sound common sense which is lacking in the critics of his generalship.[38]

§7. The Strategies of the Final Struggle

A. The Vitellian "Strategy of Penetration"—

By the time that Caecina had fought and lost the Battle of Locus

---

[38] Even Tacitus seems to approve and understand Suetonius's caution.

Castorum, Valens had at last crossed the Alps and arrived at Ticinum. When the news of the defeat reached him he acted promptly, and marched at once to Cremona, where he joined forces with his colleague. At last the Army of Germany was united. And not only were Valens' numbers by this time nearly twice as large as those of Caecina, but the misfortunes of the smaller army stiffened discipline through the entire force. It was realised that the enemy were prepared to offer a stout resistance. They had already given unwelcome proof of their valour. The crisis of the whole campaign was at hand, and the Vitellians braced themselves for a sterner effort.

In camp together at Cremona the two generals took counsel what to do. One possible plan, now that they had so large an army at their command, was to renew the direct attack upon the enemy at Bedriacum, not now by any attempt at a lure or ambush, but by an honest frontal attack down the Postumian way. But they hesitated to adopt this plan. The last fighting had gone very badly. That Otho was now himself present and was receiving reinforcements was well known. Any day might see the arrival of the whole Army of the Danube in his camp. Even if they carried the position by the dangerous method of a frontal attack before its arrival, the enemy would only fall back upon the support and shelter of this army. Caecina's energy and impulsiveness had ended in defeat. The older and more cautious Valens induced his colleague to agree to a more cautious strategy. Their Emperor Vitellius would presently arrive with large reinforcements. They must wait for him, unless themselves attacked.

On his arrival, with the whole of their resources available, they would proceed to the final struggle. But meanwhile much could be done. The assault on Placentia had been a bad failure; but the fortress still menaced both their own position and Vitellius' when he came. From it the enemy's line stretched eastwards along the southern bank of the Po, and immediately opposite Cremona Macer and his gladiators were annoying them. They decided to penetrate the enemy's line here in the centre, where very probably it was weakest, as it relied on the cover afforded by the river. Certainly the troops of the enemy here employed were not his best soldiers. Every Roman army was skilled in the art of bridge-building; therefore the engineers were set to work under Caecina's directions to bridge the Po opposite Cremona.

The attempt was vigorously opposed by Macer and his gladiators on the southern bank. Every device was employed to interrupt the building; despite direct attacks on the bridge by boats, and the use of fire-ships, the Vitellians were able, by dint of steadfast and, for the most part, successful fighting, slowly to push on the work. It appeared as if the plan of the tactical penetration of the hostile line would be achieved and Placentia hopelessly isolated. Caecina was urging on the effort when a hurried message reached him from Valens' headquarters in Cremona. The enemy had appeared in force marching for the town. He, Valens, was moving out to face them. Caecina must instantly bring all his available men up to the front to assist.

In fact, while the Vitellian commanders had been busy on their own tactical plan, the Othonians had been far from idle. If the Vitellians remained quiet at Cremona, the initiative had passed to Otho's men, so long as their general on the river made good the defence of the centre. The emperor had seized the chance offered him by Valens' cautious strategy.[39]

B. Otho's Council of War.—

Shortly after the victory of Locus Castorum, the Othonian generals welcomed the arrival into camp of the emperor and his brother Titianus. Otho had summoned Titianus from Rome, intending him to take command, when he learnt that Suetonius had displeased the troops by checking their pursuit after the battle. But, besides the full muster of the Army of Italy, the Army of the Danube was now fast approaching. Already after the victory the rest of the Thirteenth legion, under its *legate* Vedius Aquila, had arrived in camp, to join its *vexillum*, which it had sent before in time to take part in the fighting. There also came a detachment of the Fourteenth legion from Dalmatia, and a second cavalry squadron belonging to the Danube forces. To increase their numbers still further, Spurinna was summoned from Placentia with the bulk of the garrison of that fortress. He left only enough in the town to hold it against sudden surprise. In of any more serious emergency it could easily reinforced again.

By the second week of April these forces were mustered at Bedriacum. The enemy lay quiet at Cremona, trying, it seemed, to bridge the river, and Macer must frustrate this. But they certainly showed no signs of advancing to attack Bedriacum. Otho summoned a council of war to discuss the situation.

At this council of war the three generals Suetonius, Celsus, and Gallus agreed in the advice which they offered. All three had been remarkably successful hitherto by their defensive strategy. Thanks to

---

39. On Tacitus' short-sighted view of this see Note E at end of chapter.

it the victory of Locus Castorum had been won. They had, it is true, been reinforced, but the Vitellians had been much more strongly reinforced. If the enemy did not move to the attack, why should they themselves desert the safe course and take the offensive? The bridge-building was not a matter of great concern. It was an easy matter to look to this.

Suetonius therefore, supported by the other two, strongly urged Otho to remain on the defensive until the summer came. As a "second-best" strategy, if the emperor should be reluctant to wait so long, let him at least do nothing for a few days longer until the bulk of the Fourteenth legion and the "Moesian Army" arrived in camp. Already detachments of the three Moesian legions had arrived at Aquileia. But the three generals, for their part, advised the first plan, of a strict defensive until the summer. Their arguments were, in the main, three in number.

In the first place, they urged, the enemy could expect very few more reinforcements, if any. The Gallic provinces were in a ferment: Narbonensis, for instance, was seriously alarmed by the operations of the fleet. The troops in Britain had their own native foes in the island to keep them busy, and, moreover, the sea rolled between. Spain had scarcely any troops to send. The bank of the Rhine had to be guarded by some troops against the tribes over that river. The generals therefore, were of opinion that even when Vitellius himself arrived, he would bring but a scanty force with him.

In the next place, delay and defence on their own part would involve the foe in very serious commissariat difficulties. No supplies could reach him by sea. The Alps were a great hindrance to the carriage of supplies by land, and the strip of country on which he depended—at least, immediately for food and forage—that between the Po and the mountains, was laid waste and already exhausted. All that was wanted to complete the demoralisation of a hungry army of northerners was the hot sun of an Italian summer.

Very different in all respects, they concluded finally, was their own position. The longer they themselves could delay, the stronger they would become. They had vast quantities of money. In civil war money was stronger than the sword. Desertion was easily bought. Upon their side they had all the provinces of the Danube and the east, with their strong and vigorous armies, which as yet had taken no part in the fighting and were theirs to employ. Italy was theirs; theirs, above all, was the favour of the Senatus Populusque Romanus. Theirs was the rightful cause. Let them then wait till summer came. Their position was impregnable, as Placentia's resistance had shown. And men of the Army of Italy had no reason to dread the fierceness of an Italian July sun: they were used to it.

For these reasons Suetonius, supported by his colleagues, gave counsel of delay.

There is no reason whatever to suspect him of any but the best motives. A wild story, indeed, was presently afloat that the general hoped that such delay would lead both armies to weary of their emperors and depose them; that the Senate would thereupon proceed to choose another prince; that his own great reputation would then carry the election. This indeed was a wild tale enough. The soldiers of both armies were devoted to their respective emperors. Suetonius was already unpopular with his own men. Even the Roman historian, despite his pitiless insight into men's baser thoughts, rejects this story. When Suetonius counselled delay, he believed this to be Otho's wisest strategy.

And Suetonius' words would carry weight. He was "the most experienced general of the day." His fame had been early won in Mauretania, when he had been the first Roman to cross the Atlas range of mountains. If imperilled in Britain recently, that fame had been vindicated by his notable victory over the savages in the island, and he had crushed their furious rebellion.[40] He came to the council of war fresh from the field of victory; and he adduced grave arguments to support his views.

Yet a good tactician is not always a good strategist, and all Suetonius' successes had been tactical. Now, in the council of war, he was urging delay and caution as a strategical plan. That such a cautious strategy would be recommended was indeed likely.

> How greatness of intellect, which in times of peace enjoys the highest consideration, decreases in value in times of war when opposed to will, is shown by the result of nearly every council of war. It cannot be denied that in an assembly of experienced and capable men, the highest aggregate of intelligence must be collected. Yet Frederick the Great was right in peremptorily forbidding his generals to hold a council of war. That keen judge of human nature knew full well that nothing is ever gained by it save a majority for the "timid party." The intelligence collected in a council of war is wont to be productive of no other advantage but that of assiduously searching out all

---

40. See my *History of Nero*, chap, 6 §3.

the weak points of an army, and of demonstrating the danger of action.—Von der Goltz.

Suetonius had certainly produced "a series of plausible arguments for leaving well alone."[41] But indeed the emperor had reason to criticise them.[42] It certainly was not true that Vitellius would bring only scanty reinforcements. Many Gallic levies and as many as eight thousand chosen men of the Army of Britain, in spite of sea and savages, joined his march, and he was over the Alps by May.

Commissariat difficulties, also, might be foolishly exaggerated. Caecina had kept a stern control of his men on his march through North Italy, and the land had not been indiscriminately pillaged. All that could safely be admitted was that the power of the Italian sun in July is fatal to any prolonged activity at all. But despite it, the immobile defending force was more likely to lose heart because of an inactivity imposed by command than was the attacking force because of a rest imposed by the heat. It was on all accounts inexpedient to prolong the war passively till the summer. Suetonius was impressed by the strength of their line of defence; but in his admiration of the river and the forts he was forgetful of men's hearts. Otho's troops demanded to be led against the invader. They were not machine-made puppets, that they could have their keen zeal blunted, their passion disappointed, with impunity.

Therefore Otho rejected the advice offered him in his council of war. He determined to take the offensive against the enemy, and that at once. His plan embraced all his forces and was brilliant in conception. Because it failed in execution, the ancient historian failed to understand it.

C. Otho's "Strategy of Envelopment."—The Vitellian generals at Cremona were seeking to carry out the plan of the tactical penetration of the enemy's line. Otho's answer to this was a scheme for the strategical envelopment of the entire Vitellian Army. The elements of the scheme were these:—

A large part of the Army of the Danube was already at Aquileia; some of its troops were perhaps already on the road between Aquileia and Bedriacum.[43] This army was to concentrate at Bedriacum with all possible speed.

---

41. Ian Hamilton, *Staff-Officer's Scrap-Book*.
42 Tacitus adduces no reasons at all for the rejection of Suetonius' advice; for his "*imperitia properantes*" is shallow. See Note E. end of chapter.
43. *E.g.*, the *vexilla* of the Seventh legion from Pannonia and Eleventh from Dalmatia.

Meanwhile the troops already at Bedriacum were to be moved to the west of the enemy's position at Cremona, and flung across the foe's one and only line of communication and succour. Seven miles to the west of Cremona the River Adua, the modern Adda, flows from the north into the Po. This is a broad and navigable stream, the outflow of the waters of Lake Como. A strong force posted at the confluence of the Po and Adda, behind the latter river, would isolate an enemy at Cremona. The Cremona force, cooped up in the town, reduced for its supplies to the few miles of country in its immediate neighbourhood, unable to force its way over the Po to the south, would be enveloped and invested. Hunger would speedily compel it to try and cut its way out through the force posted on the Adda.

It might, it is true, find a way of retreat open on the north towards Brescia; but this way led it nowhere, save up against the barrier of the unfriendly Alps, and still the foe on the Adda lay between it and its Emperor Vitellius. If it could not cut its way through this force it must very soon capitulate. Even if it did force the passage of the Adda with heavy loss, it would be an escaping army, fleeing back to a far-off base. Its prestige would be gone and Vitellius' cause ruined. If it chose rather to force the passage of the Po, then Placentia lay like a lion in its path, and the army on the Adda could reach and notably strengthen the garrison long before the disheartened column of the Vitellians in retreat could arrive outside that fortress. The enemy at Cremona should be "enveloped" by the transferring of the army at Bedriacum to the line of the Adda, while the Army of the Danube marched to take its place at Bedriacum and complete the investment.

When Otho had once conceived the main idea, three questions arose in connection with the method of its execution:—

(1) The Route of the Flank March.—The emperor directed his army to march by the northern bank of the river. At some safe distance from Cremona, when the generals thought the time had come, the force was to leave the Postumian way, and strike off to their right flank, to circle round on the north side of the town of Cremona, and so to come down upon its intended position on the Adda. This position was therefore to be reached by a flank march in the immediate proximity of the enemy.

The dangers of this route seemed obvious. Why then did not Otho choose the route on the southern side of the Po? This would have been absolutely safe; and the army would have crossed by Placentia and turned eastwards thence to the confluence.

But this, the safer route, could not be chosen. The march from Bedriacum, in that event, would first have been an apparent retreat to cross the river at Hostilia. On the way to Hostilia the army might then have met the forces coming up from Aquileia to take its place at Bedriacum. The confusion which would have resulted would have been inextricable. There was but a single road, and the country on both sides of it was either a marsh or heavily cultivated. And the effect of the apparent retreat on the enemy at Cremona had to be considered. If the force in front of them had thus disappeared their attention must at once have been excited. Had they guessed Otho's intended manoeuvre they would have had abundance of time to occupy the line of the Adda themselves, and safeguard their line of communications to the west. The whole plan of strategical envelopment would fail dismally. Had they, however, as was far more probable, pursued after the retreating column, the feigned retreat might easily have become a real one; or if the Army of Bedriacum safely crossed the Po at Hostilia, the Danube Army, moving up piecemeal, might have met the foe hotly pursuing the others, and in that case would have been rolled up in disaster, and flung back discomfited upon Aquileia. Once more the plan of envelopment would be ruined; and the Army of Italy would find itself between a victorious foe to the east of it and Vitellius' army approaching on the west.

But if, on the contrary, the force at Bedriacum marched by the northern route, not only was this less than half the distance, but its effect on the enemy would surely be just that which was most desired. The foe was apparently quiescent in his entrenched lines at Cremona. On hearing of a forward movement on part of the force at Bedriacum, surely they would be tempted to cling all the more closely to their fortified lines, and thus give the Othonians exactly the opportunity which they desired for passing unmolested round the town on the Brescia side. Before the Vitellians recovered from their surprise the flank march would be ended, and the invaders be trapped at Cremona. There was also another consideration: the enemy were trying to bridge the Po. If they succeeded, an army marching by the southern route might be assailed violently on the flank where they deemed themselves safe. This would be fatal; for a flank march is horribly dangerous, chiefly when the men engaged upon it do not realise the nature of the movement, and any sudden appearance of the foe upon their own flank is therefore utterly unexpected.

The soldiers in the marching columns always assume that their commanders suppose the enemy straight before them. If the latter suddenly appears on the flank, the men may easily imagine that they are surprised, and this destroys their confidence. Flank marches, which even the private soldier knows to be such, are easy to execute. This is proved by the numerous marches within the investing lines before Metz and Paris in 1870, for the purpose of concentrating troops at certain points. They all in their nature were flank marches in relation to the enemy's forces stationed between and behind the works of the fortress. But here the whole situation was clear, for every soldier knew that during the march they could only be attacked from the side of the fortress, and the feeling of being placed in an extraordinary position disappeared. The troops marched quite unconcernedly along or close behind the line of investment.—Von der Goltz, *The Nation in Arms*.

No soldier marching from Bedriacum to the Adda by the northern route could have failed to realise the situation. On the southern route he might have been unexpectedly attacked and dismayed. Whereas, if the northern route were chosen, the closer the attention which the enemy paid to their bridge-building, the better the chance of passing quietly by them on the opposite side of the town. Cremona was to be the Metz of the campaign. The Vitellians were the French; the Othonians the Germans.

The northern route, then, was the one rightly chosen by Otho for the flank march of the enveloping column.

(2) The Command for Simultaneous Movement.—But why, it might be asked, was not Suetonius' advice accepted that Otho should at least wait a few days for the arrival of the Danube Army at Bedriacum? Why did he rely rather on a simultaneous movement of both armies—the one to the Adda from Bedriacum, the other to Bedriacum from Aquileia?

The answer to this, again, is not far to seek. Had the Othonians made no movement until the Danube legions had arrived at Bedriacum, the enemy at once must have heard of the arrival of these, and have been anxiously upon their guard. For the moment they seemed lulled in inactivity by a false sense of security. It was this false sense of security of which Otho could so brilliantly avail himself. Once let the Danube army arrive at Bedriacum, any forward movement after its arrival would find the foe thoroughly awakened out of sleep. There would be no chance of envelopment by a flank march without stubborn fighting front to front. The strategical opportunity would be lost. The simultaneous movement of two or more columns to the same place needs, indeed, the most careful timing to be successful. Yet it is by this that in modern warfare the most striking triumphs are won, such as that of Königgratz in 1866. More and more such a device of the simultaneous movement of converging columns will be employed. But Otho's columns had not so hard a task, as their simultaneous movement was directed on different places. There was no reason why it should not be properly carried out by both armies. Certainly the whole idea of strategic envelopment depended on this simultaneous movement.

(3) The Position of the Emperor.—Otho himself neither waited for the arrival of his Danube Army at Bedriacum, nor did he put himself at the head of the column of march for the Adda. He himself crossed the river to a place named Brixellum, the modern little town of Brescello, which lies on the southern bank of the Po, about midway between Hostilia to the east and Cremona to the west. With him he took a considerable force of Guards, light-armed troops, and cavalry. The Bedriacum column was to be led by the emperor's brother Titianus and the prefect of the Guards, Licinius Proculus, with Suetonius and Celsus to help them.

No part of the whole strategical plan has been more misrepresented and misunderstood than Otho's withdrawal to Brescello. The Roman historian thoughtlessly ascribes it to the emperor's care for his own personal safety. His troops adored him; he had endeared himself to them by a display of sterling military qualities on the march from Rome; he was presently to die with calm courage. And yet Tacitus believes that at this, the very crisis of the whole campaign, he ran like a coward. Moreover, at a time when his Army of Bedriacum was greatly inferior in numbers to the enemy, and was about to make a flank march of no small risk, he, the emperor, still further weakened it by detaching the troops which he took with him to Brescello to serve as his own personal bodyguard. "That day was the beginning of ruin to the Othonian cause," wrote the historian, Tacitus; "the spirit of the troops left behind was broken." Like the Duke of Argyle in face of Montrose, Otho, according to this view, found his courage fail him, and, when urged by his staff that his life was more valuable than his presence, was easily persuaded to withdraw. And the officers and men of the Guards felt his desertion, as did the knight of Ardenvohr that of the chief of his clan:—

> "It is better it should be so," said he to himself, devouring his own emotion; "but—of his line of a hundred sires, I know not one who would have retired while the banner of Diarmid waved in the wind in the face of its most inveterate foes!" (Sir W. Scott's *Legend of Montrose*).

Surely Otho's Roman courage and his Imperial position might well take the place even of a hundred sires, now that the very last stake was to be played. The galley on Loch Eil saved the craven chieftain's life when the battle was lost. No galley on the Po could save the emperor from the last consequences of defeat.

In actual fact, it was not Otho's duty to lead the flanking column. He was bound to take up such a central position as to be able from it to control the development of all parts of the combined scheme of envelopment. One force was to march to the Adda, another to Bedriacum, and all the while the defence of the line of the river on the south had to be maintained. The commander-in-chief was bound to occupy as headquarters a place where he could be in touch with *all* his separate forces which were co-operating to secure one end. The commander-in-chief in such a case is not allowed to take the personal command of one of those separate forces, not even of that exposed to the greatest risk of contact with the foe. He must be found in a situation whence he has a grip of the whole development of the main idea, from which he can, if necessary, send troops to any vital and threatened point in the whole area of events. Such a central position was Brescello. It was in touch with Bedriacum, with Hostilia, and with the whole southern bank of the Po as far as Placentia.

From it, as a matter of fact, Otho could send a member of his staff to take Macer's place when the latter's resistance to the bridge-building at Cremona was proving inadequate, so great was the advantage of the presence of the emperor at the central position. Because Brescello was out of harm's way, because the emperor took no share in the fighting which presently fell to the lot of the Bedriacum column, men forgot that he was commander-in-chief and not a mere general of division, and foolishly accused him of cowardice. Such easy imputations are part of the heavy burden of supreme command. "The magnitude of the personal responsibility inseparable from command against the enemy" (Henderson, *Science of War*), is surely load enough for the general-in-chief without his having also to bear such charges, lightly brought and readily believed.

> The more, therefore, that clear-sightedness and intelligent direction in the development of a battle is demanded of a general, the greater the reason that he should keep out of serious danger. The best post for a commander-in-chief is one from which he has a clear view of the lines of advance of his columns as well as of the enemy's line of battle. Such places are usually found only at a considerable distance completely beyond the range of fire; but it would be an entirely false sense of honour to reject them on that account By displaying his contempt of death, a commander-in-chief can scarcely effect more than any subordinate officer; but, by clearness and cool deliberation in his plans, he will, on the other hand, become the benefactor of hundreds of thousands.—Von der Goltz, *The Nation in Arms*.

The principle applied here in the sphere of tactics is true in that of strategy. The great scheme of envelopment meant the moving of many pieces together on the strategical chessboard. The emperor must be the player and set them all in motion from Brescello, not be himself the hardy knight to cry checkmate after its skilful moves. The flank inarch of the one column had to be entrusted to his divisional commanders. The general officer commanding must rely on the sagacity and bravery of his subordinates. If they prove incompetent he pays the penalty, as did Lee at Gettysburg.

A rough diagram, then, may illustrate the plan of strategical envelopment as it might have presented itself to Otho's mind, when the investment was completed:—

To achieve the envelopment of the enemy, Otho ordered the force at Bedriacum to advance towards the enemy upon its flank march to the confluence of the Adda and the Po.

D. The Possibility of Success.—

The crucial movement in the strategical plan of envelopment, upon which its whole fortune depended, was the flank march of the Bedriacum Army. The plan itself was a brilliant one. For modern war it has been declared that "envelopment, not mere weight of numbers, is the true secret of decisive success," (*Science of War*).

Such was the strategy by which the Emperor Otho planned to defeat the enemy, rather than stay idly on the defensive, as his older

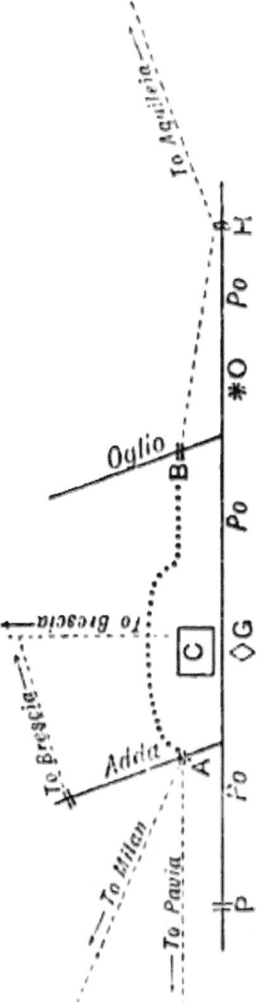

A = proposed position of the force marching from Bedriacum (B) by dotted line and based on Placentia (P), thus cutting the communications of the Vitellians at Cremona (C) with the west, *via* either Milan or Pavia (Ticinum).

B = proposed position at Bedriacum of the force from Aquileia.

C = the Vitellians "enveloped" (as a result of the flank march) at Cremona.

O = Otho's headquarters at Brescello.

◊G = Macer's gladiators defending the river against the bridge-building at Cremona.

P and H = the only passages of the Po, at Placentia (P), and Hostilia (H); both in Otho's hands.

The road to Brescia is a *cul-de-sac* for the Vitellians, as the passage of the Adda farther north (*via* Bergamo) would be easily controlled by the foe at A.

generals recommended, or make, with inferior numbers, a frontal attack on the foe. But were not the dangers of the flank march too great to allow success? The plan was a daring one. Was it not also a rash one, which merited failure? Criticism might fasten on two points—on the enormous risk of the flank march itself, and on the precarious situation of the force at the confluence even if the flank march was accomplished.

Neither, however, of these dangers was such as reasonably to deter Otho from carrying out his scheme.

(1) The Flank March.—The German expert, Von der Goltz, writes concerning flank marches:

> These have the reputation of being difficult and dangerous undertakings. Military history, however, teaches us that in the matter of flank marching one may venture more than theory would seem to allow. Frederick the Great at Prague made a flank march round the right wing of the Austrians, and at Kolin even along their whole front ... even in manoeuvres flank marches are successfully executed even within sight of the enemy.

All depended on the immobility of the enemy and, especially, on the discretion of Otho's generals. They must act rapidly and with decision, and must choose the fitting place for striking away northwards from the main road before they came within sight of Cremona or in touch with the Vitellians in the town. The object to be gained by the march was worth many risks.

> The greatest advantage of all turning movements is that, if they succeed, they finally result in the whole of the enemy's army, or a part of it, being caught between two fires. Scharnhorst expressed himself to the effect that "troops attacked upon more than one side may be regarded as defeated." This pronouncement is not true unconditionally, yet it is founded upon the fact that he who finds himself between several enemies threatening him from different directions, is constrained to eccentric action which tends to split up his forces and thus to weaken him, while the former work concentrically and gain in strength.—Von der Goltz.

If the march were successful the foe would be in the trap, and if they escaped at all, it would be only to retreat with loss and disgrace. The risks must be run. "He who would always in war be on the safe side will hardly ever attain his object."[44]

(2) The Position on the Adda.—Otho's force, if it reached the confluence, might seem to be very uncomfortably placed between the enemy at Cremona and Vitellius' approaching reinforcements; but this in reality was hardly the case. Vitellius had not crossed the Alps, and the crisis of the situation must come in a very few days after its arrival at the confluence. Valens and Caecina had not supplies enough to stay sulkily in Cremona, nor indeed would their troops be likely tamely to submit to this. This force, then, at Cremona was the danger, and the Adda was a splendid stream for Otho's men to defend even against a much larger army, especially when their comrades from the old camp would be pressing upon the rear of the attacking enemy. The strong fort which is today placed on both banks of that river at Pizzighettone, where the road and rail for Cremona cross the stream, shows the value still placed upon the Adda as a military obstacle. Here, then, the force would serenely expect the attack of the desperate foe, even though it had temporarily surrendered its own line of communications with the east.

> It never occurred to anyone in the German Army at the time that on August 18, 1870, we were fighting a great battle with reversed front, and that, in our outflanking attack upon the French right, we had completely cut ourselves off from our established lines of communication. All attention was centred forwards in victory and not backwards in retreat.—Von der Goltz.

But the Othonians at the confluence would have been more happily placed in the event of a reverse than were the Germans outside Metz; for the former could fall back on Placentia, and so regain safety and their communications once more. And they were Romans. Otho's strategical plan of envelopment was bold in conception, and needed energy and intelligence in execution. But its daring and possibility merited success; and the alternatives to it of quiescence or of frontal attack promised very little, if any, triumph for the emperor.

§8. The "Battle of Bedriacum"

After Otho had departed from the camp at Bedriacum, the generals left in command prepared to carry out his orders. Part of the force

---

44. A saying of Von Moltke's *à propos* of the campaign of 1866.

under Gallus was kept in camp to guard it, and to await the arrival of the Danube army. The rest of it marched out on April 14, along the road to Cremona. In the day's march they covered fourteen miles and halted for the night.[45] The generals judged it safe to approach within eight miles of the city before diverging to the north. The troops were marching to take up a new position at the confluence of the Adda and Po, and entrench themselves there. They therefore were naturally in full marching kit and accompanied by a baggage train. It was most desirable to keep to the broad, paved way as long as possible. Hence the generals ventured along it as far as fourteen miles, and encamped for the night. Their ultimate objective, the confluence, lay some fifteen miles away in a straight line. The next day's march would, however, have to be a longer one by reason of the detour round Cremona.

But neither generals nor troops were in good spirits. Even in April the sun can be extremely hot and the road exceedingly dusty between Calvatone and Cremona. The fourteen miles had been fatiguing, and the troops had been distressed for lack of water. This indeed was not the generals' fault, unless (which seems improbable) they had been able to improvise water-carts and had neglected to do so. For although in the flat plain to the east of Cremona there are today ditches innumerable, yet in April these were either dry or contained only a little stagnant filthy water.[46] Of rivers there were none; for every step along the road took the thirsty troops farther and farther from the Oglio, and their camp for the night in the neighbourhood of the modern hamlet of Pieve Delmona lay midway between the Oglio on the north and the Po on the south, and some six or seven miles from both. In the immediate presence of the unsuspecting enemy the men could not be allowed to straggle in search of water, either on the march or from the evening's camp. It might indeed have been better if the generals had left the main road earlier and encamped beside the Oglio for the night. But the attractions of the highway proved too strong.[47]

The soldiers were therefore in a bad temper and angry with their

---

45. See Note D, "The Distances in Tacitus ii, 39, 40." At end of chapter.
46. This at least was the case between Calvatone and Piadena in April 1906.
47 Tacitus ii.: of course, is mere nonsense if the march were only four miles. If fourteen, still it is the private soldier's view (as always) which puts his sufferings down to lack of skill on part of his generals. Tacitus never realises a military situation. He does not even tell us that the march lasted two days, although we should have inferred it from probability, had not Plutarch directly told us. For the impossibility of reconciling Plutarch's whole story with Tacitus, see Note D at end of chapter.

generals. In their discontent and impatience they loudly lamented the emperor's absence. The generals meanwhile were fiercely quarrelling among themselves. Suetonius and Celsus disliked and distrusted the whole scheme from the beginning. They now gloomily pointed out its risks to Titianus and Proculus, who were, for their part, eager and ready to carry out Otho's orders. The foe, urged the malcontents, were all but in sight. In case of attack these had but four miles to tramp (a characteristic underestimate). But their own troops were in marching order, not fighting trim, and wearied by the march. These recriminations and gloomy reflections came too late, and were indeed out of place. The troops could not but mark the acrimonious dissensions between their leaders, and these must have the worst effect upon them, especially in their present temper. There was no doubt that they had come too far along the road, too near the enemy, for safety. And now the generals were busy discussing again what had already been decided.

It was a grand error on Otho's part to entrust the column to a committee of generals in place of one supreme commander. Roman generals did not always agree together. Two were bad enough, but a council of four was indeed likely to ruin any plan. The emperor sought to remedy the evil by his own control. He despatched a Numidian mounted orderly from Brescello with the stern and imperative order to the generals to advance. It may be that they misread the order, and thought that it countermanded the original plan in favour of a direct attack upon the Vitellians at Cremona. Or perhaps Otho himself, hearing that the force had come so near to the enemy, judged that there was no room for the flank march left, and himself commanded a frontal attack instead. Or, again, the generals may have relied on the enemy's inactivity and still moved forward, intending to strike north presently, allured by the fatal attractions of the highway. Whose the blunder was can never now be determined. All that is certain is that Otho's whole strategical scheme miscarried; for when the column resumed its march, obedient to orders, on April 15, they blundered straight upon the foe. The head of the column suddenly found the enemy's horse charging full upon them.

Valens had not been caught unready that morning. Under screen of his cavalry charge he marched his army out of camp and drew it up ready for battle. Caecina and his men were quickly summoned from the half-made bridge. The full Vitellian army stood ready to fight, drawn up quietly despite the near approach of the foe. Thick brushwood on either side of the road hid the Othonian approach, and in consequence the Vitellian regiments moved to their allotted places without alarm or disorder. Their cavalry indeed came presently reeling back, for the head of the Othonian column stood its ground valiantly and repulsed them. It needed the levelled pikes and the taunts of the First infantry legion of the Vitellians to compel the shaken horse to pull bridle and rally. Then the whole army moved forward on a wide front stretching some distance on either side of the road. The repulse of the enemy's cavalry had given the generals on the Othonian side time to extend their front, and dress it to meet their opponents to some degree. But their confusion was still great. Some indeed believed that the advancing foe had abandoned Vitellius' cause and were joining them in all love and amity. Some pressed boldly on to the front seeking honour; some hurried as eagerly to the rear in search of safety. There was more uproar than there was discipline. At the height of the confusion the Vitellian line charged.

But the fighting was stubborn. Between the river and the road two legions strove fiercely. The Othonian First Adjutrix, eager to gain its first laurels (for it had been but recently levied), rushed fiercely upon the Vitellian Twenty-First, a legion of old renown, overthrew its first ranks, and carried off its eagle in triumph. In bitter anger the veterans rallied and thrust hard upon the foe. The legate of the First fell, his men were routed, and the loss of the eagle was made good by the capture of many colours from the enemy. On the other flank, the men of the Fifth legion of the German Army drove the Pannonian Thirteenth legion in flight off the field. The detachment of the Fourteenth legion, the famous legion of Britain, stood true to their absent comrades and the traditions of the regiment. But they, a mere handful, could not save the day for Otho, and they fought vainly but desperately, surrounded by a ring of foes.

It was, like Inkermann, a soldiers' battle. Otho's generals had already done their utmost to ruin his cause by their quarrels. They had ignorantly exposed their army, unprepared and in disorder, to the frontal attack of a more numerous and well-ordered veteran force. One thing only was lacking. They fled from the field. But their men went on fighting. From the southern bank of the Po, the gladiators crossed the river in boats to help their comrades. Then the Vitellians made their last supreme effort. Valens and Caecina flung their reserves into the battle-line. The enemy's centre was pierced. The Batavian auxiliaries of the German Army cut the gladiators to pieces even before they

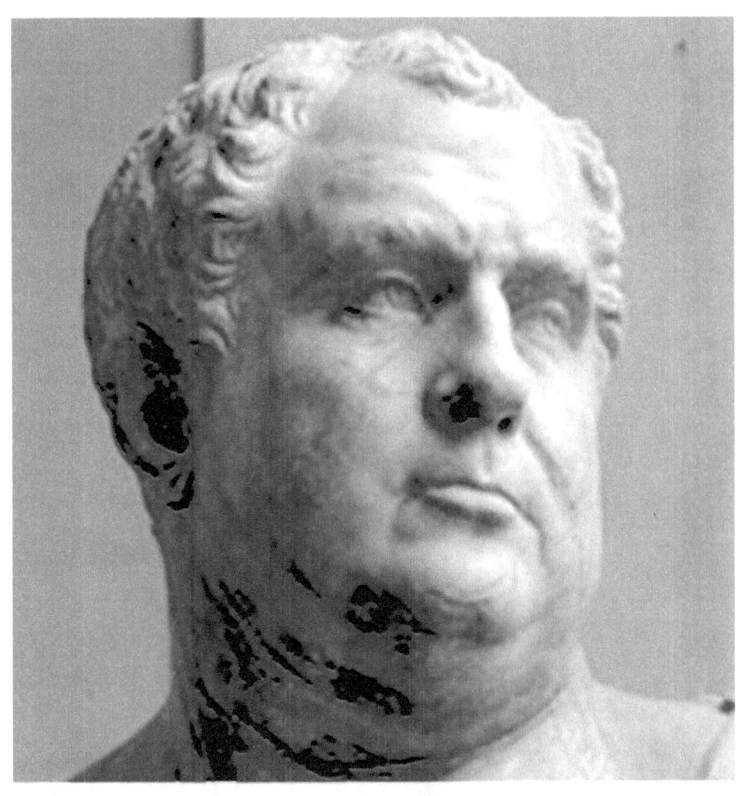

VITELLIUS

reached dry land, and, hastening in the flush of victory, came charging upon the left flank of the stubborn foe. This flank charge decided the issue. The Othonians broke and fled wildly. The battle was ended.

The pursuit rolled on for many miles. No quarter was given, for, says the Roman historian grimly, "captives in civil wars cannot be turned to profit." The ways were heaped high with the bodies of the slain. The survivors of the rout found refuge only with Gallus and the camp at Bedriacum, twenty miles away. The Vitellians checked their pursuit four miles from the camp, and bivouacked for the night just west of the modern town of Piadena. Next day, April 16, they advanced to Bedriacum, and the garrison surrendered.

Thanks to the mistakes of the enemy, Vitellius' generals had won for their master the final victory, and with it the Empire. He himself visited the scene of the struggle on the 24th of May, six weeks after it had been fought. No attempt had been made to bury the dead. Caecina and Valens showed their emperor over the battlefield and explained to him the details of that bitter fight. His one saying is recorded:—

> When hee came into the fields where the battaile was fought, and some of his traine loathed and abhorred the putrified corruption of the dead bodies, he stuck not to harten and encourage them with this cursed speech: that an Enemie slaine had a very good smell, but a Citizen farre better. Howbeit to qualifie and allay the strong savour and sent that they cast, hee poured downe his throat before them all exceeding great store of strong wine, and dealt the same plentifully about.—Suetonius, *Vitellius*, 10. Philemon Holland's translation A.D. 1606.

Vitellius is the one utterly contemptible figure of the century.

Thus the first "Battle of Bedriacum"[48] was fought, and Vitellius won his throw for Empire. A review of the military measures of both sides shows that both made mistakes, or at least failed in their intentions. Neither the plan of tactical penetration on the one side, nor that of strategical envelopment on the other, was fully carried out. As Otho's had been the more brilliant and daring conception, so its failure, which precipitated the final fight, was the more ruinous, and brought defeat and death upon him.

The great cause of its failure was the incompetence of Otho's gen-

---

48. The title "Battle of Bedriacum" is a misnomer, as the actual fighting took place just outside Cremona, twenty miles away, and that of the "Battle of Cremona" would be more fitting. But the former name is consecrate by custom.

erals. As the story of the battle shows, they clung to the main road too long, calculating too confidently upon the enemy's immobility. But the enemy gladly sallied out to attack, and Otho's troops were caught encumbered with baggage and tools, unready for a fight and not expecting it. To incompetence the generals added cowardice, of which later they blandly made a merit, and won Vitellius' pardon by this means. There was small wonder that with such generals Otho lost the day. His troops fought well for him against all possible odds. It had been better for Suetonius had he died eight years earlier amid Boadicea's war-chariots. He saved Britain. But now he had lost himself.

Otho's generals failed him, as Lee's subordinates failed to carry out their orders in the Gettysburg campaign. Decisive defeat was the result in both cases.

But the whole campaign has been misunderstood by the Roman historian. Otho's strategy was hidden from him. The reason of this blindness on Tacitus' part is easily to be found. The emperor could not explain his strategy to his troops lest the enemy should hear of it beforehand. "The one fixed law of all military experience is that whatever is believed in one's own camp is believed also to be true in that of the enemy."[49] Very little happened in the camp at Bedriacum without the foe being at once informed of it. Civil war produces a rich crop of traitors on both sides—above all when the combatants are fighting on behalf of persons and not on behalf of principles. On the very morning of April 15 itself, two *tribunes* of the Praetorian Guard sought for, and were granted, an interview with Caecina, which was interrupted only when the battle called the general away in haste.

Otho therefore, having planned to envelop the enemy by a flank march, was bound to seek to deceive them as to his intentions. If they misread his own departure to Brescello as a sign of cowardice, so much the better. They would be all the less on their guard. But by misleading the enemy, the emperor misled also the common soldier in his own camp, and in his train he misled the most unmilitary of historians. The soldier saw that Otho's orders to advance had led to the battle. He jumped to the conclusion that Otho had intended that battle from the first. Tacitus solemnly repeats his view. The soldier regretted his emperor's absence and wondered at it.

The historian explains it with great satisfaction as due to cowardice. The soldier found the battle badly mismanaged, and heavy defeat the result. The historian put it all down to a foolish order to advance

---

49. Maj.-Gen. Maurice, *Diary of Sir John Moore*.

for a frontal attack. True, the latter had discovered in his records or inquiries some faint traces of an idea of reaching the confluence. But as the direct way to it from Bedriacum lay straight through Cremona, he concluded that the troops were bound to march that way and hence would have to fight. The troops notoriously *did* march that way. The proof was complete. Otho was reckless, impatient, foolish, a coward! He had made no mistake up to the time when he issued his last orders. This was all the more reason for an accumulation of errors in them. His troops adored him after the defeat as before.

It was curious; but what will not defeated troops do? He died with unshaken serenity. Any coward can do that! He would not, as he might well have done, prolong the war, falling back on his Danube Army, where the line of safe retreat was open to him; he would not challenge Fortune's verdict upon a second field. He would redeem Italy from war's horrors by the willing sacrifice of his own life. This was conduct truly worthy of a coward. The common soldier was too ignorant to see fully his general's incapacity and shrinking. The historian took from him the tales of what befell and of what was said, and wisely added the explanations.

That the military knowledge of the common soldier, with all its hopeless limitations, should become the wisdom of the journalist is a feature of historical writing but too familiar to us of late years. Otho sought, as it were, to make a Metz of Cremona. Had his strategical idea succeeded, Tacitus might have realised its meaning if not its brilliance. It failed, and in consequence left but one puzzling trace of itself in the historian's narrative, when, that is, he speaks of the intention to reach the confluence of the Adda and the Po. But the historian does not see the meaning of this, and gives us in consequence a story of the whole campaign which is indeed "unintelligible from a military point of view," (Mommsen). Even had the Germans failed in their attempt to invest Metz—and they too came near failing—their effort would not have been caricatured. To that extent, at least, military science has advanced since the days of Otho, and left its mark even upon the intelligence of the historian.[50]

§9. The Death of Otho

When the tidings of defeat reached the emperor at Brescello, his

---

[50]. The material upon which is based the view of the campaign contained in this section, and a discussion of the difficulties of the Tacitean story, are to be found in Note D at the end of the chapter. I have judged it best to give my conclusions in the form of a direct narrative.

troops there implored him to continue the struggle. The legions from Moesia were hastening to the front and hard at hand. Had Otho willed to live, he might yet have been the victor.

But he refused to be cause of bloodshed any longer. Though his men were eager to fight—if need were, to die—for him, he would not suffer it. The wife, the children, the brother of his triumphant rival were in his power. He would take no vengeance upon them. He blamed none, neither men nor gods, for the calamity which had befallen. "Such blame rather befitted him who still longed to live." Otho had no such longing. He had played gallantly for Empire; he had staked his fortune on a throw and lost. He himself would pay the forfeit, but no other one besides. The miseries of civil war had lasted long enough, and he would not prolong them. If only his own life stood now in the way of amity and peace, the way should speedily be made open.

Intrepid in his looks, courteous in his entreaties, he now besought, now commanded, his officers to hasten to make their peace with the victor, and himself rebuked the wrath of the troops with those who obeyed and hurried from the camp. Nor would he rest until he knew that all had fled. His young nephew at his side was panic-stricken. He cheered the boy and bade him hope for the new emperor's clemency. "Be brave," he said, "and grasp life sturdily; remember that Otho was your uncle, yet remember it not overmuch." He sought out and destroyed all letters in which were written any words of love for him, of hatred for Vitellius. In such-wise and in leave-taking of his friends Otho's last day drew to evening. Then, when darkness fell, he quenched his thirst with a little cold water and lay down in his tent quietly to sleep.

The light of dawn woke him, and he called to his freedman in the tent. Had his friends, he asked, who had left him the day before, fared well upon their going? His servant answered that no ill had befallen any. "Go then," said the emperor, "and show yourself now to the troops, lest thou die miserably at their hands as having brought death upon me." The man went out. Then Otho drew from under his pillow a dagger which he had chosen and hidden there the evening before, and, turning, fell upon it. Hearing a single groan, his slaves, still faithful, and Firmus, his loyal *prefect* of the Guards, rushed into the tent and found their emperor dead. Death had come quickly to him, nor did he die with any Stoic pose. "It is the coward who talks much about his death," he had yesterday told his soldiers. He might have added, "and the philosopher." Otho was a soldier, and spent not many words on death.

His troops carried his body to the pyre, weeping, kissing, now his hands, now his wounded breast. The flame was kindled beneath the funeral pile, and, as it blazed upwards, some of his men slew themselves beside it for very rivalry of honour and of sorrow for their prince. Others too, when they heard of it, in the camps at Bedriacum, Placentia, and elsewhere, did the like. The officers might flee. The men followed their emperor through the gate of death.

> They had received nothing of great price at the dead man's hands, nor did they think to suffer any dread doom at his conqueror's. But in no tyrant ever, it seemeth, in no monarch hath there ever been begotten so terrible, yea so mad, a lust for rule as was their lust to yield obedience and submit themselves to Otho's governance. Verily that fierce longing left them not, no not though he was dead, but it abode and passed in the ending of it into loathing unquenchable for Vitellius.—Plutarch.

It is hard calmly to appraise, dispassionately to measure out, such love. It is hard to pass judgment of indifference or disparagement upon the emperor who inspired it. Otho was careless, licentious, ambitious, frankly selfish, treacherous; but he died like a true Roman when all was done. Fate gave him but thirty-seven years of life and a bare three months of Empire. He bade farewell to both unmoved, as one who goes a journey and will presently return. Like Petronius, he is scornful of life with a quiet contempt born of native courage. For him, too, the thought of death, and of the loss by death of those good things of life which he has enjoyed to the full, cannot cast a shadow on his peace when the last call sounds. Like Antony, as he answers to that call, he makes one claim to an immortality of renown, if there be any such; for he, too, has won the love of his men in surpassing measure. And to have won such love is not to have failed utterly in life after all.

Notes

A.—The Movements of the Danube Legions

Tacitus says: "*Laeta interim Othoni principia belli, motis ad imperium eius e Dalmatia Pannoniaque exercitibus. Fuere quattuor legiones, e quibus bina milia praemissa; ipsae modicis intervallis sequebant*ur." Again, in his enumeration of Otho's troops engaged in the Battle of Locus Castorum he writes: "*Tertiae decumae legionis vexillum, quattuor auxiliorum* *cohortes et quingenti equites in sinistro locantur; aggerem viae tres praetoriae cohortes altis ordinibus obtinuere; dextra fronte prima legio incessit cum duabus auxiliaribus* (MS. *vexillaribus*) *cohortibus et quingentis equitibus."*

The "Thirteenth" legion was one of the two in Pannonia; the "First" was the legion from Rome belonging to the Army of Italy.

It has been argued (*e.g.*, by Pfitzner in his *Geschichte der Kaiserlegionen*) that by the time of this battle all four *vexilla* from the Pannonian and Dalmatian legions had arrived on the scene and not the one only of the Thirteenth legion. Hence for the unmeaning MS. reading *"vexillaribus"* he would substitute *"vexillariis"* and take these two *"vexillariae cohorts"* to be two of the remaining three.

This view is to be rejected. It is clear, as Gerstenecker points out, that the *vexillum* of a legion cannot be properly described as a *vexillaria cohors*. The right form of description is already given in the phrase *"tertiae decumae legionis vexillum"*; *i.e.* the legion to which such a *vexillum* belonged is named. Moreover Tacitus, after his enumeration of the Othonian forces present at the battle, says expressly that there was no reserve, *"nullum retro subsidium."*. But he has not mentioned a fourth *vexillum* at all, supposing the two *vexillariae cohortes* were numbers 2 and 3. The proper inference is that there was no fourth *vexillum* present. Hence in we should accept the proposed *"auxiliaribus"* for the MS. *"vexillaribus,"* and take these two *cohorts* to belong to the auxiliaries, *not* to be two of the *vexilla* of the Danube legions. In this case only one of the four *vexilla* has arrived on the scene by April 6, and hence my statements in the text are based on this conclusion.

B.—The Capture of Cremona by the Vitellians

Plutarch (*Otho*, c 7) believes that Cremona remained in Othonian hands until after Caecina's vain attack on Placentia: that Caecina then marched on the town to take it; that Gallus marched thereupon to defend its garrison; and that the Battle of Locos Castorum was the result

This is certainly not Tacitus' view. According to him Cremona must have been occupied by the advance guard which Caecina sent over the Alps. It is certainly included in the phrase *"florentissimum Italiae latus, quantum inter Padum Alpesque camporum et urbium, armis Vitellii tenebatur,"* for it was "at the same time" (*iisdem diebus*) as the assault on Placentia that the Vitellian auxiliaries, fleeing before the foray of Macer's gladiators over the river, took refuge in the city. When then Caecina, on his march from Placentia, *"Cremonam petere intendit,"* the words are not to be taken in the sense of a hostile movement. Probably Cremona was taken at the same time as the "*Cohors Pannoniorum apud Cremonam*," which may have been its garrison. Gerstenecker adopts Plutarch's view and supports it by a truly quaint argument, befitting an armchair student rather than anyone with a knowledge of geography and military history. He maintains that had Cremona been captured before the attack on Placentia this attack need never have been delivered at all. "Placentia would have been completely paralysed by Cremona" (*op, cit.*). And he thinks this proved by the fact that subsequently Otho recalled Spurinna from Placentia when Cremona, without doubt, was occupied by the enemy.

This last fact, however, proves nothing in his favour, as it is the eve of the last struggle and Otho must have every man available. Yet even so a garrison is still left by him in Placentia sufficient to hold the town. One fortress does not "paralyse" another. Placentia was invaluable to Otho when there was no bridge over the Po at Cremona. Does the German student expect Placentia to take the field, like Birnam Wood? It was held to guard the great crossing of the river, and served this purpose equally well even if fifty Cremonas on the north bank were in the hands of the enemy.

C.—The Site of Bedriacum

The exact site of ancient Bedriacum has been a matter of dispute. There are three pieces of evidence:—

(a) Tacitus.

Tacitus calls it a *vicus* "*inter Veronam Cremonamque situs*." Naturally, therefore, it would lie on the Roman road between these two towns. He implies that it was situated where this road from Verona to Cremona was joined by the road along the north bank of the Po, which road he calls the Via Postumia. This was probably the road from Hostilia to Cremona.

This information is very precise, but, unfortunately for purposes of modem identification, the actual course of the Roman roads in this district has not been determined. The country here today is very flat, and well drained by modern ditches. Centuries' ruin and flood have obscured every trace of the old roads; nor do any such traces remain, it seems, even of the Roman bridges, *e.g.*, over the Oglio, which would greatly assist the inquiry. If, then, we do not know the actual course of the two roads, we are not greatly helped by learning that the village of our search lay at the point where they joined.

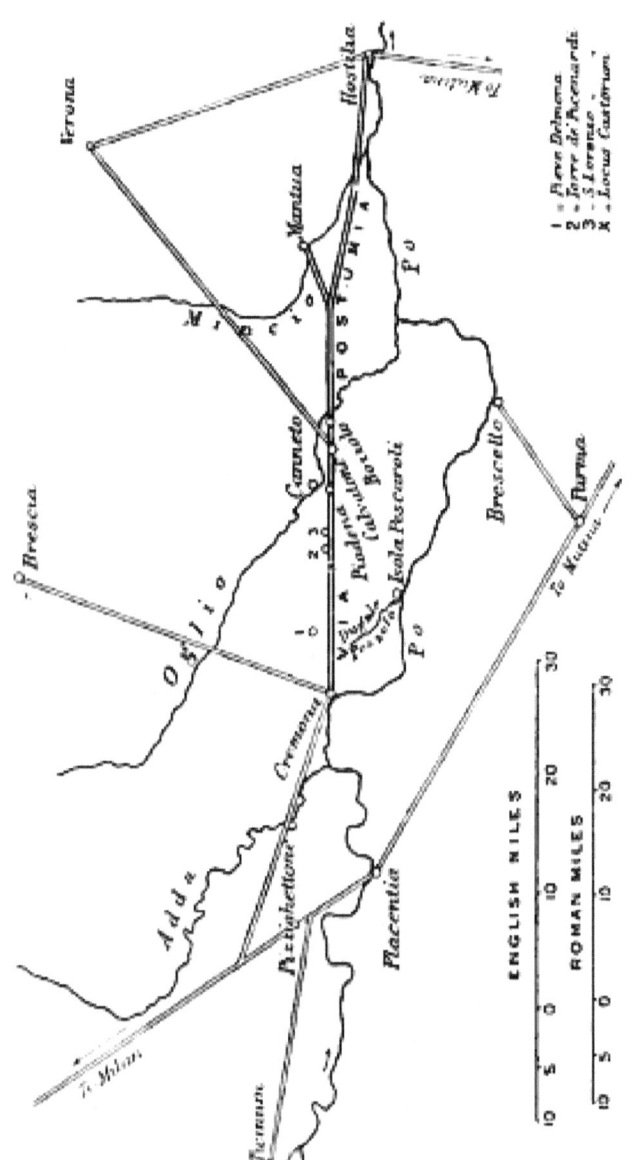

VIA POSTUMIA.

(b) The scholiast to Juvenal.

Here Bedriacum is said to have been twenty miles from Cremona, and to have lain between Cremona and Hostilia.

(c) The "Peutinger Table."

This reads as follows:—
Cremona—xxii.—Beloriaco—,,—Mantua—xl.—Hostilia.

Beloriaco is obviously Bedriacum. But there are two difficulties here: (1) No distance is given between it and Mantua; (2) The distance from Mantua to Hostilia is twice the correct number of miles. Mommsen's suggestion (*op, Hermes*, v.) is that forty was the number of miles between Bedriacum and Hostilia, and that Mantua lay on a branch road which, "as often happens," has disappeared from the map. Hence the right reading should be

Cremona—xxii.—Bedriaco—xl—Hostilia.

This would explain why the Juvenal *scholia* placed Bedriacum between Cremona and Hostilia rather than between Cremona and Mantua.

✶✶✶✶✶✶

N.B:—Conrad Peutinger of Augsburg (*A.D.* 1565-1647) possessed, it seems, a thirteenth-century copy of a Roman map of the third century *A.D.*, which he published. This gives a picture of the roads of the Roman Empire, naming the chief stations on them, and giving in figures the distances between them. It does not attempt to give any accurate delineation of shape, or to draw distances to scale. The result is a series of long strips of country which presents a very quaint appearance. But its information on vexed questions of site may of course be valuable, as in this case.

✶✶✶✶✶✶

The difficulty in Mommsen's view is that it is hard to see why Mantua, an important town, should lie on a side road which would have been an exceedingly short one, and why, even on grounds of military exigency (as Mommsen urges), it should have been avoided by the main road. The explanation, however, of the difficulty of the Peutinger Table *datum* is the only one which we have, and holds the field.

The distance of the modern village of Calvatone from Cremona tallies practically to a yard with that given by the Table for Bedriacum (33.02 kil. = 20½ English = 22 Roman miles). The scholiast's 'twenty" is less trustworthy. The distances from Cremona of other villages suggested—Carneto, Cividale, S. Lorenzo Guazzone—suit neither of the figures. I have little doubt that Calvatone lies on the site of Bedriacum, and that the Roman road ran a quarter of a mile north of the modern high-road from Cremona to Mantua.

D.—The "Distances" in Tacitus

Two statements of distance in Tacitus' account, when put together, present very great difficulties:—

(1) "*Promoveri ad quartum a Bedriaco castra placuit, adeo imperite ut quamquam verno tempore anni et tot circum amnibus penuria aquae fatigarentur.*"

According to this the troops reach the fourth milestone from Bedriacum, *i.e*, a point eighteen miles from Cremona. See above. Note C, Position of Bedriacum.

(2) When the troops resume their march from this point—

"*Non ut ad pugnam sed ad bellandum profecti confluentes Padi et Aduae fluminum sedecim inde milium spatio distantes petebant.*"

Celsus and Paulinus, in the next sentence, remonstrate against exposing their tired troops—"*militem itinere fessum*"—to an enemy who—"*vix quattuor milia passuum progressus*"—would be likely to attack them with vigour.

The crux here is that the confluence is seven miles *west* of Cremona, and thus some twenty-five miles from the position in (1), not sixteen miles.

Other difficulties of explanation are added, *e.g.*:—

(1) How can a four-mile march distress the troops for want of water? It seems absurd, however hot the sun.

(2) Why do the troops want to get to the confluence at all? No motive is given for this extraordinary objective.

(3) How can the troops possibly expect to get to the confluence without fighting, as the road lies in a Cremona? What, then, is the meaning of "*non ut ad pugnam sed ad bellandum profecti*"?

Plutarch, it is true (*Otho*, ii.), has a different and straightforward account which presents none of these difficulties. According to him, the troops march first day fifty *stades* from Bedriacum, *i.e.* about six miles, and then encamp. The want of water is due to the "ludicrous" position chosen for the camp. 100 *stades* = 12 miles. This would bring the force to a point some four miles short of Cremona. Plutarch appears to have thought Cremona nearer than it actually was, or, more probably, the battle actually took place here. (See below.) But Suetonius and his party objecting, nothing is done until Otho's orderly arrives with orders. Immediately the scene shifts to Caecina and Valens and the battle, without any further hint of its precise position on the road.

This account is in itself not altogether satisfactory. But it does not raise the difficult questions presented by Tacitus. There is no word of the confluence in it, no hint that the troops were not marching out to make a frontal attack upon the Vitellian position at Cremona. On the contrary they marched along the road to fight, and, reasonably enough, did fight as soon as they met the enemy, at or near the city: four miles away, if we insist on Plutarch's distances, but he allows us some margin to play with.

But if Plutarch has (on the whole) a simple straightforward view of events, this does not help us in the least to solve the perplexities of the Tacitean story, unless it induces us to reject the latter altogether in favour of the alternative. We have no right, and small inclination, to adopt this heroic course.

Various solutions have been suggested of the perplexities of the second passage in Tacitus:—

(a) Gerstenecker proposes a remarkable translation for it:"*Nicht wie zu einer Schlacht, sondern wie zu einem Feldzuge aufgebrochen, befanden sie sich auf dem Marsche nach der Mündung der Adda in den Po, sechzehn Milien davon entfernt*" (*op, cit*.), *i.e.* "having set out, they found themselves at a distance of sixteen miles from the objective of their march, the confluence."

This version separates "*confluentes*" and "*distantes*"; makes "*distantes*" agree with the subject of "*petebant*"; and translates "*petebant*" as the equivalent of "arrived at" instead of "were making for." All this is surely impossible as a mere matter of the general run of a Latin sentence. It also gives no answer at all to the question of the reason for the objective, or to the question why the troops did not expect a battle. And it brings the army nine miles from Cremona (= sixteen from the confluence) for the battle site, which agrees with no other *datum* of any kind and is intrinsically wildly improbable. Gerstenecker outrages Latin and only makes confusion worse confounded.

(b) The new Kiepert map of North Italy (Berlin, 1902), to my amazement, I find escorting the Adda into the Po through the very town of Cremona itself. I can only infer that this is Kiepert's effort to solve this very problem. Bedriacum to Cremona as twenty miles (according to the scholiast's account): the troops march four miles: they are then sixteen miles from the confluence. It must follow that Cremona is at the confluence and the confluence at Cremona! If Tacitus will not suit the course of the river, then the course of the river must suit Tacitus! Dr. Grundy's recent map of Italy (Murray, *n. d,*) avoids this error. Of course this solution cannot be entertained for a moment.

(c) The words "*Confluentes Padi et Aduae*" give all the trouble. How simple, then, is the remedy of rejecting the words "*Padi et Aduae*" entirely as an addition by a very ignorant scribe which has crept unluckily into the text! The troops are making for a "confluence" sixteen miles away. What confluence is the proper distance from their first camp? At this point a stream, the "Caneta" by name, is produced by Nipperdey, flowing from the north into the Po. Nipperdey's "Caneta" is cheerfully quoted by Professor Bury (*Students' Roman Empire*), and Mr. Hardy believes in "a small stream from the north" (*Plutarch's Lives of Galba and Otho;* cf. his whole note on the matter, with its despairing conclusion). On this view of the situation the troops intend to diverge from the main road southwards towards the Po "to get into touch with Macer's gladiators." But they all mean to fight, and the words "*non ut ad pugnam sed ad bellandum profec*" are merely meant as a picturesque description of the general carelessness and disorderliness of their march.

This indeed is a violent remedy, when a puzzled scholiast is invented to create the whole difficulty. Not even a scholiast would lightly have thought that the Adda joined the Po *east* of Cremona. Why in the world should he have inserted an impossible river into the narrative? Why should an impossible insertion have been accepted ever since? *Praestat difficilius?* Not a bit of it! We get rid of the words which cause the whole difficulty and build our hopes on the River Caneta!

Veritably they are built on sand and not on a river at all! The large scale Italian ordnance map of Cremona lies before me as I write (Fo. 61, 1897, scale 1: 100,000). For the twelfth time I search seventy-five square miles of country east and south-east of Cremona to find the name of Caneta. There are plenty of "Ca," but this presumably stands for "Casa." There is no Caneta. Very wisely Mr. Hardy wrote of his "small stream from the north" without naming it. But there *is* a brooklet or a ditch called, it seems, Dugale Pozzolo, with a course (so far as I can track it) of some seven miles, which enters the Po from the north at Isola l'escaroli. Its beginning seems to be four miles away from Cremona. Its "confluence" is nine miles from the camp, "fifty *stades* west of Bedriacum." This distance refuses to suit anything. Is this "Dugale Pozzolo" (if that be its name) the notable stream which makes a confluence? Is the "confluence" an error for the source of this noble river (9 + 7=16)? What then befalls Macer's gladiators, who could have jumped this ditch here? All this Caneta-erratic scholiast story is a mere tissue of silliness.

(d) Mommsen (*Hermes*, v.) proposes to regard the distance, sixteen miles, as due to a confusion in Tacitus' own mind between the ultimate objective of the whole march, *viz*. the confluence of the Adda and Po, and the proposed end of the first day's march on the way to the objective. In his view the army did not set out to fight, nor did it intend to march for the confluence by way of Cremona. But the plan was that, after marching for some distance along the main road, it should diverge to the north-west and plant itself astride the Cremona-Brescia road to the north of the former town. The proposed end of the first day's march is sixteen miles away from the camp, four miles from Bedriacum. (This would not have reached the road to Brescia.) But the troops do not get so far. For after marching along the road twelve miles (Plutarch's one hundred *stades*) to the point where they mean to leave it, at this point they meet the enemy come out from Cremona to fight Tacitus' whole account is unintelligible because he misunderstands the military situation. The army is ordered to provoke a fight, not by marching straight on the enemy but by threatening their communications; and the distance of the intended end of the first day's march is confused with that of the confluence, the ultimate objective.

Mommsen thus accepts the objective and propounds briefly the idea of a flank march, but rejects the number sixteen as given for the distance of the objective. He regards, it seems, Brescia as being of some importance, whereas this road, as I have explained in the text, mattered little or nothing to the Vitellians. And the whole march is treated in isolation instead of as part of one great strategical idea. The criticism of Tacitus' failings as a military historian must win the acceptance of every student of the historian. To Mommsen's whole paper the student of the *Histories* owes much, and not least in the consideration of the difficulties of these particular passages in Tacitus' account

I have endeavoured in the text of this chapter to develop my view of the whole strategy of the battle. But with regard to the special difficulties of the Tacitus sentences mentioned at the beginning of this note, I would suggest that one simple alteration of a numeral in the first passage will clear most of them up. To alter the "*sedecim*" (as has been proposed), of course, would get rid also of the main crux of the second passage, but leaves the "*water*" difficulty of the first unexplained. But an alteration of "*quartum*" to "*quartum decumum*," if allowed, solves both. The plan works out as follows:—

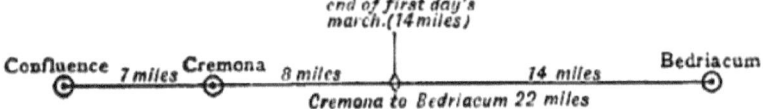

The first day's march is fourteen miles. This is eight miles from Cremona (22-14) and thus fifteen from the confluence. The discrepancy of a mile (roughly) need not trouble us greatly. The force is then "fifteen miles from the confluence" in a straight line. Perhaps the sixteenth mile allows for the circle round the city; for of any wide turning movement Tacitus has no notion. The troops are naturally distressed for want of water after fourteen miles, as well as because where they encamp there is none (Plutarch). Next day Suetonius urges that the enemy will have "barely four miles to march." It looks as if he thought both sides would set out to march at the same time, and so would meet in the middle of the eight miles which then separated the Othonians from the city.

Tacitus seems to believe the whole march and fight took place in *one* day, which accounts best for his making Suetonius insist on the weariness of his own men. Plutarch definitely says the fight was on the second day after leaving camp. This is more probable. But I can make nothing of Plutarch's figures. They disagree entirely with Tacitus' whether we read four or fourteen, save that, if we read fourteen and then make the force advance four miles farther next day for the battle (the "half eight" required by Suetonius' statement of the distance to be marched by the enemy), then in Tacitus' account as well as in Plutarch's the battle takes place eighteen miles from Bedriacum (150 *stades*) and four from Cremona.

My whole account in the text of the movements of the troops is based on my "fourteen miles" suggestion and on the importance of the mention of the confluence of Adda and Po. Of course, the view there taken of Otho's strategy as a whole is entirely independent of the difficulty of the figures (names are far more valuable than figures) and of the proposed alteration of these.

E.—Tacitus as Military Historian

In my preface I have stated my view that Tacitus' information "in matters military represents the common gossip of the camp, the talk of the private or of the subordinate officer."

The narrative and the notes to it have given not a few instances in support of this contention. A bare summary of the more important of these from chapter 1 may be presented here, in proof of the contention, for clearness' sake:—

(1) Caecina's hesitation as to his route to Italy: described by Tacitus as a choice between an invasion of Italy and an attack on Noricum. See above, §4.

(2) Otho's motive for sending the fleet to Narbonese Gaul: Tacitus fails to understand its bearing upon the general strategical situation. See above, §5.

(3) Valens' despatch of the Batavian cohorts to the coast to guard his flank: Tacitus reproduces the complaints of the common soldiers. When the private marching east sees his comrade detached to march south, he does not think of strategic necessities, the safety of lines of communication and retreat, etc. etc. When he murmurs secretly, or, in the time of civil war when discipline has gone to the dogs, grumbles openly, he is thinking that the enemy, of unknown strength, will have twice as good a chance of disposing of his own valuable life. Hence he enunciates in exactly the wrong place a splendid principle of strategical concentration, "Let the whole army stick together," etc. Tacitus himself sees in Valens' action only his desire to "guard his allies and to get rid of mutineers from his army"; both only primary and not ultimate strategical reasons, if true. See above, §4.

(4) Spurinna's reconnaissance in force from Placentia: according to Tacitus forced by a mutinous soldiery on a reluctant general. See above, §6.

(5) Caecina's attack on Placentia: Tacitus explains it as due to his desire to score an opening success—a motive of very secondary weight. See above, §6.

(6) The Battle of Locus Castorum: a most confused tale in Tacitus. But he does seem to understand and appreciate Suetonius' reasons for recalling his troops from pursuit. See above, §6.

(7) The bridge-building at Cremona, and—

(8) Otho's order "to attack."

According to Tacitus, Caecina and Valens hear of the Othonian intention to attack, and so "like wise men stay quiet to take advantage of others' folly": "*Caecina ac Valens, quando hostis imprudentia rueret, quod loco sapientiae est, alienam stultitiam opperiebantur.*" But in order to give their idle troops something to do, they begin their mock bridge-building—"*ne ipsorum miles segne otium tereret.*" Even Mommsen himself agrees that the bridge-building "cannot have been seriously meant" (*Hermes*, v.).

This entirely fails to realise the whole strategical plans of both sides. It is a shallow conclusion from results. Because the bridge was not finished, it was not meant to be finished. Because the Othonians' advance led to an attack, they meant to attack. Because they were defeated, their attack was folly.

I have endeavoured to show the deeper significance of the plans of both sides, the evidence for them, and the reasons why Tacitus failed to understand them, in the whole of §7, 8.

(9) Otho's withdrawal to Brixellum with a considerable number of troops: described by Tacitus as a step urged on him and agreed to by him in order that he might not incur the risk of the battle. I have commented on the improbability of this in § 7. Apart from its inconsistency with all that we know besides of the emperor's character and acts, he did not need so large a bodyguard if all that he and others were thinking of had been his own personal safety.

Tacitus' whole account of these closing scenes of the campaign makes the Vitellians act like babies ("Satan finds some mischief still," etc.), and Otho a strategical idiot and a craven as well. He becomes himself again only just in time to die.

The picture of Vitellius, however, is harmonious throughout and a masterpiece. So simple a character could hardly be misunderstood.

In the following two chapters Tacitus' failings are those of the lack of strategical insight upon more than one occasion. They lend themselves, however, less easily to the purposes of a catalogue, and may be left to the discovery and appreciation of the reader.

CHAPTER 2

The Flavian Invasion of Italy

How oft, indeed,
We've sent our souls out from the rigid north
To climb the Alpine passes and look forth,
Where booming low the Lombard rivers lead
To gardens, vineyards, all a dream is worth.

E. B. Browning: *Casa Guidi Windows.*

§1. Vitellius and his Army in Rome

The first "Battle of Bedriacum" was fought on April 15, A.D. 69, and Otho slew himself next morning. The news of the victory reached his rival Vitellius at Lugdunum, where he was met by his victorious generals Caecina and Valens as well as by the fugitive leaders of the defeated army, Suetonius and Proculus. The former were suitably honoured by the new emperor; the latter, when they pleaded that their own treachery to Otho had lost him the battle, were acquitted of the charge of honour and received pardon. From Lugdunum Vitellius went on his way slowly to Rome, escorted by his generals, who showed him the battlefield, (on May 24), and entertained him with gladiatorial shows at Cremona and Bononia. To his large and triumphant army which accompanied him was given on the march every license of plunder and debauchery, and it did not hesitate to follow the example set by its emperor.

News speedily reached Vitellius that the legions of the East, under Mucianus in Syria and Vespasian in Judaea, had accepted the fact of his victory and recognised him as emperor. His last anxiety, therefore, was allayed, and he gladly abandoned himself and his army to the full enjoyment of the sweets of power. His mercy and his cruelty were alike capricious. Otho's brother, Salvius Titianus, was pardoned.

Galerius Trachalus, the orator, who was suspected of writing Otho's spirited harangues for him, happily enjoyed the protection of his relative Galeria, Vitellius' second wife.[1] But some of the *centurions* of the enemy's army, whose crime was that of military loyalty to their dead prince, were executed in cold blood. They had not the wit of their generals to plead treachery as their reasonable apology. Thus dispensing favours to some and punishments to others, and always chiefly intent on the pleasures of the appetite, the glutton emperor made his slothful progress to Rome. He entered the city in great state at the head of sixty thousand troops and a larger rabble of camp-followers.

The troops spread themselves over the city, lodging where they liked and doing what mischief they pleased. All discipline was at an end. The officers had no control over the men, the men none over their appetites. The torrid heat of the Roman summer, the unhealthiness of the city, the self-indulgence of the troops, completed a demoralisation begun by victory and plunder. Many of the men encamped on the right bank of the Tiber, upon the low-lying plain of the "Vatican." This flat land, now occupied by the crowded "Leonine City," St. Peter's, and the Papal palace, has always been notoriously unhealthy; and then, when the troops new come from the cold north hastened without self-restraint to quench their raging thirst with the foul, polluted river water, disease took an ominous toll of life.[2] Even regimental *esprit de corps* was suffering; for Vitellius, having disbanded all Otho's Praetorian Guards, set to work to enrol twenty new regiments of Guards (sixteen Praetorian *cohorts* and four Urban, each a thousand strong). The men were chosen at haphazard, with scant regard to their merit or their services, and as a result the legions were depleted, but no really efficient corps of Guards was created to compensate for this.

Such thoughtless army reorganisation did but corrupt and spoil a fine force in its attempt to remedy an existing deficiency. Recruiting also for the legions was stopped, with intent to save money, and many of the troops were invited to accept their discharge from the ranks. The Gallic auxiliaries were sent off home, and the unruly Batavian *cohorts* despatched to Germany, there soon to kindle savage rebellion. Death and folly played havoc with the splendid Army of Germany, and at the end of six months' loose living in Rome it seemed to be

---

1. His first wife was Petronia, now divorced and married to Dolabella—who was presently slain for his temerity.
2. I see no reason to suppose that this disease was malaria, as suggested by Mr. W. H. Jones in his essay on *Malaria*. This disease is not rapidly fatal, even to northerners.

going to rack and ruin.

Meanwhile the emperor played at "constitutional government," and devoted his more serious thoughts to problems of the palate. When he was at Lugdunum, it was said, men heard the roads which led to the city ringing with the hurrying feet of those who came carrying the dainties of all lands to whet his appetite, his "foul insatiable maw." But the capital offered him nobler opportunities of delicacies, and during his few months' stay in Rome he is said to have spent nine hundred millions of *sesterces,* (over £7,000,000). He had at least the merit of a consistency of taste, whether the object of his extravagance was large or small. Nero had built a palace for his soul's delight, famous and hated as the "Golden House." For it he had clothed the squalid slopes and dusty purlieus of the Esquiline with woodland glades and garden greenery, refreshed them with cool waters and with quiet shade, and made the arid desert of Rome's hovels blossom as the rose.[3]

Otho, the "second Nero," had added to its beauties and extent. Vitellius complained at it: he felt himself cramped by such a meagre habitation. But if he himself could not roam afield as widely as a fitting pleasaunce might have suffered him, no such limits could fetter the activity of his mind's intelligence. A new recipe for hotchpotch was the child of that intelligence, planned on so vast imperial a scale that no mere potter could fashion a dish large enough to contain it. The silversmith alone succeeded where the potter failed, and his silver dish remained an object of wonder to succeeding generations until the thrifty Hadrian melted it down for coin. In drunkenness and revelling, in gluttony and foulness, the Emperor Vitellius spent his few months of rule.[4] And all the while his splendid army was decaying and its two victorious generals grew more jealous each of the other every day. "Truly it was to the State's good that Vitellius was vanquished."

§2. The Gathering of the Storm

Meanwhile heavy storm-clouds were gathering on the far horizon to east and to north-east. Vitellius' treatment of the victorious army was senseless enough, even though he believed all danger of further war at an end; but his method of dealing with the vanquished army was not of such wisdom as to warrant such a belief. Some small efforts indeed were made to remove the defeated legions from the neighbour-

---

3. See my *Life of Nero.*
4. Tac. ii. Cf. Suetonius, *Vitellius,* 3, 10-13. There is no reason to discredit these accounts.

hood of Italy. The First Adjutrix legion, which had fought gallantly for Otho in the recent battle, was sent to Spain. The veteran Fourteenth legion was known to be in a most dangerous temper. Only a detachment of the regiment had taken an active part in the war, and this had stood its ground to the last outside Cremona in the centre of a ring of foes. The legion as a whole had not been defeated, and indignantly disowned a share in the blame for the defeat. It was promptly ordered to return to its old quarters in Britain. At the time it lay at Turin, fretting and rebellious, quarrelling as usual with the ferocious Batavian *cohorts* attached to it. So anxious was the government to dispose of it without the chance of further friction of any kind, that the Batavians were finally detached from it and sent off to Germany, and it itself was bidden avoid the town of Vienne on its march through Gaul.

The townsfolk of this city had always wished Vitellius so ill that it was feared the *legionaries* might be encouraged to make a stand here and refuse obedience any more. Hence they were made to march by the Little St. Bernard Pass over the Graian Alps to Montmélian and thence, instead of pursuing the usual route by Grenoble to Vienne, to strike away to Chambery, and so direct to Lyons.[5] These prudent precautions were of avail, and the legion arrived in Britain. It had done no damage on the way, except that it had left its camp-fires burning on the night when it marched from Turin, and by some means or other, thanks to this, part of the unlucky colony was burnt to the ground. This was a small price to pay for riddance of the legion.

Its Batavian comrades also duly reached their homeland on the lower Rhine. But fortune had not separated the cohorts and the legion for long. The folly of the Roman Government had sent the Batavians, now proud and experienced troops, back to their tribesmen to add fuel to their discontent and strength to their plots. The "Indian Mutiny" of Roman history was, within a few months, the result. Then when the tide of massacres and Roman defeats at last was ebbing, and Vespasian's Government set grimly to work to crush the mutineers, the men of the Fourteenth legion came gleefully from oversea to take vengeance upon their ancient enemies and old-time false comrades for all the insults endured at their hands, (see chapter 3).

These events were quickly to happen. But for the moment Vitellius had rid Italy of two of the "conquered legions." With this, however, his stock of wisdom was exhausted. The Guards and the Danube Army had also belonged to Otho's strength. These he now treated with less

---

5. The use of the modern names is perhaps justified for clearness' sake.

prudence. The Guards were disbanded, with the exception of two *cohorts* which had done good service in helping to overawe the Batavians while these were still in camp with the Fourteenth legion at Turin. Though the disbandment was well managed, the *cohorts* being separated before the order was issued, and though the men were given the customary rewards on retiring from the service[6] (a treatment indeed which was more generous than perhaps they had any right to expect), yet they regretted the loss of their career, and gladly seized the chance of taking up arms again, which Vespasian's rising so soon gave to them. These Guardsmen formed "the strength of the Flavian cause."

If Vitellius had been able to retain them under arms and attach them by interest to his service, they might have forgiven and forgotten their own defeat and Otho's death. But the new emperor judged that he had too many troops of his own. How then could he find room in his army for those who had fought against his cause? Moreover, there was the risk of treachery in case of disturbance. The problem of dealing with Otho's Guards was certainly a delicate one for Vitellius, but the event did not justify the easy solution which pleased him.

The Danube Army was differently treated. This had consisted of seven legions: two in Pannonia (VII. Galbiana and XIII. Gemina); two in Dalmatia (XI. Claudia and XIV. Gemina); and three in Moesia (III. Gallica, VII. Claudia, and VIII. Augusta). The Fourteenth legion had now been sent to Britain. Of the other six, only the Thirteenth legion from Pannonia had been present at the Battle of Bedriacum. The survivors of this regiment were at first set to work to build amphitheatres at Cremona and Bononia, in which Vitellius was to be entertained when he arrived in Italy. Such work was inglorious, and the strain was not relieved by the gibing of the townsfolk who, at Cremona at least, sharpened their silly wits upon the vanquished and labouring soldiers.

That merriment was presently to be recompensed, and the men of the Thirteenth exacted the full price, and more, when autumn came. But now it was summer, and the soldiers performed masons' work till the buildings were done. Then they were sent back to their old headquarters in Pannonia at Poetovio (now Pettau on the River Drave). Their comrades of the Seventh legion had preceded them on their return to the province at Vitellius' orders. There the two legions waited, nursing wrath in their hearts, longing for the hour of requital for Otho's defeat and for their damaged reputation. The Eleventh legion

---

6. The "*honesta missio*" probably carried with it the pension paid by the *Aerarium militare*.

had in the same way returned to its province Dalmatia. It too had had no glut of fighting, and was ready to strive again.

But the three Moesian legions, the Third, the Seventh, and the Eighth, were bolder, and refused any parleyings with their triumphant rivals, the men of the German Army. They were in full strength, marching for Aquileia, standing, as it were, on the very threshold of the war, at the moment when the battle was being fought at Cremona a few miles to the west. Had they come so far to find the door shut violently in their very faces upon all their hopes of merry battle and the soldier's sure reward? Messengers came bringing the tidings of Otho's defeat. They chased them roughly from the lines, and hastened forward to the frontier town as if scornful of the rumour of disaster. Colours were found bearing Vitellius' name. They rent them in pieces. If they had not enjoyed the fighting, at least they would not forgo the plunder. They seized on the legions' military chests, broke them open, and divided up the money. They sought spoils on every hand. They were in the enemy's land, and as the enemy's land it should be treated. Vitellius was leading his placid and gross life at Rome.

Caecina and Valens were contending there for the prize of greater honour at their master's hands. But on the north-east frontier of Italy were three legions, which still defied them all, and formed the centre for the gathering storm. News reached the *legionaries* from the distant East. The Empire was not at peace. The provinces did not all rest quiet under Vitellius' rule. It was but the German Army which had won him the victory. The great army of the Eastern frontier would acquiesce no more in a triumph so lightly won, would accept no longer so despicable an emperor. Vespasian had risen. Mucianus, Governor of Syria; Alexander, prefect of Egypt; all the kings, princes, peoples, and soldiers of the Eastern Empire were leagued together under his banner against the glutton, the puppet nominee of the savage German Army. The legions at Aquileia heard the news and embraced the opportunity. They had disowned allegiance to Vitellius: this then might be counted loyalty to Vespasian their prince. They had plundered Italy: this was clearly a land hostile to his cause. With speed they sent to their comrades in Pannonia.

The Seventh legion, swayed by desire for revenge and by the promptings of their legate, Antonius Primus, gladly answered to the call. The Thirteenth legion had still better reason to join the growing army. The Dalmatian Army, the Eleventh legion, hesitated. But the Army of the Danube was so far united that five legions were ready to

Vespasianus

strike in Vespasian's name against their old enemies and conquerors. Letters were at once sent to the other remnants of Otho's army. Surely they would not now hold back from the cause which had revived again. The First legion in Spain, the Fourteenth in Britain, received from their old comrades the news of the great rising and the call to arms. Manifestoes were scattered broadcast through Gaul. The little cloud in the East had become a rushing tempest. "In the twinkling of an eye the flame of a mighty war leapt up." The banner of the Flavian cause was waving on the north-eastern frontier of Italy.

Flavius Vespasianus, the general then busy with the Jewish war, was at this time nearly sixty years old. Neither his age nor his blunt soldierly character of good-humoured common sense encouraged him to embark upon so desperate an enterprise as that of challenging Vitellius, the emperor now recognised in Italy and Rome, for his Imperial power. Vespasian had survived the shock which his untimely gift of sleep had once given to Nero's artistic sensibilities, (my *Life of Nero*). He had placidly accepted Galba as his prince, and sent his elder son Titus from Judaea to do the old emperor homage on his father's behalf. He was not inclined to quarrel with Otho, and his army in due course took the oath of fidelity to him. Even Vitellius' victory had been recognised in the same way. Left to himself, Vespasian might well have been content to smoke out the hornets' nest in Judaea, whatever prince ruled at Rome.

The burning of the Capitol at Rome might have been spared, and the burning of Jerusalem have been the chief glory of the Flavian leader, not of Titus his son. But the Fates of the Roman Empire pressed hard upon him. Every influence was brought to bear to move his caution and provoke him to defy Vitellius. His own army and the great Army of Syria demanded the right to challenge the insolent troops of Germany for the mastery. Mucianus, Governor of Syria, who had become his close friend through Titus' willing offices, was instant in his urging that not even safety could now be won save by accepting the last risk, and promised him his powerful support. Men worked upon that superstition which in him was so curiously interwoven with a hardy scepticism and healthy vigour of thought—a purple strand in a thick grey robe.

The towering cypress tree which rose above the ancestral mountain-farm in far-off Samnium, and in Vespasian's youthful days had fallen only to rise again the following day more green, more beautiful, and all unhurt; the statue of the murdered Julius at Rome, which, as

Galba's star was setting, turned to face the rising sun; the two eagles which, before the armies clashed together on the battlefield of Bedriacum, were seen contending in the air, when, behold, from the eastern quarter of the heavens a third came speeding and chased the victor from his victory,—how could omens such as these, remembered from the past or carried to his credulous ear by eager faithful friends, how could they be mockeries without meaning?

His Jewish captive, Josephus, was always whispering promises of coming Empire to his master. The very gods of the mysterious land which he held in iron grip knew of his coming glory. Again, there was an altar built on Mount Carmel to the unknown, unseen God; again, the priest stood to offer sacrifice upon it, and the Deity vouchsafed his answer, not now by fire from heaven to confound the impious, but by quiet promise through the priestly assurance that the Roman general who stood with hidden thoughts offering the sacrifice should have full fruition of his secret hopes.[7] That nothing should be lacking to rouse Vespasian to put his fate to the touch, letters were, it was said, brought to him, purporting to be written by Otho in the brief time between his defeat and death, commanding him to take vengeance on the victor for his emperor's ruin, and imploring him to help the State in its bitter need.

Still the general hesitated, counting the strength and valour of the legions of Germany. How could he pit his own less war-worn troops against those flushed with so notable a victory? But his friends' impatience brooked no longer delay; his soldiers' enthusiasm for their general cast for him the decisive throw. Tiberius Alexander, *prefect* of Egypt, proclaimed Vespasian emperor to his troops at Alexandria on July 1. His own army acclaimed him emperor on the 3rd, and the three legions of Syria, with Mucianus the governor, saluted the name and ensign of the new prince a fortnight later. How the Danube Army welcomed the news has been related. The fire of revolt was kindled again on the frontiers of Italy.

§3. Flavian Plans of War

A. The Muster of the Eastern Army,—Even apart from the six legions on the north-eastern frontier of Italy which had declared for

---

[7]. This extraordinary tale finds a place in both Tacitus and Suetonius. It evidently made a deep impression on the Roman mind, which always loved to toy unintelligently with Jewish rites and mysteries. The very priest's name—Basilides—is given. For the omens in general, of which I give only a selection, cf. Tacitus, ii. 78; Suetonius, Vespasian, 5.

him, Vespasian's army in the East was a truly formidable one. In Syria were the three legions—the Fourth Scythica, Sixth Ferrata, and Twelfth Fulminata. The fourth legion which properly belonged to this province was the Third Gallica, but this had recently been sent to Moesia, and was now with the other troops of Moesia at Aquileia.[8] It was indeed a curious chance that a habit acquired by this legion during its stay in Syria should help largely to decide the issue of the desperate battle which was soon to be fought in the plain of the Po, (see §6).

The Syrian legions were as devoted to Vespasian's cause as were his own veteran troops in Judaea, not only because they felt themselves part of the whole Army of the East, whose interests were not divisible, but also because Mucianus in his guile had warned them that it was Vitellius' intention to remove them to the German frontier, and to send his own legions of Germany to enjoy the climate and luxuries of Syria in their stead. The mere thought of the bleak north, of the savage wilds of the German marches and their barbarian inhabitants, of the black forests and cold, wind-swept marshes, of the unceasing toil and pitiless, inclement weather, which were the unfailing lot of those encamped upon the Rhine, and the contrast of it all with their own peaceful, happy life under the warm Syrian sun, amid the groves and fountains, the thronging, busy streets and booths, the never-ceasing merriments and festivals of Antioch, excited in the breasts of the *legionaries* of Syria the direst feelings of resentment against the emperor at Rome. Very reasonably Vespasian might count all the Syrian legions as "his own."

Equally eager, splendidly disciplined, and better acquainted with their general were the three legions in Judaea—the Fifth Macedonica, Tenth Fretensis, and Fifteenth Apollinaris. These had borne with him the burden of the ferocious Jewish war, a struggle stained by every horror that the savagery and brutality of the religious fanatic could devise. Weary marches, desperate sieges, merciless pursuits, had led the veteran troops at last within sight of the goal of the bitter enterprise, and only the walls and precipices of Jerusalem itself still defied the Roman arms. There is small wonder that the soldiers in Judaea would follow the general who had redeemed the Roman honour and re-

---

8. Hence Tacitus speaks loosely of the Syrian legions as four: "*Quattuor Mucianus obtinebat in pace*" (ii.), and counts the Third Gallica as one of the "*novem legiones integrae e Judaea et Suria et Aegypto*" (ii.), for there were three legions in Judaea and two in Egypt.

dressed disgrace, who had given them unfailing victory and immeasurable spoil, even to the gates of Rome itself with devotion and proud confidence.

The two legions in Egypt—the Third Cyrenaica and Twenty-Second Deiotariana—brought the number of the legions of Vespasian's Army of the East to eight. But in addition to the *legionaries* there were to be counted the auxiliary forces of the Roman provinces and subject princes of the Eastern Empire. Sohaemus, Prince of Sophene (the strip of land which borders Upper Euphrates on its eastern bank and surrounds the sources of the Tigris), came with his native levies. Antiochus, King of Commagene (the district on the great river wedged in between the Roman provinces of Syria on the south and Cappadocia on the north), who was the richest of the princes of the East owning Roman overlordship, offered Vespasian the resources of his kingdom. Herod Agrippa II., ruler of Peraea, was secretly summoned from Rome, to which he had gone in the early part of the year, and sailed swiftly back to Syria, leaving Vitellius ignorant of his flight from the city. His sister and Queen, the beautiful Berenice, then "at the height of her beauty,"[9] eagerly embraced the Flavian cause. Titus, still an impressionable youth at twenty-eight, was young enough to be enamoured of her mature charms; Vespasian was old and wise enough to be pleased by the magnificence of her gifts.

There was, finally, no portion of the Roman world from Greece to Armenia, from Egypt to the Black Sea, which did not swear allegiance to Vespasian. New troops were levied. The veterans were recalled to the standards. The mint at Antioch poured out new gold and silver. Cities rang with the clank of hammers and the forging of arms. The rich contributed their wealth of free will or compulsion. And the chiefs of the party, the officers and more experienced veterans of the army, the princes of the East with brilliant retinues, gathered together at Berytus for a council of war. The massing of the infantry and cavalry, the emulous rivalry of the royal pomp and trains, made the Syrian seaport indeed present the appearance of a city of the Imperial Court.

B. The Council of War at Berytus: the "Strategy of Exhaustion."—The council of war, assembled at Berytus to discuss and choose a strategy for the coming campaign, had to take into account not only the distance between the Syrian Army and Italy, but also that between

---

9. Her first husband (and uncle), Herod, Prince of Chalcis, had died twenty years before this. But the Romans in the matter of beauty were Venetian rather than Florentine or English in taste.

it and the Army of the Danube. The Flavian forces were strong and their resources adequate; but they were in two widely separated halves, and, moreover, the unfinished Jewish war could not be neglected. John of Gischala and the Zealots were not men to wait upon Vespasian's convenience. But the council was confident that their numbers were large enough for both wars. Happily, there was no other danger on the Eastern frontier.

The kings of Armenia and Parthia alike were friendly to the Flavian cause, and the latter. King Vologeses, the hero of the great struggle with Rome in the days of the Emperor Nero, actually made Vespasian the offer of forty thousand Parthian cavalry, the most famous horsemen in the world, to help him against his enemies. Nothing serves so forcibly to illustrate the wisdom of Nero's final solution of the problem of the Eastern frontier as does this peace on that frontier during the Roman civil wars. It was exactly the time when the Parthian might have been expected to take advantage of the discord which was rending in twain the strength of his hereditary enemy. But neither Vologeses, nor his brother Tiridates in Armenia, showed any desire to break the peace and friendship recently secured by the Neronian policy. The Flavian leaders could therefore devote part of their forces in the East to quell the rebellion of the Jews, and could direct the rest to Italy undisturbed by any fear of an invasion of the frontier or of a sudden attack upon their rear. Titus and the greater part of the Army of the East were set apart to end the Jewish war. This policy determined, the council turned its thoughts to the war with Vitellius.[10]

Vespasian himself, it was decided, should not conduct the campaign in person. He departed to Egypt to seize and secure firmly the "keys of the country," Alexandria and Pelusium. No corn-ship could sail thence to Italy without his pleasure. From Egypt as a base he intended to proceed by sea and land against the other granary of Rome, the province of Africa. By this means he thought that the enemy in Italy could be put to great distress, and that discord would be the result of it, even though no single Flavian soldier had set foot in Italy. Meanwhile, Mucianus was to march by land through Asia to the Bosporus. The best ships of the Pontic fleet, forty in number, were summoned to Byzantium to effect and secure the passage of his army. Mucianus himself led the van of the column, consisting of light armed troops; but there followed as its main strength the Sixth legion and thirteen thousand veterans besides. At Byzantium he halted, hesitating between

---
10. Jerusalem was not taken and destroyed by Titus until September A.D. 70.

two strategies.[11]

Two plans of campaign, in fact, seem to have been considered by the Flavian leaders. The first was that of offence pure and simple. In pursuit of this strategy, Mucianus should march from Byzantium by the well-known military road, the Via Egnatia, through Macedonia to the seaport of Dyrrhachium on the Adriatic. There, if he had the ships to cross to Italy, he could threaten a landing at any one of the harbours within reach as opportunity offered. Not only Brundisium, the Dover of Italy, lay opposite and open to his landing, but Tarentum, and all the coast-line of Lucania and Calabria were equally exposed to a hostile descent. Vitellius would be in sore perplexity, not knowing how to guard so long a coast-line, and already threatened on his north-east frontier by the Danube Army.

If he sent his troops to defend the line of the Po or the Julian Alps, which lay to the east of Aquileia, surely then Mucianus could make a dash on Southern Italy, even on Rome itself; for the road over the Apennines from Brundisium to Capua and the capital had been used before now by many an army. If, on the contrary, Vitellius massed his troops round Rome, he surrendered all North Italy to the Danube Army, and with it the courage and confidence of his men. If he divided his army and sent one half northwards, keeping the other to watch the coast, his resistance to the vigorous attack on both sides was likely to be but an enfeebled one. The march to Dyrrhachium from Byzantium involved the strategy of offence and co-operation between the Danube and the Eastern Army.

But this was not the strategy which Vespasian himself wished his troops to adopt. He preferred to rely upon slower means for exhausting and wearing out the enemy. If his own strategy were followed, Mucianus was to march from Byzantium by the valleys of the Moritza and Morava through Moesia, and up the valley of the Drave through Pannonia and over the Julian Alps to Aquileia. The Army of the Danube was to wait there until Mucianus arrived. So the whole Flavian force would be concentrated to threaten Italy on the north-east, and meanwhile all supplies of corn to the enemy would be cut off by Vespasian's activity in Egypt and in Africa. Hunger and despair, the would-be emperor hoped, would do the work. The Vitellians, starved and desperate, would submit without fighting. The strategy of exhaus-

---

11. Tac. The withdrawal of the ships and the Roman troops in the province to join Mucianus' column gave the opportunity for a local rising in Pontus, which was, however, easily suppressed by a small force sent later for the purpose by Vespasian.

tion and combination, not that of offence and co-operation, should be employed. And at Byzantium Mucianus definitely chose this plan. He sent bidding the Danube Army not to move from its lines at Aquileia, and marched himself with his whole force for that city. The other strategy, that of offence, was indeed attractive. The plan of a "double objective" always perplexes the enemy, and when skilfully used, as by the Japanese in the war of 1894, may always lead to notable successes.

Such a plan was involved in this Flavian strategy of offence. But apart from its greater risks, which might well have been ventured, two difficulties in its way were serious. From the middle of July to the middle of August the prevailing wind in the Adriatic is that from the north-west, and this greatly hampered naval operations from Dyrrhachium as a base. A still more weighty objection was the fact that the command of the sea was as yet by no means ensured to the Flavians. About the very time that the plan of invasion oversea was being discussed at Berytus, a Flavian general, at the council of war held by the officers of the Danube army at Poetovio, pointed out that the enemy had two fleets, those of Ravenna and Misenum, and that these might easily take the offensive by sea, for there was no Flavian fleet in the Adriatic to stop them. At the outset of the campaign, indeed, the command of the sea rested with the Vitellians.

It is true that the Ravenna fleet quickly proved treacherous to their cause; but its coming treachery was not an element in the strategical situation on which plans could be built, or by which strategy could be determined, either at Berytus or at Poetovio. In old days Sulla had crushed the democrats at Rome by his strategy of attack oversea from Dyrrhachium. Later in the century, Julius Caesar, for fear lest the like strategy should be used by Pompey against him, had been forced to risk the passage of the Adriatic in face of the enemy's superiority at sea, and to seek out his foe in Epirus. Still later, Antony had threatened Octavian with the same strategy. But both Sulla and Pompey had had command of the Adriatic. Antony had been master of a powerful fleet. Mucianus neither possessed the command of the sea, nor had as yet any means of gathering a fleet to secure it. The familiar strategy of offence by sea had therefore to be abandoned by him.

But it by no means followed as a consequence that no strategy of offence could be tried. Vespasian's proposed "strategy of exhaustion" deserved hearty condemnation. Apparently he intended his army at Aquileia to do nothing, even after Mucianus and his force had joined the Danube legions there. The Vitellians were to be starved into submission and blockaded during the process on the north-east frontier. From a political point of view it might be urged that this plan would save bloodshed. From a military point of view there was nothing to be said for it at all. Many losses have been caused, many campaigns wellnigh ruined, by the interference of the politician with the conduct of military operations. Virginia, Natal, the Yalu, have all recently enforced again this lesson, which is as old as the history of war. But Vespasian hitherto had been far more of a soldier than a statesman, and his plans for the campaign against Vitellius remain all the more a puzzle; for how could it be expected that this "strategy of exhaustion" would end the war in his favour? Sextus Pompeius had tried the plan of starving Italy before now, but Octavian had defied even this risk; and Octavian was far less popular with his troops than was Vitellius with his army, which was still devoted to his interests. The civilian in Italy might suffer if no corn-ships came from the South; but the soldier would find a way, even at the civilian's expense, to feed himself And not even today are the issues of war decided by the clamour of civilians; still less would this have been the case during the civil war of *A.D.* 69.

Neither was Italy so barren of food, so dependent on sea-borne corn, so pitifully unable to feed her own children, as England is today. The *proletariate* in Rome might have felt the pinch of need, and its anger was doubtless dangerous enough to an emperor in Rome; but there was no need (other than the excellence of the palace kitchen) for Vitellius to stay in the city and listen trembling to the howling of the hungry mob. There is no evidence that the corn from Egypt or Africa was necessary for any place save Rome, or even ever sent up country at all. Italy fed herself even though Rome starved. There was no transport for corn, no commerce in corn, from Rome to the other districts of the land any more in *A.D.* 69 than there was in the days of the Gracchi. Vespasian's "strategy of exhaustion" was not in the least likely to exhaust the Vitellian Army.

Its ultimate base of supplies was still the western part of the Empire, Germany and Gaul. Neither Vespasian in Egypt nor Mucianus at Aquileia threatened in any way the safety of the enemy's communications with the lands which were still the source of their strength, the place of replenishment for their resources. The strategy of masterly inactivity, if pursued in this way by the Flavians, would not discourage the temper of the Army of Germany. They, after all, were the men in possession. Rome and Italy were the sign of Empire, the crown of conquest. It must be the Flavians' part to attack and evict, for theirs had been the challenge. If they rested quiet, the Vitellian Army in high scorn might take the initiative themselves. They, by means of the fleet, might descend upon the motionless force at Aquileia, land in their rear, and cut them off hopelessly from their base and line of retreat, while the Vitellians could always use the fleet as a base. The value of the possession of the strategical initiative in war cannot be set too high. The force which possesses the command of the sea is the more likely to possess this initiative if numbers are equal; and, possessing it, such a force compels the enemy to make his dispositions conform to its own plans for the campaign.

But the Flavians, if the attacking party, might seize at the outset the strategical initiative, thanks to the fact that a large army lay already on the frontier of the enemy's country when the war broke out, whereas the defending army was slowly moving north from Rome. If they let the opportunity slip, the initiative would naturally pass to the Vitellians. The "strategy of exhaustion," which would have been no exhaustion at all of the Vitellians, wilfully abandoned this the Flavian great military opportunity. It made a present of the strategical initiative to the foe. This strategy, in fact, is appropriate only to the weaker side, and then under very special conditions. Fabius Maximus used it at a crisis and saved Rome. But it was not this strategy which gave Rome at last the victory in the second Punic war.

Pericles used it against the Peloponnesians, and thereby ran the ship of State hard on the rocks, whence more skilful pilots had to rescue it. Frederick the Great saved his kingdom by its use, and had indeed no other choice. But the quarrel was not of his seeking, and his prize of victory was not conquest but his country's preservation. Such a strategy might have been appropriate to the Vitellians: the choice of it by the Flavians, whose part it was to conquer, not to preserve, must have gone far to ruin their cause. The Danube Army meant to fight. Were they to be told that fighting was too dangerous? For what other purpose were they at Aquileia?—To wait attack by the hated foe? To be cut off by an enemy landing from the sea in their rear, and a chain of fortresses in a hostile land to their front? Roman war is fought with men, not with automata. The Flavian was the challenger. He had flung down the gauntlet. Was he to retire to his tent until the other champion came to turn him out with ignominy, scarcely leaving him time to mount his lazy steed?

Offensive strategy alone can quickly end a war. The passive

attitude may eventually induce the weary enemy to seek for peace; it can never produce the same effect as the offensive crowned with tactical victory. Hence in strategy the defensive should never be assumed except as a temporary measure, or by the weaker side, to be changed to the offensive as soon as opportunity offers. A nation which declares war and acts on the defensive shows that it does not understand the condition most essential for success.—James, *Modern Strategy*.

Whether in reality this "strategy of exhaustion" would have been pursued by Mucianus after his arrival at Aquileia or not cannot be determined; for despite his orders sent to the Danube Army there, and long before his arrival, this had taken the bit in its teeth and charged furiously upon the foe.

C. The Council of War at Poetovio: the "Strategy of Annihilation"— While at Berytus Vespasian and Mucianus were discussing plans for the war, the officers of the Danube army met at Poetovio, the town near the western frontier of the province of Pannonia, to deliberate on their own account. The actual governors of the three provinces—Pannonia, Dalmatia, and Moesia—took but a small part in the council and in the military operations which followed. The Legate of Pannonia, Lucius Tampius Flavianus, does indeed seem to have been present, and he presently accompanied the army of invasion as far as Verona; but he was cautious by nature, old in years, and, moreover, a kinsman of Vitellius, and at first, when the disturbance began in Pannonia, fled hastily to Italy to be out of the way of danger. The persuasions of Cornelius Fuscus, *procurator* of the province, induced him to return. The *procurator* desired for his party the prestige attaching to the name of one who had been consul; the governor hoped to pluck some profit from the rebellion.

But the troops naturally mistrusted him, and at Verona they made an excited attack upon him, which nearly cost him his life, and got rid of him away from the army for good and all.[12] Marcus Pompeius Silvanus, Governor of Dalmatia, was, like Tampius, old, rich, and more of a financier than a general. He certainly was not of any weight in the council, if present; for the one legion of his province, the Eleventh Claudia, was still hesitating, and, in fact, the legion and its governor appeared in the Flavian camp only after the first great victory

---

12. He was consul about *A.D.* 46 and again under Vespasian in 74. He seems to have given his name to the *ala* I. Pannonionim Tampiana, CI.L, iii.

had been won and Cremona had fallen. These were incidents which relieved the anxiety of general and private concerning the probable issue of the struggle, but gave them matter for anxious thought concerning their reception in the victors' camp if they delayed longer to join them. Silvanus, a man "apt to waste in words the hour for deeds, and a sluggard in war," was wholly ruled by the legate of the Eleventh legion, Annius Bassus, who by judicious deference to the old governor won his assent to all his own plans and carried them out quietly and ably.

Thus neither Tampius nor Silvanus added any strength to the Flavian cause except the lustre of their names and the benefit of their actual insignificance. The third of the three *legates*, M. Aponius Saturninus, Governor of Moesia, was absent from the council of war.

He had indeed written hurriedly to Vitellius the news that the Third legion in Moesia had mutinied against his authority. Later, however, he had seen fit to follow the lead of his troops, and declare for Vespasian, and early in the campaign he appeared in the Flavian camp with one of the three legions of his province, the Seventh Claudia. But some letters which he was supposed to have written to Vitellius were one day published in the camp, and the fiery and suspicious troops indignantly joined in an eager hunt for the traitor through the gardens where he was staying. Aponius saved his life by hiding promptly in the furnace of some disused baths, and, when the storm blew over, retired to Padua and took no further part in the war. It was not to such time-servers as an Aponius, a Tampius, a Silvanus, that Vespasian owed his Empire. Three men of lower rank, whose military energy was spoilt by no politic caution, whose zeal on his behalf was hampered by no considerations of their own dignity, swayed the counsels of the Danube army and led irresolution captive to daring.

Cornelius Fuscus, the procurator of Pannonia, had as a mere youth preferred the Imperial Civil Service to the Senatorial career which, as a lad of good family, he would naturally have followed. Renouncing the rank to which his birth entitled him, he chose the career which, if of less repute, gave greater opportunities of a fortune. But the tempestuous days of the civil wars afforded him chances of action which he loved better even than money-making. To him, now in the vigour of his early manhood, battle was a delight, risk more joyous than certainty, peril than the rewards of peril. His services in the war won him honour and promotion. Under Domitian he was prefect of the Praetorian Guard, and he perished at the head of his troops, trapped and destroyed by the barbarians in the second Dacian war of *A.D.* 89.

Arrius Varus was probably an older man, but the military experience which he had gained while serving under Corbulo in the Parthian war twelve years before served him in good stead. The rapidity with which the column of invasion swept down upon North Italy showed that he had not forgotten the lessons taught him in the field by his old master in the art of war. His very success earned for him, later, Mucianus' suspicion, and he had to suffer degradation from the office of Praetorian *prefect*, which had been his reward, being given instead the inferior position of *prefect* of the Corn Supply.

Such energy was exhibited also in an equal, if not in still larger, measure by the third of the three leaders, M. Antonius Primus. This officer is the hero of the successful Flavian invasion of Italy. His earlier career, indeed, did him little credit. Eight years before, he had been condemned at law as one of the witnesses to a forged will; but Galba had restored him to his senatorial rank and given him the command of his new legion, the Seventh Galbiana. Antonius had a happy confidence in his own ability, and men said that he had written to Otho offering himself as general-in-chief for his war with Vitellius. That emperor was already plagued by too many general officers, and took no notice of the offer. But now at last Antonius' chance was come. He was an able speaker, and, when the news of Vespasian's rising reached Pannonia, he at once harangued the troops on behalf of the Flavian general, and that in no ambiguous terms.

Others might strive to face both ways, but Antonius was impatient of such shallow cowardice. The blunt soldiers found in him a man after their own heart. His unscrupulous dexterity might bring disgrace upon his rivals; he might rob with the one hand and fling money broadcast with the other; but he was a stalwart soldier who knew his own mind, and if he advertised his own merits, at least they were merits which his fellow-soldier loved, and he really possessed them. The men of the Seventh legion knew that they had found a man to lead them, however hazardous the enterprise, and were impatient of any other general.

When such officers met in council at Poetovio, it is not surprising that a vigorous strategy found favour. There were indeed some who urged that they were bound to wait for the arrival of Mucianus and their comrades of the Syrian Army. They dwelt upon the strength, the fame, the recent victory, of the enemy. Their own position, they urged, could easily be made impregnable against attack until the reinforcements came. The high road from Poetovio by Emona and Nauportus to Aquileia, a hundred and fifty miles away, had to cross the mountain chain of the "Pannonian Alps" to the north of the Istrian promontory. The passes of the ridge, they argued, could be blocked, and their army would then rest in safety under cover of the mountains. "Conquered troops," they asserted, alluding to the recent defeat which some of their army had suffered at Bedriacum, "may talk as boldly as they please, but they have not the courage of their conquerors for all that."

A fiery speech by Antonius consumed this advocacy of delay in a moment. The council of war was held in open air, and the centurions and even private soldiers came thronging up to assist the deliberations of their officers. Antonius' clear loud voice rang through the camp, and he carried even the more cautious away by his fierce eloquence. In bitter terms he described the demoralisation of the Vitellian soldiery. " Scattered through the townships of Italy and no longer under arms, sluggard guests dreaded only by their hosts, draining the cup of new, strange pleasures with a wild zest, a zest as great as was that rude ferocity which once was theirs and was theirs no longer, these erstwhile soldiers of Vitellius had lost their hardiness in the circus, the theatre, the allurements of the capital. Yes, but they were soldiers still. Give them but time, and the very thought of war would brace them again to valour. Germany and Gaul, Britain and Spain, Italy and Rome itself, would send out new armies to fill their ranks. Nor would their own position be safe behind the ramparts of the mountains. Vitellius' fleets commanded the Adriatic, and it would be easy to land an army in their rear. Where then would be the service of their delay, and where the food and money for the troops if they lay idle till next year's summer came? They had not been defeated, but tricked into submission.

The day for vengeance for this trickery was come. Their comrades of the Moesian Army had lost no single man. What did it matter that they were inferior in *legionaries?* In discipline, in sobriety, in very numbers, if men of every arm were counted, they had the mastery of the foe. Above all, in cavalry lay their own great strength. In the battle lately fought two little squadrons had charged and broken the enemy's line. Were these defeated troops? But now sixteen squadrons of horse would overwhelm with the thunder of the onset of their serried ranks, would bury beneath the rushing wave of their furious charge, horses and horsemen forgetful of battle.

"Keep back the legions," he cried, turning scornfully to the advocates of caution; "keep back the legions, you who risk nothing by defeat,[13] and give me the *cohorts* only.[14] I have planned, and I will carry out the plan. You will be glad enough to follow in my steps when the victory is won."

After such a speech there was no room left for moderate counsels. The soldiers cheered "their one and only leader" to the echo, and the council broke up intent on an immediate advance into Italy. A message was sent to Aponius Saturninus bidding him hasten to bring the Moesian Army into the field.[15] Certain precautions also were taken to ensure the safety of the northern frontier when the provinces south of the Danube were stripped bare of troops. There was, in fact, danger all along the Danube frontier. West of Pannonia lay the district of Noricum, which was threatened by the procurator of Raetia, who was firmly loyal to Vitellius. On the north of Pannonia, occupying the district north of the Danube between the Rivers March and Waag, lay the tribe of the Suebi, ruled by two princes jointly, Sido and Italicus. Though vaguely in the sphere of Roman influence the Suebi were practically independent of Rome.

The Danube, after flowing in an easterly direction for many miles, turns abruptly to the south at a point about a hundred and forty miles east of Vienna, and continues on the southerly course for not far short of two hundred miles. This reach of the river formed the eastern boundary of Pannonia. Some fifty or sixty miles to the east of it the Theiss flows parallel to the Danube, and joins it from the north after the greater river has turned eastwards again. The strip of land between the Danube and the Theiss, some two hundred miles therefore in length, was occupied by a tribe of Sarmatian stock, the Jazyges, which always maintained its independence of the Roman Empire

---

13. "*Quibus fortuna in integro est*," *i.e.* who have not compromised themselves fatally with Vitellius, but still hope to be able to sit on the fence.
14. *I.e.* the auxiliaries.
15. Tacitus, whose account of the Flavian invasion is far more satisfactory than that of the war of Otho and Vitellius, leaves us, however, in great perplexity as to the actual position of the three Moesian legions at this time. In April they have already "entered Aquileia", and are there when they refuse allegiance to Vitellius, "*Aquileiam progressae*". But the council of war at Poetovio sends bidding Saturninus "*cum exercitu Moesico celeraret*", and Antonius' first act is to occupy Aquileia with his auxiliaries. When he moves on to Verona, it is some days before the Moesian Army joins him there, and then they arrive in two detachments, the Seventh legion first, and then the Third and Eighth. It is possible that they were at Aquileia all the time, as Vespasian appoints this town for the general rendezvous (iii.). But iii. seems to imply that they had withdrawn again to Moesia. Tacitus, however, never tells us this directly, and this is characteristic of the looseness of his military narrative.

even after Trajan's conquest of Dacia many years later. A tribe of hardy horsemen, they could defy any attempt of the slow-moving legionary to subdue them in their native wilds. East of the Jazyges, north of the Danube and the province of Moesia, lay the powerful and restless tribesmen of the Dacians, and the lower course of the river to the sea had roving Sarmatian tribes, such as the Roxolani, upon its northern bank.

So far as was possible, the Flavian leaders secured the safety of all this vast length of frontier before they directed the army which garrisoned it upon Italy. A special expeditionary force was sent under an able officer to assist the native levies of Noricum to defend the line of the River Inn against attack from Raetia. This force, consisting of eight *cohorts* of auxiliary infantry and one squadron of Spanish horse, the *ala* I. Hispanorum Auriana, under Sextilius Felix, was unmolested by the enemy over the river. Sido and Italicus, princes of the Suebi, with a cavalry bodyguard of their own people, actually joined the column of invasion, and fought for Vespasian's cause at Cremona. In like manner the chiefs of the Jazyges offered their services and those of the horse and foot of the tribe. The latter offer was declined, since the Flavian leaders could not trust such allies' loyalty, if it should be tempted by bribes from the enemy. But they prudently secured pledges for the peace of that section of the frontier by taking the chiefs themselves with them.

By such measures the safety of Pannonia was guaranteed in the absence of its garrison; but the longer Moesian frontier was left dangerously denuded of Roman troops. The Governor of Moesia may have relied upon the effect of the crushing blow which had in the previous winter been dealt to the raiders of the Roxolani in the province.[16] But the Dacians were but eagerly watching for their opportunity. As soon as the legions marched for Italy, they crossed the river and fell upon the Roman camps on the southern bank. Happily for the Roman province, Mucianus was already in Moesia on his march to Italy, and sent off the Sixth Ferrata legion of the Syrian Army in hot haste to the rescue. For a short time the Dacians were repelled, but the situation on the lower Danube grew more and more ominous.

But, meanwhile, Italy had been the scene of fighting. Antonius and his fellow-generals had taken such precautions as seemed to them necessary or possible to guard the frontier from Passau to the sea. But for the main enterprise every *legionary*, despite Antonius' vaunt, must

---

16. See Chapter 1 §2.

be called to the war. Antonius himself, with Arrius Varus at his right hand, led the advance of the invading column. If the orders from Syria to await Mucianus' arrival ever reached him, these were blandly disregarded. At the head of a picked band of auxiliaries and part of the cavalry Antonius and Varus crossed the Pannonian Alps and swept down upon Aquileia, leaving the rest of the army and the legionaries to follow with what speed they could. They seized Aquileia, and pressed at once on westwards. The strategy of instant attack had carried the day. The Flavians would seek out the enemy to annihilate them, if it might be so, in battle. While their supreme leaders in far-off Eastern lands were devising schemes of "exhaustion" and devious strategies of war, the Danube Army flung caution to the winds and rushed to the attack.

Thus the Flavian invasion of Italy led to a struggle once more between the old enemies of the war in the spring of the year—the Rhine Army and the Danube Army. In April the Danube Army had had but a part of its strength engaged, but it had enjoyed the co-operation of the Army of Italy, upon which indeed the chief brunt of the fighting had fallen. In April the Rhine Army had been the army of invasion. In October the Danube Army was at full strength, but there was no friendly army marching from the south to combine with it. The relics of the former Army of Italy were either enlisted in its ranks or scattered to the four winds, and some were even fighting for the enemy. The Rhine Army had become the army defending Italy against invasion. It had itself suffered in strength, thanks to Vitellius' discharge of many of its troops, and in efficiency, thanks to six months' loose living in Italy. But it had added on to it all available soldiers in Rome and Italy, and the two victorious generals of the first campaign, Valens and Caecina, were once more in command of it. The strategy of the October campaign is more simple and therefore less interesting than that of April; but the struggle was a fiercer one, even to the death. In April the seeds were abundantly sown of bitterness and passion. Now the late harvest-time had come, and the furious soldiery were the reapers.

§4. The Strategy of the Defence

The tidings of the mutiny in Moesia against his authority had first reached Vitellius at Rome in a letter from Aponius Saturninus, governor of the province. But Saturninus sent word only that the Third legion had revolted, and flattering friends in the Imperial Court made light of the whole disturbance. Trustworthy news was indeed difficult to obtain as soon as the Danube Army had blocked the road over the Pannonian Alps, for if the northwest wind in the Adriatic hampered any naval movements on part of the enemy, it at least also hindered the coming of despatches from the East overseas. Vitellius, however, sent to Britain, Spain, and Germany for reinforcements. But his summons were tardy, nor were they very urgent. Vespasian's spies and agents were everywhere, and men had no confidence in Vitellius' chances of victory. Three of the four legions in Britain did indeed send detachments in time to take part in the struggle.[17] The fear of troubles in the country and the half-heartedness of its governor restrained the rest. The legates of the three legions in Spain with one consent held all their troops back.[18]

They would not help to prop a falling cause. In Upper Germany was an old and timorous governor, Hordeonius Flaccus, whom Vitellius had left there to guard the bank of the Rhine. But he by this time was alarmed at the signs of revolt against Rome, which were now but too clear lower down the river, and wisely kept the few troops at his disposal in the province. Only the one legion in Africa,[19] and the provincial troops here were ready and eager to fight for their old governor Vitellius, but their legate, Valerius Festus, wavered, and they did not cross the sea. When, therefore, the instant and alarming approach of the danger soon put its reality beyond question, Vitellius had to confront it with such troops as he had in Italy, together with the timely, if weak, reinforcements from Britain. Alike the West and the South were happy to be spectators of the combat, and were ready to applaud the victor heartily enough. Self-interest in such a civil war was bound to be men's ruling instinct.

But no such reproach of timorousness or indifference belongs to the emperor's old troops, the soldiers of the former German Army. They from first to last were loyal and devoted to Vitellius. Nor, indeed, were their numbers small. Their old generals, Caecina and Valens, were ordered to march at once to the seat of war in North Italy as soon as the general revolt of the Danube Army was beyond doubt. Valens was handicapped by illness, and unable to leave Rome at once. But Caecina, after taking an affectionate farewell of the emperor, whom he

---

17. *Viz.* II. Augusta, IX. Hispana, XX. Valeria Victrix. The Fourteenth legion was, of course, hostile to Vitellius, and sent no aid, see §2 above.
18. *Viz.* I. Adjutrix, VI. Victrix, X. Gemina.
19. *Viz.* III. Augusta.

intended to betray, marched for the north at the head of an imposing column of infantry, preceded by a cavalry detachment. In the van of the foot there marched the veterans of four legions—the First, Fourth Macedonica, Fifteenth Primigenia, and Sixteenth. The centre consisted of the Fifth Alaudae legion and the Twenty-Second Primigenia. In the rear of the column came the First Italica legion, the Twenty-First Rapax, and the detachments from the three legions of Britain—the Second Augusta, Ninth Hispana, and Twentieth Valeria Victrix. The whole number can hardly have fallen short of forty thousand *legionaries*. Four of these legions had belonged to Valens' old command in Lower Germany,[20] and he sent bidding them wait upon the march until he could overtake them. But Caecina overruled the order, and he had every possible military justification for so doing.

The writers of the *principate* of Vespasian loved to paint in gloomy colours the appearance which the soldiers of his defeated rival presented as they marched to the front from Rome by the great north road, and the Roman historian of a later age had no choice, it seems, but to tell their story over again. If these writers dared to ascribe honourable motives to men, Tacitus' critical faculty was at once aroused; but the mere record of supposed facts, if they were picturesque, excited no suspicion in his mind. Yet the soldier's trade is war, and many an army has marched out to defeat as cheerfully and made as brave a show as have the coming victors in the battle. When the defeat is history of the past then the curious scribes find presage for it in the imagined demeanour of the troops as they marched for the front. The change in the bearing of the German Army, says the Roman writer, was indeed great as it left the city. There was no strength in their bodies, no fire in their hearts. The column rolled heavily along, sluggish and scattered, the weapons dull with long neglect, the very horses moving listlessly. The soldier, grumbling at the sun, the dust, the weather, shirked his duty, and made up for it by quarrelling with his comrade.

It is a sombre military picture. Yet this is the army which, after a march of three hundred miles in summer heat, is ready, in spite of the desertion of its general, to march some thirty miles on a short October day, and, without taking rest, fight strenuously in hand-to-hand combat with the enemy the whole of the following night until the sun rose! Moore's Englishmen, Blücher's Prussians, young General Bonaparte's ragged troops, happy in their desperate victories, happier still in their generals, would yet find comrades to their heart in the

---

20. *Viz*, I. Italica, V. Alaudae, XV. Primigenia, XVI.

Romans of Caecina's leaderless army—soldiers, in truth, for all their grumbling, and no craven, no undisciplined, mob of recreants.

The force of circumstances compelled the Vitellians to adopt the strategical defensive. To this Caecina now chose to add the tactical defensive as well. He contented himself with the occupation of a strong position guarding the line from Cremona to the sea. The thrust of the assailants would come from the north-east. Caecina made due preparations to repel this attack upon his lines. North of the main stream of the river Po, between the marshes of Mantua and the lagoons of Maestra, two rivers at no great distance apart flow through the level plain. The first of these, the Tartaro, is distant some five miles, at an average, from the Po for the greater part of its course. North of this again the splendid stream of the Adige, which comes foaming down from the Brenner Pass and sweeps in a magnificent semicircle round the fortress of Verona, leaves the hills at that city, and for the rest of its course cuts through the marshy level to the sea by Chioggia with a quieter flood.

In Roman days there was no bridge over the Po from Hostilia for over forty miles to the east. From the passage of the river at Hostilia the main road ran north-east through Ateste (Este), Patavium (Padua), and Altinum (Altino) to Aquileia. This road crossed first the Tartaro at three miles' distance from Hostilia, and then the Adige eight miles from its crossing of the Tartaro. Here, guarding the passage of the Adige, is today the fortress city of Legnago, one of the four great fortresses of the "Quadrilateral," famous in the times of the Austrian domination of Italy.[21] In the first century of our era a little Roman market-town, by name Forum Alieni, lay on the site of the fortress of Legnago.[22]

The advance guard of cavalry was sent on at once to occupy Cremona, and it was followed to the town by the First Italica legion and the Twenty-First Rapax. The rest of the large army was directed straight upon Hostilia. Caecina himself turned aside to visit the naval station at Ravenna, where lay the fleet under the command of its prefect, Sextus Lucilius Bassus. Ravenna, indeed, was necessary to the completeness of the defence. For although the invaders had no fleet able to cope with the Vitellian fleet at Ravenna, yet there seems to

---

21. The four fortresses were: N.W. Peschiera; N.E. Verona; S.W. Mantua; S.E. Legnago.
22. There cannot be reasonable doubt as to this identification. The suggestion that Ferrara is Forum Alieni is impossible in view of the military operations of this campaign.

have been a coast road leaving the main road from Aquileia to Padua some miles short of this latter city, and striking due south by Adria to Ravenna; and if the enemy had chosen this road, the defenders' position from Cremona to Hostilia would have been outflanked and turned. But the presence of a friendly fleet at Ravenna would make any such scheme of advance far too dangerous to adopt. Thus the line of defence ran from Cremona to Hostilia, from Hostilia to Ravenna. And thrown forward at Forum Alieni, guarding the bridge over the Adige, was a small outpost, consisting of three *cohorts* of auxiliary infantry and a squadron of Gallic cavalry, the *ala* II. Gallorum Sebosiana. The breadth of the river and the single bridge should make its defence possible even by so small a force if it observed the elementary duties of an outpost, constant scouting by the cavalry, and watchful pickets at night.

The first blow dealt to the defence fell upon this force at Legnago, which the enemy successfully rushed at dawn. The camp was completely surprised, and many were cut down before they could reach their weapons. This disgrace was the result only of inexcusable carelessness on part of the sentries, or of the commander, if no sentries were posted.

> Men on the line of defence cannot sleep at ease at night, or kindle fires to warm themselves. The night is the time when they must be most vigilant and wide awake. The patrols on the picket line and the scouts far in front must try to take in everything. However tired they may be from their day's work, at night they must not even allow a singing insect or a flying bird to pass unnoticed.[23]

The outposts of the camp on the Adige, if there were such, incurred great dishonour. But the reverse was partially redeemed by some of the troops who, though surprised, held their ground long enough to allow the destruction of the bridge, and by this means checked for the time the pursuit and advance of the invaders. But when the news of this reverse reached Caecina, and his outposts also came into touch with the enemy's skirmishers, who presently crossed the Adige, the Vitellian general moved his main camp at Hostilia a few miles forward, and entrenched a strong position on the northern bank of the river Tartaro. To its rear, therefore, lay this river, crossed by a bridge; on both flanks the marshes of that muddy stream safely

---

23. *Human Bullets*, by Lieut. Sakorai. The Japanese siege of Port Arthur puts most warfare, ancient and modern, to shame.

guarded it.[24] With its front only exposed to attack and this strongly fortified, secured on the west of the whole line by Cremona, on the east by the fleet at Ravenna, the camp on the Tartaro might surely defy the assaults of the enemy.[25]

While Vitellius' legions lay upon the Tartaro or at Cremona, maintaining a strictly defensive attitude, the emperor's second general, Fabius Valens, in due course left Rome and moved slowly northwards along the northern highway, following in the steps of the army towards Ariminum (Rimini) which lies on the road thirty miles south-east of Ravenna, and one hundred miles from the camp on the Tartaro. In his train he seems to have brought more women than soldiers, more eunuchs than *legionaries*. The march of so soft a column was naturally slow. Valens possessed military ability; but, at a time when there was crying need for it at the front, he preferred to postpone its exercise to the gratification of an unbridled and horrible lust with which he amused himself at his frequent halts along the road. The army at Cremona and the Tartaro could look for small reinforcements to arrive with this general when he came, and might look for his coming for long in vain.[26] Caecina's army was, in fact, the emperor's one hope. It had marched swiftly to the north. Now it lay sullenly in its lines waiting attack by the foe. To the strategy of attack, chosen by Antonius Primus and the Flavian generals of the Danube Army, the Vitellians opposed a strategy of defence. Such a strategy may be executed by a tactical offensive as well as by a tactical defensive. But Caecina chose the latter, and destroyed his emperor by his choice.

§5. The Strategies compared

The comparison between the advantages of the offensive and the defensive in strategy is a favourite theme with military scientists, and Clausewitz's expressed preference for the latter has produced a rich

---

24. This position is described by Tacitus in as "*inter Hostiliam et paludes Tartari fluminis.*" From this it would appear as if it lay on the south bank of the Tartaro and that the "*flumen*" at its rear (*loc. cit.*) is the Po. But when the troops evacuate it, Tacitus describes the movement as "*relictis castris, abrupto ponte Hostiliam rursus, inde Cremonam pergunt.*" Therefore the bridge broken down lay between the camp and Hostilia, and as this latter place lay on the north bank of the Po, it can only have been a bridge over the Tartaro. As this bridge lay in rear of the camp, the camp must have been on the north bank of this latter river.
25. Movements of the Vitellians.
26. Tacitus' account of Valens' actual movements is the vaguest and worst possible. See Note F, "Valens' March to the North" at end of chapter.

crop of explanations, interpretations, even apologies. Certain advantages of the attack are indeed evident, and are as visible in strategy as they are in tactics. The attacking army is the more likely to be keen, even enthusiastic; its confidence is probably greater; its sense of daring stimulates courage and at the same time enforces discipline. "The greater vitality resides in the attack," (Von der Goltz). The invasion of a hostile country especially fires the imagination and stimulates the vigour of the soldier. An advantage in numbers over the enemy is indeed greatly to be desired by the invader. Lines of communications have to be guarded, and these are always increasing in length. Fortresses have to be seized and garrisoned, or blockaded; important strategical points have to be secured. Supplies are obtained with greater difficulty in a hostile than in a friendly land.

Losses in battle are made good less easily. Stragglers are cut off and cannot rejoin. The sick and wounded cannot be left to the care of the inhabitants, but must be tended and guarded by the invading army. To supply these many demands for men, and yet to retain a force strong enough to push ever deeper and deeper into the heart of the enemy's country, and able to defeat the foe when these choose to stand their ground rather than to surrender still more of the homeland to their foe,—these requirements make a superiority of numbers on part of the invader and his constant reinforcement well-nigh essential.[27] "Armies acting on the offensive melt like fresh snow in spring," (Von der Goltz).

> It is thus plain that the offensive is only possible when large numbers enable a leader to overcome the difficulties it offers, and good organisation ensures the rapidity necessary for carrying it out. But, given these, there can be no doubt of its advantage. The moral gain is great; the soldier feels he is superior to his adversary when led with determination against him; and this mental attitude leads more than halfway along the road to victory.—James, *Modern Strategy*.

There are few generals who would not prefer to conduct rather

---

27. Of the drain in men suffered by an invading army there are stock examples in the military text-books: Napoleon in 1812 crossed the frontier of Russia with over three and a half million troops: at Moscow he had barely a hundred thousand; in 1877, 450,000 Russians crossed the Danube: 43,000 arrived outside Constantinople; the Germans in 1870 invaded France with three and a half million men: six weeks later they had only half the number before Paris. Cf. James, *Modern Strategy*; Von der Goltz, *The Nation in Arms*.

than to resist an invasion; who would not choose to attack rather than to defend. Even though, on the actual field of battle, the lot of the defender may seem to have fallen in pleasanter places, to act on the defensive in the whole theatre of the war is but a gloomy business. There are indeed no generals who would not desire to have for their invasion or attack an efficient army larger than that of the defender. And yet the brilliant genius of the commander has in times past more than made good even an inferiority of numbers possessed by the invading army when it crossed the enemy's frontier. Hannibal in Italy, Cromwell in Scotland, Lee and Jackson in Maryland, took no account of the general rule that the invader must greatly outnumber the field army of the defender.[28] But the world sees few commanders such as these. And even so, alike in Italy and in America, the brutal weight of numbers had in the end its revenge.

The Flavian invading army was far from enjoying any such superiority of numbers. But the leader of the invasion, Antonius Primus, was a, commander, as the event showed, who won the admiration and devotion of his troops to a high degree, and inspired them with his own self-confidence and energy. The troops which he led across the frontier were spirited and ready for any desperate enterprise. No invading army could in temper have been better fitted for its work. Neither did the general lack ability or a keen insight into the possibilities of a military situation. The German general would have his brother-officers go to school of Goethe's Mephistopheles:—

An Kühnheit wird's euch auch nicht fehlen,
Und wenn ihr euch nur selbst vertraut,
Vertrauen euch die andern Seelen.
      —Von der Goltz, *The Nation in Arms*

It was just this supreme confidence in himself which, added to his courage and "dash," endeared Antonius to his men, and seemed to make him an ideal leader of an invading army.

The invasion of Italy by the Danube Army was clearly a daring, even a perilous, strategy to adopt. But when invasion is conducted by such a general, when in itself it has such advantages over the defence,

---

28. Of course this rule applies only when the hostile nations and their armaments are of similar character and their troops display similar qualities. It does not hold good in contests between European troops and most Asiatic nations, or barbarians; *e.g.,* an Alexander or a Caesar, a Cortex or a Clive, is not an example to the contrary of this rule. Nor does it apply to mere raids across the frontier where no fighting or occupation of the enemy's land is intended.

surely the plan might seem justified?

> In the zeal to inflict injury upon the enemy, a resolution must not aim at the unattainable, though it should venture to go to the extreme limit of the permissible. In war, nothing rational must be considered impossible as long as it has not been tested; and we may dare everything we believe we can carry out.— Von der Goltz.

"In war, nothing rational must be considered impossible." The Flavian invasion of Italy as conducted in the autumn of *A.D.* 69 had no rational prospect of success. It ought to have been hurled back in ruinous defeat and panic-stricken disgrace over the Pannonian Alps.

For the Flavian forces struggled over the mountains down to the plain of North-east Italy in widely separated detachments. Those who arrived first flung themselves forward regardless of any co-operation with those who were to come after them. Here came a band of auxiliaries; then, after a gap, came a legion; then, after a pause of some days, other legions. The whole conduct of the enterprise in face of a foe who knew how to use his opportunities was mad. Even when concentrated, the invading army was hardly equal in numbers to the Vitellian forces on the river. If the defenders had taken the tactical offensive as soon as the foe appeared in the plain south and east of Aquileia, there was no hope for the invaders but that they would have been swallowed up piecemeal. The legions which came tardily down over the mountains, because encouraged by the unopposed progress of Antonius and the advance guard, would have hesitated longer had a few frightened fugitives come speeding back to them for refuge from the pursuit of a victorious foe. Antonius' numbers for the first few days after he had come into touch with the enemy were contemptible. But the legions of Vitellius lay passively in their entrenchments, looking dully at the stream of the enemy which flowed past their front in intermittent waves.

The procession of the Flavian troops passed gaily along day after day, always exposing their flank. They seized town after town, fortress after fortress, a few miles away from the torpid Vitellian Army. They concentrated undisturbed, unopposed, in high spirits, and at leisure, at the powerful fortress of Verona. Even after this, their whole line of communications lay open to attack. If the enemy fell on them they must of necessity have formed front to a flank outside Verona's walls, and their defeat would have meant annihilation for them. During the weary days while they were mustering, a single victory (and it was impossible that the Vitellians should not gain it) would have ruined the whole scheme of invasion—at least until Mucianus arrived, and would have given even him much cause for thought.

So sensitive is the barometer of men's inclinations in days of civil war to the storms of failure or the sunshine of success that the mere rout of the advance guard of the Danube Army might possibly have wrecked Vespasian's whole enterprise. This, perhaps, would have been too much to expect. Hardrada is routed at Stamford Bridge, but the Norman still lands at Pevensey and Harold falls at Senlac. But, even so, the Northman did not invade on Duke William's behalf. At least the frontier of North-east Italy might have been securely guarded had Vitellius' men quitted their stagnant lines and advanced to battle. Mucianus' heart might well have failed him, or his discouraged troops have refused to follow him; and then the victorious army might have marched south again, as did Harold's men, and have defied the Eastern invader to make good his landing from overseas, or, if he landed, have fought him to the death. Antonius' invasion would have remained on record but as a monument of rash folly. The real struggle for Empire might once more have been waged outside the walls of Rome. And who then would with surety forecast the victory for Vespasian?

It was treachery which defeated Vitellius' soldiers and their emperor, not the strategy of the enemy. Two men were faithless to the cause. Caecina, the general, of subtilty kept his splendid army idle in its entrenchments. Lucilius Bassus, prefect of the fleet at Ravenna, sought to entice the sailors from their loyalty. Both men's motives were despicable. However unworthy their emperor, it was not for these men who had received honours at his hands to plot craftily against him. Happy indeed was Rome and fortunate the Empire which lost Vitellius to gain Vespasian as emperor; but the traitor's taint is not therefore sweet-scented. Bassus, a mere cavalry captain, had hoped for the prefecture of the Guards at Rome. Preferred to the lower post of Admiral of the Fleet, he sought in a dastardly perfidy the remedy for his disappointment.

Caecina, vain and ambitious, ever craving popularity, secretly resentful at the greater fame which his colleague had won in the recent campaign, believed that Valens enjoyed the greater share of Vitellius' esteem. The two had indulged in envious rivalry of pomp, parade, and self-advertisement during the last few months at Rome. Caecina had yielded himself a slave to indolence and luxury. His ambition waxed as his self-control waned. Envy preyed upon him, jealousy mastered him. The man brooded over his wrongs until, as often happens, he lost his sense of honour. He who first should make terms secretly with the Flavians would doubtless receive the greater rewards at their hands. Without shame and without scruple Caecina and Bassus conspired together at Padua to bring fleet and army over to the enemy.

There was little difficulty with the fleet. The sailors, loyal to Otho, had accepted Vitellius' rule with chagrin. Many of them were drawn from the provinces of Dalmatia and Pannonia, now in arms for Vespasian. In a night the mutiny was accomplished. The Ravenna fleet declared for the Flavians with Bassus' full approval, and chose Cornelius Fuscus as their new *prefect*. Bassus gained little by his treachery save the loss of his command and a short stay in prison at Adria. Later he was employed by the victors again as cavalry captain on petty operations in Campania. His ambition had sorely overleapt itself, and he had this excuse for his treachery that he had failed to profit by it.

But Caecina had a harder task with the army. The general could urge with truth that the mutiny of the fleet had made their position on the Tartaro untenable, and that Vitellius' cause had suffered a grievous blow. With some success he laid insidious siege to the loyalty of the centurions and a few of the soldiers, who at last allowed his arguments and their fears to prevail over their fidelity. But though for a moment's space Vespasian was proclaimed in the Vitellian camp, the bulk of the soldiers and the higher officers held firmly by their emperor. They passionately asked:

> What did the miserable fleet count in comparison with eight legions? Were they, the proud, victorious army of Germany, to be handed over to an Antonius Primus as so many cattle, so many slaves, for sale? Caecina and Bassus might seek to rob the army of its emperor; but how could they, soldiers who had in this campaign tasted nothing as yet of bloodshed, make answer to their enemies or look them in the face when asked tauntingly of their victories or defeats?

The Fifth legion Alaudae overthrew Vespasian's standards with bitter indignation; the others swiftly followed suit. Caecina was put by the men in irons. The army on the Tartaro was loyal to its emperor. Its inactivity, its hopeless reliance upon the tactical defensive, had been forced on it by guile and by treachery. Its opportunity for avenging the folly of the invader on his head was indeed lost. The mutiny of the fleet must force them to retire from their useless lines. Their general, too, was lost to them. But honour was not lost, and they were still eight legions with arms in their hands and burning anger in their hearts.

The strategy of invasion should have been met and defeated by the tactics of offence employed by the strategical defensive. Success crowned Antonius' rashness. If he had reason to hope that Caecina would play the traitor, the prize was worth the risk, and Antonius who ventured it was truly a great general. But if, when he descended from the mountains upon Aquileia, he knew nothing of the temper of the sailors at Ravenna or of Caecina's meditated treachery (and the scanty evidence points to this conclusion), he cannot be acquitted of an impulsive rashness which properly deserved defeat. For in this case he was presuming upon a degree of sloth, ignorance, and incapacity on part of the enemy which it was incredible that they should display. Judged by results, the Flavian strategy of invasion was a notable success. Yet there are victories in war as in games which rightly give small satisfaction to the victors. Every general makes mistakes; but it is not scientific strategy which is built upon nothing but the expectation of the foe's mistakes. When Antonius rushed to knock his head against the enemy's wall, he deserved a headache rather than the discovery that the wall was lath and plaster.

And on the other side, Valens, so far as he was able, completed the ruin begun by the traitor general and admiral. When the Vitellian army quitted the position on the Tartaro and concentrated, ably enough, at Cremona, it lacked nothing even then but a general. One fatal error gave the hard-won victory to the foe. From this Valens' ripe wisdom would surely have saved the army. But Valens was not at Cremona. While still on his slow march to the north, he received the news of the mutiny of the fleet. He was then already probably north of Ariminum, not very far from Ravenna, to which city he was marching to cooperate with the fleet. [29] The harbour now was hostile, and he could not venture to march forward. His disorderly rabble was not an army. But still he might have turned aside by a cross road to the main road from Ariminum to Bononia, and, if he travelled with great speed, have perhaps reached Caecina on the Tartaro in time to dissuade that wavering general from his treachery. Bassus' action seems to have be fallen before Caecina expected it, and the general was still hesitating. Or, Valens might certainly have reached Cremona, had he pushed on fast, before the critical battle was fought.

---

29. See Note F, "Valens' March to the North" at end of chapter.

But Valens never at any time in his career showed resolution or rapidity of movement. He halted his column in miserable indecision, and finally sent to Rome begging for reinforcements. A poor little force was sent him, of no avail for any useful purpose. These he despatched to Ariminum. He himself gave up all thoughts of taking any part in the campaign on the Po, and crossed the Apennines to reach the Arno valley and the sea at Pisa. Great schemes of future warring at the head of the forces of Gaul and Germany floated through his mind, and he took ship at Pisa for the coast of Gaul. This plan ended lamentably. At Monaco on his voyage he heard that all the coasts had declared for Vespasian. Most of his comrades promptly followed the example set them, and Valens himself with but ten companions, setting out upon the unfriendly sea, was driven by a gale upon the Stoichades islands.[30] There he was captured and sent as a prisoner of war to the Umbrian hill-city of Urbinum.[31]

Long ere this, the Vitellians in North Italy had fought their final battle there without a general to lead them. When so many were the blunders of the defence, when the defending army had for its generals a Caecina and a Valens, the traitor and the faint-heart, there is small wonder that the strategy of offence and invasion prevailed against it. A combination by the Vitellians of the tactical offensive with the strategical defensive must have given them, at first at least, the victory. The Imperial Army was wilfully sacrificed by incompetence and treachery.

§6. The Second "Battle of Bedriacum"

A. The Flavian Advance to Verona.—Antonius led the van of his invading army rapidly down upon North-east Italy. The towns which lay upon the roads leading west and south-west from Aquileia, far from resisting him, even welcomed his coming. Opitergium, the modern Oderzo, forty-five miles from Aquileia, and Altinum (Altino) to the south of it, fifty-five miles from Aquileia, opened their gates to him. Altinum was a position of importance, as a few miles to the west of it the road from Ravenna which crossed the Po at Adria joined the road from Padua and Hostilia to Aquileia. It was Antonius' intention to press rapidly forward down this latter road. While then the fleet at Ravenna belonged to the enemy, there was a danger lest a hostile

---

30. The Iles d'Hyères, off Toulon rather than (as Tacitus describes them) off Marseilles.
31. See Note F end of chapter.

force should advance by the former road from the seaport and throw itself astride of the road by which the Flavian vanguard had come after these had passed by. In this event, their van would be cut off from the rest of their army and from their communications.

Its position would be perilous. Antonius knew nothing as yet of the intention of the fleet to desert from the enemy. He therefore left a garrison in Altinum to guard the communications, and pressed on with the main body to Padua, and beyond it to Ateste, the modern Este. Both of these towns admitted him. At Ateste he was but some seventeen miles from the enemy's outpost which was guarding the bridge over the Adige at Forum Alieni. This outpost, as has been seen, was successfully rushed at dawn and dispersed. But it found time to destroy the bridge and check the pursuit.[32]

While Caecina the enemy's general, upon news of this reverse, moved his army from Hostilia forward to the camp on the Tartaro and entrenched himself there, Antonius lay quiet at Padua. The first wave of the invasion had swept forward eighty miles, and had for the moment spent its force. But the news of the advance and of the success gained on the Adige was quickly carried back to Poetovio, and the two legions of Pannonia, the Seventh and the Thirteenth, started out forthwith with much greater confidence, and joined Antonius in due course at Padua, meeting with no difficulty on the way. Here they were given some days' rest to recover from the march.

Antonius and the other Flavian leaders had now to consider their next movements. The enemy lay quiet in their lines beyond the Adige, and showed no sign of advancing themselves to the attack. This left the initiative still comfortably in the invader's keeping. To assault the position on the Tartaro, however, seemed most unwise. It was an exceedingly strong one, and, moreover, was held by a veteran army which was far stronger in numbers than were the troops who had up to that time arrived at Padua, It was also becoming evident that Caecina's heart was not towards Vitellius any longer, and it was far better to give him time for quiet thought and a furtive correspondence with the Flavians than to hurry him into a loyal resistance by an ill-timed attack. And two other thoughts had weight with Antonius.

The strength of his force lay largely in its cavalry. If Caecina should make up his mind after all to advance his standards against the invader, Antonius needed a battle-ground where he could deploy all his horse

---

32. See Chapter 2, §4.

to best advantage. There was, indeed, plenty of level ground round Padua at the foot of the green Euganean Hills. But these hills might screen the advance of the enemy, and, besides, to stay at Padua would seem a confession of fear. The advance must continue.

The second consideration which influenced the Flavian general was the very lively dread lest large reinforcements should reach the enemy from Germany by way of the Brenner Pass. Raetia, on the northern side of the Alps where this pass began, was loyal to Vitellius, and the Flavian forces already sent to the line of the Inn might indeed defend Noricum against an attack from Raetia, but were too weak to intercept the coming of reinforcements to Italy over the Brenner.[33] If there were an army on the march by this road—and Vitellius had certainly sent to Germany for help—and if it reached Hostilia, little would be heard henceforward of Caecina's wavering.

One town, however, guarded the issue of the Brenner Pass from the mountains, the strong and important city of Verona, across the River Adige, some forty miles up stream above Legnago. To the south of Verona was a plain suited in every way for cavalry manoeuvres. If he seized this town, Antonius would have not only the prestige of holding one of the greatest cities of North Italy, but also a suitable base for his future operations. Moreover, at Verona he would be able to intercept any German reinforcements coming to the enemy from the north; and Verona was halfway from Padua to Cremona. Poised at this central point he could swoop down upon any part of the enemy's long line of defence, which reached from Cremona to Hostilia and beyond.

As soon, therefore, as his men were ready again for marching Antonius marched from Padua to Verona. On the road lay the town of Vicetia, the modern Vicenza under the Monti Berici. Today this busy city numbers nearly half as many inhabitants as Verona herself; but in Roman days it was a small place of little importance. It gave, however, peculiar pleasure to the Flavians to take possession of the town, since it happened to be Caecina's birthplace, and they gleefully thought how the news would be spread abroad that "*patriam hostium dud ereptam,*" ("the enemy's general had been despoiled of his native land.") The town, however, was of no military importance, and Caecina, who was pondering matters of greater moment, was not likely to be greatly moved by so trivial an incident. From Vicetia the army moved forward

---

33. See chapter 2, §3.

to Verona, thirty miles away, and the town gladly received them. Entrenchments were thrown up and a halt of some time was called.

From this position, says the Roman historian, Caecina could doubtless have hurled them, had he so chosen. But the traitor kept his army quiet, and soon the coming of the Moesian Army relieved Antonius from the more instant peril of defeat First the Seventh Claudia legion arrived under command of a stalwart tribune, Vipstanus Messalla, and accompanied by the Governor of Moesia himself, Aponius Saturninus. The tribune had taken direct command himself of the legion, since its *legate* was at this time fleeing for his life over the Balkans from the private vengeance of the governor. Messalla, says Tacitus, "was the one and only man who brought an honest heart to that war." Later he wrote the history of it, and Tacitus has certainly thanked him gracefully for the use which he himself made of his history.

After the Seventh legion came the other two, the Third and Eighth. By this time at last the Flavian leaders had assembled a truly powerful army at Verona. It cannot have been greatly, if at all, weaker than the enemy's force on the Tartaro. One thing was lacking to its strength, namely, perfect discipline. And it enjoyed too many possible generals. The one evil remedied the other. The turbulence of the men scared away the governors of Moesia and Pannonia from the camp. Antonius was left in undisputed command, so far as any man had command over the unruly spirits of the soldiers, and he could rely on Arrius Varus to help him.

B. The Race for Cremona.—Then to the Flavian camp at Verona there came exciting news. Antonius had for some time past been in correspondence with Caecina. The latter had doubtless assured the Flavian commander that he could induce his army to follow his example in renouncing its allegiance to Vitellius. Caecina tried and failed. His indignant troops put him in chains; but they wisely judged their position on the Tartaro to be no longer tenable. The Ravenna fleet threatened their rear; the Flavian Army at Verona, within a few miles of their front, was now strong, and might advance against them when they were in confusion and had no leader to inspirit their defence. To the west at Cremona, however, lay two legions and a force of cavalry of their comrades. The troops resolved to march to join them at once. The direct road to Cremona from Hostilia lay north of the Po, and ran by Mantua and Bedriacum. By this route Cremona was not quite sixty miles away from Hostilia. But if they marched by this route they would be perilously near the Flavians at Verona, and their right flank would be exposed to attack by these at any point along the road.

If the Verona Army marched down upon their column (and Antonius would certainly not miss such an opportunity) they would have hurriedly to deploy into order of battle by the right with the enemy's cavalry rushing down upon them, and they would fight with flanks unprotected, without cavalry of their own, and with their backs to the broad and unfordable stream of the Po. Though they now lacked Caecina's guidance, the legate of the Fifth legion and the Camp Prefect, to whom the soldiers had entrusted the command, were able to realise that such a position must mean ruinous defeat. The march by Mantua was impossible. Their only alternative was to cross to the south of the Po, and march by Mutina, Parma, and (possibly) Placentia. It was a terribly long detour and a long and trying march of a hundred and ten miles.[34] But at least their right flank would be safe, and distance would be their only enemy. They must trust to speed of marching to bring them to Cremona in time. And, in truth, never did troops merit better the praise which belongs to the Roman soldier than do these betrayed and leaderless men of the Vitellian Army. Placed in so disheartening and critical a position, the modern European soldier might but too easily lose heart entirely, or lack the initiative and foresight which the Roman at this time displayed. There have been few troops in the world to equal those of Rome.

The Vitellians abandoned their camp on the Tartaro and fell back to Hostilia. They crossed the Po there, broke down the bridge behind them,[35] and disappeared entirely from the range and ken of Antonius' scouts. The crisis of the campaign evidently was hard at hand.[36]

Antonius understood at once the meaning of the empty camp. There was now to be a race for Cremona and its small garrison be-

---

34. Distances: Hostilia to Mutina, 30 miles; Mutina to Parma, 30; Parma to Placentia, 35; Placentia to Cremona, 15. 35. An obvious inference from military requirements. The broken bridge in Tac., of course, that over the Tartaro.

36. Tacitus has not the least interest in the march. He merely remarks, "*Abrupto ponte Hostiliam rursus, inde Cremonam pergunt.*" That they marched *via* Parma, as Mommsen suggests, is shown by the fact that Antonius, on their departure, makes a forced march of two days from Verona to Bedriacum (some thirty-three miles), but never gets in touch with the Vitellian retreating army, and he arrives outside Cremona after a day's fighting as soon as they do. And these have marched with desperate haste, thirty miles on the day before the night of the final battle. Verona to Cremona is fifty-five miles. If the Vitellians found a road striking off straight to Cremona at some point on the main road short of Placentia, the distance from Hostilia to Cremona, *via* Parma, may be reckoned at about ninety to ninety-five miles.

tween his own and the Hostilia Army. The two divisions of the enemy must not be allowed to join. Cremona must be taken before the eastern division could march to it, and before it could be reached by Valens, who surely (so judged the soldier Antonius) would hasten to join the enemy's army on hearing of Caecina's betrayal. Vitellian reinforcements, too, were said to be mustering from Britain, Gaul, and Germany. He had the shorter march by fifty miles. But the garrison of Cremona was strong enough to offer a sturdy resistance. Without hesitation or delay, Antonius led his entire force south from Verona. The race for Cremona had begun.

By the evening of the second day Antonius and his army had marched thirty-five miles from Verona to Bedriacum, where the road from Mantua to Cremona joined their own. Cremona itself lay twenty-two miles away by the Via Postumia to the west.[37] There had been no sign of the enemy on the march. Evidently he had not risked the direct route from Hostilia to Cremona.

Next day, October 27, A.D. 69, Antonius left his legions at Bedriacum with orders to complete the defences of that camp. He himself rode out at the head of four thousand cavalry eight miles along the road in the direction of Cremona. His auxiliary infantry were sent out on both sides of the road to plunder and taste beforehand the sweets of victory, which could only be fully theirs when they had won the battle. This strange order could not be justified save by the character which civil war breeds in the troops; and, in fact, it was quickly punished. At eleven o'clock a mounted scout, who had been sent forward by Antonius, came riding back in hot haste with the news that the foe were advancing along the road. He had himself seen but a small body of their horse, but "the noise and the movement of the enemy could be heard far and wide."

This somewhat vague report[38] caused Arrius Varus, with part of the cavalry, to ride on to investigate its truth. Antonius, with greater foresight, halted and drew up the remainder, leaving room on the road to receive Varus and his troopers into the shelter of the centre should they be driven back by weight of numbers. Messengers were at once sent off to bid the legions march forward from Bedriacum, and signals were displayed to summon the plundering auxiliaries to the spot. Very soon Varus and his company were seen galloping back at full speed along the road, hotly pursued by superior numbers of the enemy's

---

37. For the site of Bedriacum-Calvatone see Note C at end of chapter
38. It is a report more worthy of the historian than of the scout.

horse. The garrison of Cremona had boldly sallied out to the attack. The runaways plunged madly into the midst of the Flavian battle-line. All Antonius' precautions were vain, and the whole mass of his four thousand cavalry fled back along the road in hopeless panic and confusion, their general swept along in the rout, vainly protesting, imploring, reproaching. Their flight was checked only by a small stream with steep banks and dangerous to ford, which crossed the line of the road.[39] The bridge over it had been broken, and Antonius seized the last chance of rallying the fugitives here.

A standard-bearer came wildly riding in flight down upon him. He thrust the coward through with a lance, grasped the standard, and himself turned it to face the pursuing foe. A handful of his men, not more than a hundred, saw the sight and made a stand round their general upon the streamlet's bank. The mass of fugitives, their flight checked, rallied round them. Discipline had already been restored and some kind of order formed when the pursuers came in sight, following the rout recklessly in a long scattered line. They were roughly handled, and the tide of pursuit turned. Back towards Cremona hurried the Vitellian horse, and in their wake followed the Flavian Army, now continually reinforced by legionaries from the camp and auxiliaries from the fields. A confused mass of horse and foot, like a muddy tide, rolled along the Postumian way for at least ten miles, until it presently dashed upon the enemy's infantry. The two legions had marched out under cover of their cavalry's advance, and halted four miles from Cremona. Their steadfast array and standards glittering in the sun gave promise of a firm resistance as of a line of stubborn cliffs against the flood.

But the Flavians were not to be denied. Their camp lay eighteen miles behind them; they had fought and pursued breathlessly the last ten miles. But the Vitellians had no general to marshal them to admit their fleeing horse within their ranks, or to take advantage of the enemy's weariness. They stood stolid and perplexed, and when Vipstanus

---

39. Heraeus, quoting one Rycke, calls this stream "the Delmona, a tributary of the Oglio." There is today a "Dugale Delmona" south and east of Piadena. But the Tacitean stream may be a brook more to the north, running (*sic*) from near Drizzona to the Oglio near Isola Dovarese, which probably crossed the line of the ancient road from Calvatone westwards. Precise identification is impossible, owing to the modern drainage channels. There is a marsh north of San Lorenzo dei Picenardi and, a mile to the west, a moated *castello*, and lakelet at Torre dei Picenardi, and there may well have been a stream here in old days. The "Delmona" (*sic*) is too far to the east and much too near to Calvatone.

Messalla hurled himself upon them, they broke and fled. Shelter was near. Outside Cremona's city walls lay their own fortified camp. They quickly found refuge in it, and the road up to its very gates remained in possession of the Flavian troops.

The evening shadows were falling when the mass of Antonius' army was gathered on the scene of the victory. His troops clamoured to be led to the final assault. Thoughts of the sack and gluttonous rapine of a helpless city when night covered every deed of darkness spurred on the infuriated soldiery. Their general knew well that to assault the enemy's position that night was a task fraught with the greatest peril. His men were tired with the busy day's fighting and pursuit; they had no siege implements; they knew nothing of the nature of the fortifications which confronted them. While he opposed their demands, he sent the least wearied of his horsemen back to the camp at Bedriacum to bring supplies and a siege train up to the front as speedily as possible. But that night he would advance no further.

All Antonius' entreaties and arguments, however, could not prevail over the impatient ardour of his troops. They were on the point of advancing madly forward when scouts were seen speeding back from the direction of the city. The tidings which these brought hushed the clamour in a moment and gave the soldiers food indeed for saner thought. The whole Hostilia Army, the scouts reported, was even now within the city walls and preparing to march out at once to the attack.

The veterans of Caecina's army had indeed accomplished a feat well-nigh beyond the possible. In four days[40] they had covered a hundred miles. That morning they had quitted camp thirty miles away from Cremona, and now, as evening fell, they marched into the city, as their comrades came fleeing back under its shelter. The whole army was at last united. Once more the scale of victory seemed to incline towards the Vitellians. They needed but a general of their own to throw his sword into the scale and the day was theirs.

Had that night been allowed to pass without fighting, the Flavian Army must on the morrow have been in sorry plight. Hungry and stiff and anxious, encamped all night long upon the open road within striking distance of the enemy, constantly alarmed and ever under

---

40. I allow a day for the news of the evacuation of the camp to be brought to Verona and for Antonius to make his dispositions for the march to Cremona. Not even Vitellians could have marched a hundred miles in three days and fought on the evening of the third.

arms, without food or fires or entrenchments, they would have passed the night in as miserable a state as that of an army expecting attack could well be. Meanwhile the Vitellians, safe within their lines, warm and with abundant supplies, would have rested from their long day's march, and risen for the battle on the coming day with a fresh energy and confidence equal to their courage and determination to conquer. One charge of theirs, it might be thought, would have broken the cold and wavering Flavian line, and then there remained for them but the grimmest and the most savage of pursuits.

What spell of Fortune's weaving was it that bewitched the men of the German army? Surely Heaven was resolute that Vitellius' rule must end, though his foes in the field sought by their mistakes to maintain it. Once Antonius had offered the enemy victory on the plains by Padua and Verona, and had been saved by treachery. Now on the morrow he promised them easy victory again. They had only to wait for it. But now Folly came to Treachery's aid and finished the work. The Hostilia Army, weary and footsore, impatiently brooked no single night's delay. They had no general to compel them to be wise. At nine o'clock that night the whole Vitellian force marched defiantly out from their camp under the walls of Cremona and challenged their hated foe to the final struggle. The hour for which they had been waiting so long had come at last; the prize they had toiled so heavily to gain seemed at last within their grasp. A night's delay might let it slip. But now there should be no escape for the enemy.

C. The Battle of Cremona.—Thus *"indigus rectoris, inops consilii,"* the Vitellian Army marched out and drew up in order of battle. On the left of the raised Postumian way were stationed the men of the Twenty-Second, Sixteenth, and First legions; on the road itself the Fifth and Fifteenth legions, with the detachments of the Second, Ninth, and Twentieth behind them; on their right flank stood the Fourth legion. Men of the First legion Italica and the Twenty-First legion were scattered along the entire line. No precise position is given for the cavalry and auxiliaries, but the former at least were doubtless posted on the extreme wings. The Flavians were already drawn up in line of battle to meet them. On the road in the centre was the Thirteenth legion. North of the road, forming the Flavian right wing, and drawn up along a cross road, were the Eighth legion next the main road; then the Third legion, distributed in the intervals of thick brushwood; and next to them the band of Otho's old Praetorians who had joined Antonius' standard. On the left wing were the men of the

Seventh Galbiana legion next the road, beside whom stood those of the Seventh Claudia legion, whose front was protected by a ditch. The auxiliaries were placed beyond the legionaries on both wings, beyond whom again were some of the cavalry, while the rest were kept in reserve in the rear. The battle plan can therefore be represented by the following diagram:—

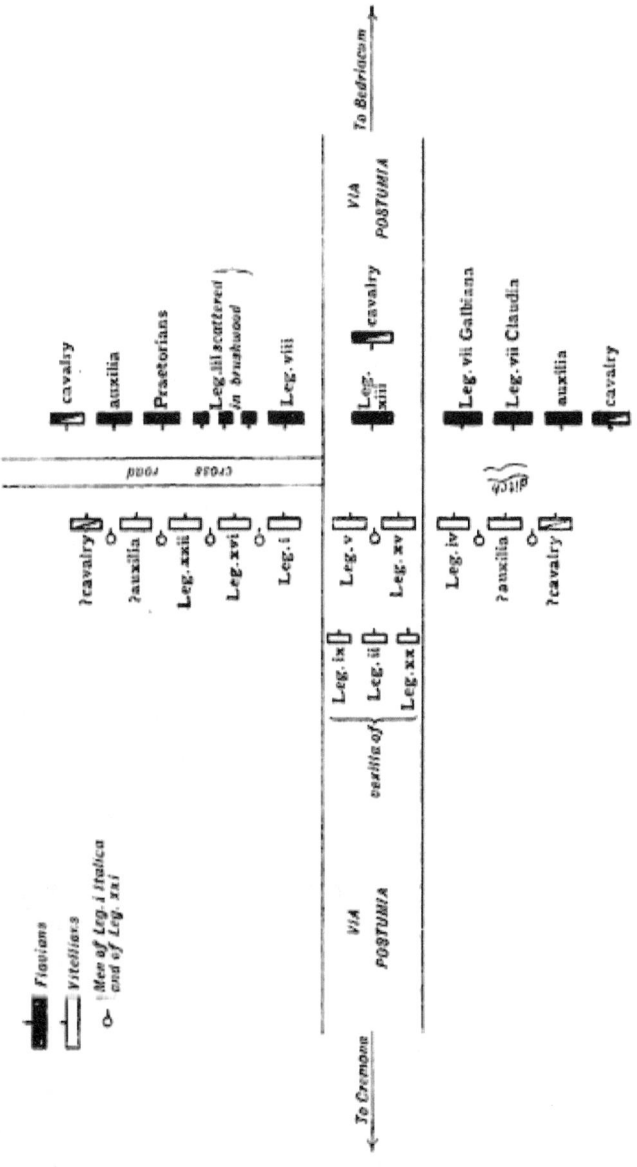

Fighting began about nine o'clock at night, and, as always happens in battles by night, was confused. Order was quickly lost, and hand-to-hand conflicts were waged all over the field. The two armies were armed alike; the watchwords quickly became known to the men on both sides; and captured standards displayed here and there by both combatants increased the perplexity and disarray. The Flavian left was hard pressed, and the Seventh Galbiana legion lost men quickly. Its very eagle was all but taken, and rescued only by the desperate valour of a centurion, who died to save it from the enemy. Antonius summoned the Praetorians from the right wing to strengthen the wavering line, and the battle, now restored, swayed to and fro in alternate advance and retreat. The Vitellian artillery had at the beginning of the fight been scattered up and down the line of battle, and its missiles had gone hurtling among the bushes opposite without doing great hurt to the enemy. But later all the engines were massed together on the high-road, and their fire, concentrated on the clear space in front of them, made the Flavian centre suffer heavily.

Here again the tide of war seemed setting against Antonius, when two of his soldiers found a remedy. Their names are not known, but their deed is not forgotten. Snatching up shields from two of the enemy's dead, they made their way undetected over to the hostile line, and cut the ropes of the engines. At once they fell, pierced with wounds; but they had saved their comrades and their general, for now the enemy's artillery was useless. Presently, late at night, the moon rose in the east, and shone full upon the faces of the Vitellians. The moon-light, disabling their own sight, exposed them to the sure aim of the foe, while they themselves smote vainly at the shadows which the dark figures of the soldiers opposite cast far on the ground before them. Ever and again clouds drifted over the face of the moon, and then, as by common consent, the fighters drew apart and rested, leaning on their weapons, until the moon shone out full again.

Women came out from Cremona, some themselves to plunge into the battle and be slain, fighting fiercely for the cause; some to carry food and drink to the soldiers of their army. The Vitellians ate and drank, and offered of the fare also to the enemy. "Come, comrades," they cried. "Here is meat and drink: take and eat; take and drink; that we may slay and be slain, but strong and not fainting." Then arms were grounded, and the men ate and drank together. But, the short rest over, they fell again to fighting with bitterness and anger all the greater.

All through the long autumn night the battle raged with unabated fury. Here son slew father unawares; here brother cut down brother. Men shuddered at such sights, and, hastening, did the like. The Flavian general was to be seen everywhere in his battle-line, encouraging, taunting, rebuking, cheering his soldiers on to yet stronger blows and a more stubborn stand.

> On that same battlefield, yet cumbered with the relics of their dead, the Pannonian legions must redeem their honour from the stain of the defeat which they had once suffered there. The men of Moesia had been bold enough of speech against the foe: could they not show the deeds to match? Dared the men of the Third to shame the records of the regiment? Had it not fought under Mark Antony in Parthia, under Corbulo in Armenia? Had it not but newly crushed the wild Sarmatian invader and saved their province? Why above all, he fiercely demanded, were the Guards hanging back in the final hour of trial? Had they not even yet drained ignominy to the full? Boors and peasants that they were, soldiers no more, did there remain for them yet another Emperor, another camp, to shelter them? Their standards, their arms, were with the enemy; for them death alone was guerdon of defeat.

Everywhere the men wildly cheered their fiery leader as he rode up and down the line, and grimly they held their ground, until at last the sun rose upon the scene.

Then the Third legion, lately come from Syria, saluted it, as was their wont, and the chance salute decided at last the day. The word ran fast down the Flavian line that Mucianus and their comrades of the Eastern army had come at last. Their hopes rose high. The enemy caught the rumour and wavered. In one final heave of massed column the Flavians thrust desperately at the Vitellian line, now ragged, thin, despairing. The line bent and gave. There was no rally. Ensnared, inextricably involved, among the broken engines, the waggons, the heaps of slain, the Army of Germany broke up into a rout of fugitives, and the enemy's horse, cutting, hewing, butchering, drove them to their camp. The battle on the open field was ended.

The tide of victory surged up against the gates and ramparts of the camp. The troops had marched and fought for twenty miles and twenty hours. Still Antonius gave them no rest, but called on them for the last great effort, and, as one man, they answered to the call. A very storm of missiles raged for some time on either side. Then two columns of assault rushed at the ramparts and the gates on the eastern and the northern roads, towards Bedriacum and Brixia. The men were hurled back. Antonius flung himself among them. With significant gesture he pointed to the city: Cremona was theirs to sack, if they would rally. Himself at the head of the storming column, he led the Third and Seventh legions again up to the Bedriacum gate. Down crashing on their heads came the great engine of war itself, hurled by the desperate defenders, and they recoiled once more. It was but for a moment. The engine's fall had torn away with it part of the rampart. Fresh assailants swarmed to the breach, the men of the two legions vying with one another in eager regimental rivalry. The gate was hewn down with axes and with swords. Volusius of the Third was the first man in. The others poured over and through the defences. The Vitellians leapt despairing from the ramparts as the foe rushed in. The camp was cleared of the living among the enemy up to the city's walls.

D. The Sack of Cremona.—The actual town itself seemed still to defy assault. It was crowded with citizens and many strangers who had gathered there for the fair, which had chanced upon those very days; and many of the defeated troops had escaped within the city and thronged its lofty walls and towers, menacing the foe. But Antonius never hesitated. Soon the inhabitants saw the fairest of their buildings outside the walls in a blaze of fire, and others, which overtopped the ramparts, crowded with soldiery. A rain of missiles and flaming brands again began to descend upon the walls, and under its cover the legionaries were seen moving to the assault. For nearly three centuries the proud and stately city had been queen of the valley of the Po. In her earliest years the fierce Gallic tribes had raged round her walls in vain.[41] Temples and palaces gave her beauty; walls and iron-clamped gates glorified her strength; the river bestowed riches on her fields and prosperity on her citizens. Now at last an enemy sterner than the Gaul, fiercer than the barbarian, was at her gates. And the garrison played her false. The officers, hopeful of mercy for themselves, surrendered the city. The soldiers sullenly allowed it, or, careless of the end, roamed through the streets, plundering or fighting.

Caecina, who had been hurried there by the army which once owed him obedience and cast into the city prison, was released from his dungeon, clad in the robes and decorated with the insignia of his consular office, and the men begged him humbly that he should plead

---

41. 200 B.C. The city was founded as a Latin colony in 218.

for them with the victors. "It was the last of evils that so many valiant men should implore the traitor's aid." The gates were thrown open; the garrison laid down their arms, and marched out between lines of jeering troops. But soon mockery was changed to pity. The victors had been vanquished by the vanquished of today, and as they had received mercy at the others' hands, so now it should be shown these in return. Only when Caecina came proudly out from the gate, glittering with his train of *lictors*, did a fierce cry of scorn and hate arise. Antonius checked it, and sent the traitor under guard to Vespasian.

For the moment the city itself was spared, but only for the moment. The soldiers had not forgotten the insults which the citizens a few months earlier had heaped upon them.[42] And never did city promise richer plunder. At the crisis of the struggle the general had spurred his troops on by the thought of spoiling it. He should not restrain them now. Already the flames were spreading, and one chance word did the rest. Antonius hastened to the baths to wash off the blood and grime which covered him. The water was cold.

"Were not the fires lit?" he impatiently demanded.

An anxious slave hastened to him with the assurance: "It will soon be warm."

Question and answer ran from mouth to mouth. The time had come to light the fires of rapine: this was their general's meaning. Forty thousand armed men, and a yet larger and more horrible army of sutlers, camp followers, the refuse and sweepings of the vilest, broke into the city. For four days it was given up to their maddened lust and rage. The chapter in which the Roman historian tells the story of the sack equals in ghastliness the tale of the sack of Rome by the forces of the Constable de Bourbon, of heretic Antwerp by the fanatic Spaniards. When four days had passed, fifty thousand had perished by the sword and torture, by fire and by lust. Flames consumed the city. Only a solitary temple, that of Mefitis outside the city walls, remained untouched by them. The very spoilers were driven to encamp three miles away by the reek of the blood which rose from the poisoned soil. In this way Cremona came to its end.[43]

There are wars, even civil wars, which inspire devotion and self-sacrifice; this struggle of A.D. 69 displayed the horrors of war in all their nakedness.

---

42. See chapter 2 §2.
43. The city was rebuilt under Vespasian, but the disaster remained proverbial.

§7. The Advance to Rome

A. The Halt at Fano.—The sack of Cremona ended on October 31; there were still nearly two months to pass before the end of the war came.

News of the victory was sent at once by Antonius to the western provinces, Spain, Gaul, and Britain. All three presently declared for Vespasian, the First Adjutrix legion in Spain setting the example. This legion had never forgiven Vitellius' rise to power and Otho's fall. Next, the defeated army had to be sent away to a safe distance, lest it should still take a part in the resistance which the emperor would offer. The men were sent to the Danube provinces, save for a few cavalry who took service with the Flavians. Distributed skilfully through Dalmatia, Illyricum, and Moesia, they gave after this no cause for anxiety, and in Moesia were of excellent service against the marauding Dacians. There then remained only the fear lest Germany should still send men to Vitellius' aid.

Antonius therefore at once sent troops to occupy the Alpine passes. The mutiny against Rome which shortly afterwards broke out on the Rhine was already so far afoot (under the guise of a war in Vespasian's interests against the Vitellian troops on the river) that the army in Germany was but too busily occupied, and not a man was sent to cross the Alps. It was Antonius who, by letters, had provoked this rising on Vespasian's behalf, and his scheme was so far magnificently successful.[44] But, in very truth, to encourage those who were little better than barbarians to rise against the Romans, even though these last might be of the opposite faction, was nothing else than to play with fire, and brought quickly a terrible retribution in its train. It was as if the English had let loose the Basutos upon their enemy in the recent Transvaal war. To this extent Antonius lacked the true Imperial feeling which, if it delayed sorely the coming of peace, yet gave us the chance of goodwill when peace at last did come.

No such thoughts troubled Antonius the Roman. The immediate military need was his only care, and for this at least he had made most wise provision. That he had opened the floodgates to rebellion and savagery in the far North, and that the flood would not hereafter be arrested at his word, he refused or was unable to perceive. At least he had stayed the coming of all reinforcements from any quarter of the Empire to Vitellius. And with this he was well content.

Having taken these precautions, the general turned his thoughts

---

44. See chapter 3 for the history of this rising.

to the enemy in the South. The emperor at Rome might be inert and torpid, but at least he would not, like Otho, save his foes the need of further fighting by slaying himself, because his army had been vanquished on the banks of the Po. Moreover, he still commanded troops of excellent quality and by no means contemptible in numbers. Twenty-five thousand infantry, and most of these the veterans whom he had made his Guards, could not be played with as if they had been a toy army or a rabble of recruits. The campaign had opened for the Flavians well indeed, but much work yet remained to be done. The invading army must of necessity advance towards the capital.

Yet such an advance promised many difficulties. From Cremona to Ariminum the road was easy all through its length of one hundred and fifty miles. It ran over a perfectly flat plain, skirting the mountain chain upon the right hand. But after Ariminum the troubles began. The great highway to Rome, the Via Flaminia, crossed the ridge of the Apennines at its lowest point. From Ariminum it ran along the sea-shore to Fanum Fortunae (Fano), and there struck inland up the stony winding channel of the Metaurus, entering the hills at Forum Sempronii, a name corrupted today into that of Fossombrone, the last comfortable village of the lowlands. From that point the climb began, by Cales (Cagli) and the wild ravine of Cantiano to the top of the pass, which lies at a height of 2400 feet above the sea. The rise to this was very steep. Thence it dropped to Nuceria (Nocera Umbra) and Fulginium (Foligno). From Fulginium it crossed the five-mile expanse of level plain to Mevania (Bevagna) opposite, and the chief natural difficulties of the road were ended.

But if at places this road runs through a fair and smiling land, adorned with fields and lanes, flowers and fruit-trees, worthy of the county of Devon, at others it pierces rocky ravines, crawls up through gorges and rocky mountain sides black with oak-woods or bare to all the blasts of heaven. The mountains shoot steeply up first on the right hand, then on the left, rugged, inhospitable, cleft by great red ravines and strewn with broken rocks and screes. The hamlets are squalid and miserable, the mountaineers in appearance a rude and lowering race. Other tracks cross the central ridge, but there is none which can so easily be traversed as this of the main highway. Many miles to the south the Via Salaria crosses the central heights of the Abruzzi from Ascoli to Rieti, but the difficulties of the Flaminian way are as nothing to the toils which await the traveller who plunges by this route into the heart of Italy's wildest mountains.

More than a hundred and eighty miles separate Ariminum and Rome; for the first hundred miles the road is mountainous. And to Antonius and his army the late season of the year increased the difficulties. Already in November snow had fallen on the mountains, and bad weather had set in. There was little food to be obtained along the road until he reached the great central Umbrian valley at Foligno, and December would be upon him first, even if the enemy made no effort to block the way. Even Vitellius could hardly fail to seize this great chance which the winter offered him. And if the pass were blocked by the emperor's army, with a strong force at its summit, and fifteen thousand men in camp at Foligno, Antonius could never force the passage of the mountains in that year.

Other causes also made the general hesitate. There was dissension in his staff, some urging the advance, some bidding him delay till Mucianus came. Mucianus himself wrote to him in ambiguous terms. He doubtless desired himself to lead the victorious army into Rome. Antonius, somewhat of a braggart, a veritable soldier of fortune, it might seem to the other, had gained success enough. The two men hated and distrusted each the other, and on Antonius' staff were many who looked to the greater man for their promotion, and sought now to thwart the general who had led them to victory. If Antonius gave the order to advance, all the penalties of failure would be visited on his head. Mucianus clearly washed his hands of all responsibility. The very troops, knowing well the quarrels in the staff, were turbulent and clamorous for "shoe-money." Jealousy and insubordination, difficulties of supply, perils of the road, defiance by the enemy,—all these troubles, actual or possible, pressed heavily on Antonius.

He moved forward to Ariminum. The town was still in the enemy's hands, but the fleet under command of Cornelius Fuscus had by this time closely invested it by land and sea. There was therefore no army upon the eastern side of the mountains and down the Adriatic coast to oppose his advance. And the timely capture of Valens on the Riviera was in every way most fortunate.[45] Yet even the march to Fanum Fortunae, twenty-eight miles beyond Ariminum, was not without its difficulties. Heavy autumn rains had swollen the Po and its tributary streams, and the low country of the valley at foot of the mountains was flooded to such an extent that the heavy baggage of the soldiers had to be left behind. Commissariat troubles, too, began early. Antonius failed to keep his troops in hand, and they indulged in

---

45. See §5 above.

indiscriminate plunder on the way. This of was neither a strong one nor in good temper. All the sick and wounded had been left behind at the base, Verona, but also the greater part of the legionaries remained there, and Antonius at Fano mustered only picked troops from these, together with auxiliary infantry and cavalry. The mountains rose before him, and he halted.

Further advance was not possible until his force was strengthened, supplies were collected, and the country in his front was explored. Antonius set his hand resolutely to all three tasks. The legions were summoned, supplies hurried up by sea, and cavalry scouts sent forward to discover if the enemy had occupied the pass.[46] But all this involved delay, and winter was fast approaching. Vitellius had his opportunity, if he had the wit to use it. course at once doubled the difficulties of supply. The force which arrived at last at Fano

B. Movements of the Vitellian Forces.—The emperor had meanwhile been waiting on circumstance, and this at last had roused him to action. At first, as soon as his army had marched for the north under Caecina, and when Valens had presently followed after it, Vitellius took no further interest in the war. In the pleasant shade of his gardens, or under the trees of the woods which clothe thickly the sides of the Alban hills at Aricia, a few miles south of Rome, the ruler of the Empire dozed the days away, heavy with food and slumberous, torpid as a fat and well-fed toad, (*"ut ignava animalia quibus si dbom suggeras jacent torpentqae."*—*Tac.*) The news of the mutiny of the Ravenna fleet scarcely moved him. Valens' urgent request for reinforcements was answered by the sending of a petty force which was far too weak to be of any use.[47] Only at last the tidings of Caecina's treachery and the troops' loyal requital of it woke him from his slumbers in the greenwood. "With that dull soul joy had a greater weight than trouble," (*"Plus apud socordem animum laetitia quam cura valuit"*—*Tac.*) Vitellius came to Rome and harangued both Senate and people. When the news came of the Battle of Cremona the orator's powers abruptly failed him. Everyone at court went about silently, and no one made any allusion to so unfortunate an incident. They whispered in the anterooms and streets, but in the emperor's presence no one had heard anything of the battle. The government ordered silence on the topic, and, if it were possible,

---
46. Tacitus explains that he sent the cavalry on to explore the whole of Umbria: "*si qua Appennini juga clementius adirentur.*" That the Via Flaminia was the easiest route could hardly be in question.

47. See §5 above.

the disaster was magnified in consequence.

The spies sent out were courteously welcomed by the enemy and escorted round their camp. Vitellius blandly shut his ears to their reports. At last a brave centurion, Julius Agrestis, convinced his emperor that it was time to be up and doing. Allowed at his own request, so ran the tale, to go out from Rome to discover the actual facts of the situation, he went openly to Cremona and straight to Antonius, avowing his mission. That general readily gave him guides and showed him everything—his army, the battlefield, the prisoners of war. Back came Agrestis to Vitellius and told him all the truth. The emperor refused, as usual, to believe a word of it, and suggested that he had been bribed to bring such news.

The centurion was indignant. "Since," he cried, "you have need of a sure proof, and have no longer any other use whether of my life or death, I will give you proof verily to believe." With these words he hastened from Vitellius' presence and slew himself. Then at last, "as one roused from sleep," the emperor took measures of defence.

His available forces consisted of sixteen *cohorts* of Praetorian, and four of Urban, Guards—twenty thousand men in all. To these was added a new legion, hurriedly levied from among the sailors of the fleet at Misenum, which may have numbered five thousand more.[48] Besides these he had a small force of cavalry at his disposal. With such forces he still might defend Italy, at least unless Vespasian came at the head of all the armies of the East. And of him there was no sign.

The greater part of this force was sent northwards along the Flaminian road to defend the ridge of the Apennines. Fourteen of the sixteen Praetorian *cohorts*, the new legion, and the cavalry marched out promptly as far as Mevania (Bevagna), eighty miles from Rome, near the issue of the road from the northern mountains. The other two Praetorian *cohorts* with the four *cohorts* of Urban Guards were left in Rome, under the emperor's brother Lucius, to garrison the city. Vitellius himself still dallied for some time in Rome, but at last, at his army's urgent entreaty, joined the camp at Mevania. No enemy as yet had been seen upon the pass. He had even men and time enough to cross it and descend upon the scattered enemy from the hills, hurling

---

48. This "*legio e classicis*" is of course not Legio I. Adjutrix, which was then in Spain, but the nucleus of the legion later formally enrolled by Mucianus in the name of Vespasian under the title of Secunda Adjutrix. There is a military diploma of March 7 *A.D.* 70, applying to some who have seen service with this legion. Hardy, *Studies in Roman History*.

them, if fortune served, back in rout from Fano towards the flooded valley of the Po. The Roman historian himself maintains this strategy to have been the right one for him:—

> It was open to Vitellius to cross the Apennines with the vigour of his army unimpaired, and to fall upon the foe while these were weary with the winter's cold and hunger. But he divided up his strength and scattered it; he gave over to slaughter and captivity troops of the keenest courage and faithful to the last Though the most skilful of his centurions opposed his plan and would have told him the truth had he but inquired of them, his friends held them back from coming to his presence.—Tacitus

Not only did the emperor refuse to advance over the mountains, but very soon "he divided up his strength and scattered it." Dire omens, indeed, were seen at Mevania, but, as the historian grimly says:

> Vitellius was his own worst portent. . . . Ignorant of soldiering, improvident of counsel, here asking one concerning the drill of marching order, there another concerning a scout's duties; here questioning whether it were well to hasten on the final issue, there whether to delay it; in his face and limbs alike making manifest his fear when each new messenger arrived; and at the last reeling drunken round the camp—(such was Vitellius the emperor among his troops).

> *He alone*
> *Dealt on lieutenantry and no practice had*
> *In the brave squares of war.*

The very camp became wearisome to him; doubtless the camp kitchen pleased him ill; and when one more message of disaster reached him he left Mevania and returned to Rome. The fleet at Misenum had mutinied against him. The rebels had seized the city of Tarracina, where the road creeps round between the sea and the sheer cliff which towers many hundred feet above it and all but bars its passage. The city's walls and strong position made it a fortress all too hard to storm. And now it too was in an enemy's hands, and Campania, south of Rome, in a ferment. The emperor at this lost the last portion of military wisdom which was his. In that desperate situation one with cool head would have seen that Campania mattered very little. The enemy there were still but a sorry band, and the fierce local jealousies between its cities preserved the loyalty of some and thereby hampered the hostility of others. A very small force sent from Rome would have been enough to keep the rebels of Campania in check. The true danger lay, as always, north of the Apennines.

But now Vitellius issued his last and most fatal orders for the redistribution of his troops. The emperor himself took seven *cohorts* and part of the cavalry with him to Rome. A poor seven only, with the legion and part of the cavalry to help them, were left to defend Italy against the attack from the north. On arriving at Rome, Vitellius sent his brother with six *cohorts* and five hundred horse to Campania, keeping with him in the city three Praetorian *cohorts*, and probably the Urban *cohorts* as well.[49]

Thus, instead of concentrating his army where it was above all needed, the emperor made three divisions of it; instead of advancing, as a bold general might perhaps have advanced, over the pass to search for the enemy, he recalled the division now left at Mevania back to Narnia, thirty miles in the rear, and only some fifty miles from Rome; instead of at least attempting to block the pass by which the Flaminian road crossed the mountains, he left it bare of all defence, opposing the foe's advance over it by nothing save by the snow which had fallen upon it. "Fortune," comments the historian, "helped the Flavian leaders not less often than did their own counsels,"—"*Fortuna quae Flavianis dudbus non minus saepe quam ratio adfuit.*" The cup of Vitellius' blunders was now indeed full to the brim.

The diminished army of defence now amounted to some twelve thousand infantry and a handful of cavalry, some four hundred in number. Certainly, now that the pass was surrendered to the enemy and Mevania evacuated, the position occupied at Narnia was the best possible for defence. The river Nar here tears through a narrow rocky ravine, hurrying south to join the Tiber, and the Flaminian way spanned the valley by a great bridge of three enormous arches. An army posted above the ravine might easily make the passage of the bridge most hazardous to an enemy.[50] From Mevania again two roads

---

49. The figures work out as follows: there were 16 *cohorts* of Praetorians (Tac.); of these 14 go to Mevania (*ibid*), thus 2 remain in Rome. Later there are 6 with L. Vitellius in Campania (*ibid*), and 3 at Rome storm the Capitol (*ibid*). If these 3 were Praetorian and not Urban *cohorts*, which is probable, this leaves 7 only for the force at Narnia. These would be the "*pars copiarum Narniae relicta*" (*ibid*). Of the original 14 at Mevania, therefore, 7 go back to Rome, making with the 2 left here 9. Of these 9, 6 are sent to Campania and 3 stay behind in Rome, where also the Urban *cohorts* probably remain and take part in the defence of the city.
50. So the actual position taken up was above the "*subiectos Narniae campos*," Tac.

led to the south—one the Flaminian way itself; one a longer road running up the vale of the Clitumnus to the picturesque little fortress city of Spoletium (Spoleto) at the head of it, and thence crossing a low ridge to Interamna (Terni), a few miles higher up the Nar than Narnia. From Interamna it ran downstream to join the Flaminian road at this city. Thus an army retreating from Mevania was bound to retire as far as Narnia before it made a stand again, or its flank could be turned and its retreat intercepted by a force which followed the longer road. The cavalry of the Vitellians were pushed forward up this road as far as Interamna; the infantry remained at Narnia. In this position the small army which was the emperor's last hope awaited the coming of the enemy.

C. The Capture of Rome,—That coming was not long delayed. Antonius' cavalry scouts, whom he had sent forward to explore the pass, returned to him at Fano with the welcome if unexpected news that it was clear of the enemy. The general thereupon ordered an advance, and his troops made their way over the ridge, encountering no worse foe than the snow of mid-December which lay upon the pass. There was still the fear lest the unoccupied pass should be a snare of the enemy's setting, and that, as the Flavians emerged exhausted from the mountains, the Vitellians would fall upon them from Mevania.[51] But no such danger was encountered. Without any opposition the army crossed the pass, came down into the central Umbrian plain, and advanced down the Flaminian way as far as the town of Carsulae.[52] Here the army was halted. Ten miles away the enemy were reported to be holding a strong position in their front at Narnia. Carsulae served the Flavians very well for a place of encampment. From it two roads sloped gently down hill to the valley of the Nar, the one on the right hand to Narnia, the other on the left to Interamna, and the position commanded a wide and uninterrupted view.

Moreover, the countryside was friendly to them. The retreat of the Vitellians from Mevania had convinced the flourishing little Umbrian towns that the emperor's cause was a losing one. Prosperous cities on the line or on the flanks and rear of the Flavian advance, such as Foligno, Spello, Assisi, Todi, hastened to send supplies. There seemed to the Flavian leaders no need for hurry. The mountains had been crossed. Vitellius might submit without a blow, and surely there had been

---

51. For the strategical method for defending a mountain ridge see chapter 1, §3.
52. Now ruins only.

enough of bloodshed and rapine. The sack of Cremona, it was felt, had sorely besmirched their fair name. Heaven forefend that Rome herself should run any such risk, if Vitellius would spare both her and himself by making terms with the conqueror while there was yet time.

Indeed there seemed a good hope that the war might end in this way. Vespasian's elder brother, Flavius Sabinus, had all through these months of war stayed unmolested in Rome. He had been thirty-five years in the public service, of which seven were spent by him as Governor of Moesia, twelve as prefect of the city. A man much esteemed and honoured, he was far from ambitious, and would welcome a peaceful and friendly settlement. In Rome also was Vespasian's younger son Domitian, now a lad of eighteen summers. He, too, might serve as a pledge of friendliness.

Negotiations between the emperor and Sabinus were already afoot. Vitellius' lethargy seemed now not unlikely to be his salvation. The Flavians had little fear of him personally, nor was he himself unwilling to lay aside the cares of Empire and the dangers of an unstable princedom for a modest competence which should secure him comfort and good fare for the rest of his life in some luxurious Campanian country-house. It would not assist the hopes of so genial a settlement if the Flavian Army advanced in hostile guise up to the city. But the emperor must be made to realise that he had no chance of prolonging a successful resistance. "Out of the whole world nothing was left to him save the land which lay between Narnia and Tarracina." Yet still he might be tempted to put trust in his armies. It was indeed hard to drive sheer facts home into a brain so dull.

For some days Antonius remained in camp at Carsulae. He was waiting for the arrival of the main *legionary* force, which was following in the steps of his advance guard over the pass. Until this arrived, he had no wish to provoke a fight. Its coming made his army strong enough for any enterprise and alarmed the enemy at Narnia. The hearts of the defending force sank within them. The sailor legion was raw and had seen no fighting; the Praetorians must have known that events in Rome were tending towards peace. Theirs is indeed a hard fate who without need or gain die upon the last battlefield in the war—fighting when all reason for fighting is ended, slain in the darkness of the valley when the day of peace is already dawning on the mountain-tops. It needed but a little to turn the scale of the defenders' wavering. From the hill at Carsulae, Varus and his cavalry rushed upon the enemy's horse at Interamna and dispersed it utterly.

The infantry at Narnia were isolated. Antonius again and again sent offers of welcome and good treatment to the officers if they would submit, and these passed over one by one to the Flavian camp. Still, however, the common soldier remained stubbornly loyal to his emperor. His own prefects and officers might desert him, but he trusted yet that his old general Valens with a new army from Germany would suddenly appear, coming down the ridge to his succour. To this hope Antonius made a grim reply. He sent and beheaded Valens in his prison at Urbino. As the general Claudius Nero in old days had hurled into Hannibal's camp the head of Hasdrubal his brother, so now Antonius sent the head of Valens to the force at Narnia.

Then the Vitellian soldiers, long hoping against hope, saw at last that such hopes were vain. They surrendered, but with honour. Proudly, in military array, with standards and colours and all the panoply of war, they marched down from their lines on the hillside to the plain beneath, where the Flavian army was drawn up in battle order to receive them between their lines. Antonius spoke kindly to them, and bade them remain at Narnia and Interamna. He left with them some of his troops—as many as would be able to suppress any rising on their part, yet not so many as could terrify or maltreat them. For the remainder of his force the path to Rome lay open.

With this he now moved forward a few miles farther down the Flaminian way to Ocriculum (Otricoli), a place in the Tiber valley, thirty-five miles north of Rome. The days of the Saturnalia, the great December festival of the Romans, were at hand, and Antonius determined that his army should celebrate the feast at this small town. The news from Rome was promising: the emperor, as soon as he had heard of his army's surrender at Narnia, had practically consented to resign, and to entrust the government at Rome to Sabinus until Vespasian should come himself. The soldiers were better kept away from the city, and the war seemed ended. But though Antonius himself kept the infantry in camp at Ocriculum, he sent a thousand cavalry forward under the command of a kinsman of Vespasian, Q. Petilius Cerialis.

Cerialis was a tried soldier, who eight years before had seen service in Britain as legate of the Ninth legion. He had just escaped from Rome disguised as a rustic, and had joined Antonius during the march over the mountains. As an officer of experience (whose chief fame, however, was speedily to be won in the far north), he could be trusted to lead the cavalry forward. But so small seemed the need for haste, that Antonius bade him ride by cross-roads to the Via Salaria and enter Rome by the

Colline gate, to which this road led, instead of following the direct road by the Flaminian way.[53] By passing through this gate the cavalry might attract less notice, and the risk of opposition or disturbance be lessened. The greater time which this route would require seemed not worth consideration, when all at Rome was said to be so quiet.

The mistake made by the Flavian commanders led to the gravest and most terrible results. Had they arrived outside the gates of the city forty-eight hours earlier, their strength would have been enough to overawe the numerous partisans of Vitellius within the walls, and the indignation which these in ever-increasing measure felt for the emperor's pusillanimity would without doubt have been checked. The stormy day would have sunk to rest in a calm and tranquil evening. But the Fates willed that Vitellius' sun should set in gloom and raging storm, in a consuming fire of slaughter and grim vengeance.

Antonius and Cerialis had failed to realise the passionate anger of Vitellius' soldiers in the city, their dogged determination of despair. On the morning of the 19th of December a messenger rode at full speed into the Flavian camp at Ocriculum, demanding to see Antonius at once. He was the bearer of tidings sent the evening before from Rome, thirty-five miles away. From him Antonius learnt that the day before, while he and his men were keeping jollity, the soldiery and mob in Rome had risen, compelling Vitellius to do after their own pleasure: that Sabinus, Vespasian's brother, Domitian, his son, and a little band of adherents, were blockaded and besieged in the Capitol by a Vitellian rabble, howling for their blood. If he would save them from massacre, Antonius must march at full speed to the rescue. Even so, it might be too late.

Not a moment was lost. The Flavian general issued orders for an instant march, and he and his army hastened at top speed for Rome. There was life to save and treachery to be requited. The fall of evening never stopped them, and it was deep night when they reached a point on the road known as "The Red Rocks," six miles only from Rome. They had marched nine and twenty miles without ceasing. But all their speed was vain. There the news came to them that all was over. The Capitol had been stormed that day, and its garrison cut to pieces. Sabinus had been taken and butchered in cold blood at Vitellius' very

---

53. Perhaps Cerialis was sent off earlier, from Narnia, when he could reach the Via Salaria by marching to Interamna, climbing the height by the magnificent falls of Terni to the valley of the Velinus, the "Rosy Vale," and so to Rieti, at the great bend of the Salarian way. This road crosses the Apennines from Ascoli on the Tronto to Antrodoco and Rieti. It pursues a mountainous route, and is rough going as far as Rieti.

feet. The great temple itself, the glory of Rome, towering up to heaven on its sheer rock with the busy Forum at its feet, the home of the greatest of the gods of Rome, had been destroyed by fire. Glutted with blood and fury, the Vitellians had manned the walls and held the city.

The army of rescue became an army of vengeance. Swift and keen as a beast of prey terrible in his wrath, the soldiers, when morning dawned, leapt upon the doomed city. Cerialis, too, had heard the news, and, pushing faster forward, had been ensnared among the gardens and orchards at foot of the Pincian hill by the enemy's horse and foot, routed with loss, and pursued back for some miles as far as Fidenae. But when the pursuit drew off, he rallied his troopers and advanced again towards the city.

There was not a man in the Flavian Army who would lightly now withhold his hand from the work to be done. Messengers came out from the city to Cerialis and Antonius, speaking of terms to be agreed upon. Cerialis sent them hurrying back, answering with scorn and insult, Antonius with courtesy but with equal firmness. No truce was henceforth possible. A Stoic philosopher judged it the time to preach to the troops of mercy and of peace. His "untimely wisdom" came near to costing him his life, and he was contemptuously brushed aside. The Vestal Virgins came in procession from the city to bear to the Flavian general a letter from Vitellius, begging the respite of a single day. He sent the Vestals back with all honour, but instantly refused the emperor's request. The murder of Sabinus, the burning of the Capitol, had made the war a "truceless war" for ever.

The army swept forward over the Mulvian Bridge,[54] which crossed the Tiber. Antonius here, it is said, would have halted them awhile, but his men brooked henceforth no restraint. They moved to the assault in three columns of attack, the cavalry leading and driving back the Roman mob before them. The centre column advanced by the main road upon the gate under the Pincian hill.[55] To its right, another column moved along the bank of the river to storm the wall. To the left the third column moved round outside the wall to the Salarian way to assault the Colline gate, the scene of Sulla's desperate battle a century and a half ago.[56] The Vitellians defended gates and walls with the fierce courage of men who knew that for them there was henceforth no pity.

---

54. Now the Ponte Molle, two miles from the gate.
55. Now the busy Porta del Popolo.
56. Hard by the Porta Pia, the scene of the far more famous entry of the troops of the kingdom of Italy into Rome on September 20, 1870.

From the garden walls of the "Hill of the Gardens," today the pleasure resort of the Romans, the defenders hurled javelins and stones upon the Flavian troops, who struggled in a network of lanes upon its outer slope and suffered heavy loss. Here the assailants gained no ground till late in the day. But then the cavalry forced at last an entrance by the Colline gate, and rode round to take the enemy in the rear. The Vitellians broke and fled, and the hill was carried. Meanwhile their comrades of both the other columns had also forced an entrance, and pushed through to the Campus Martius, fighting their way forward inch by inch. At last the Flavians were inside the very walls of Rome.

But still the soldiers of Vitellius fought with fury, as they fell slowly back along the narrow streets. The unarmed citizens of Rome crowded to look on as at some gigantic gladiatorial contest waged for their marvelling and applauding. Wounded and fleeing soldiers who sought refuge from the pursuer in shops and houses by the way were hounded out again to meet their doom, and the base civilian reaped the harvest of the plunder of the dead while the *legionary* sped forward, always bent on slaughter. Among the heaps of the slain, which cumbered every way, roisterers and harlots made merry in riotous glee. One last stand was made by the defenders at the Praetorians' Camp hard by the Porta Pia. And there, in one last splendid sally out upon the swarming foe, Vitellius' soldiers perished to a man, all their wounds in front, and their faces to the enemy. Night fell, and Rome was taken.

§8. The Death of Vitellius

Thus the Emperor Vitellius lost the greater cantle of the world with very sloth and gluttony; he had slept away kingdoms and provinces. The end of this his pitiable life may be told in the words of Suetonius, the biographer of the Caesars. Suetonius' father had fought in Otho's army at Bedriacum in the spring of the year as tribune of the Thirteenth legion from Pannonia, (*Otho*), and may himself have seen and told his son the scene which the latter tells as follows:[57]

> Word was brought unto him by his espiall that the enemie approched. Immediatly therfore shutting himself close within a bearing chaire, accompanied with two persons onely, his baker and his Cooke,[58] secretly hee tooke his way to the Aventine

---

57. Suetonius, *Vitellius*. I use the translation of Philemon Holland, A.D. 1606. The notes to the translation are his, not mine.
58. "That made his deinty pastry works and sweet meates: meete grooms to accompanie such a glutton."

hill and his fathers house: minding from thence to make an escape into Campania. Soone after, uppon a flying and headlesse rumour, That peace was obtained, he suffred himselfe to be brought backe to the Palace. Where, finding all places solitary and abandoned: seeing those also to slinke from him and slip away who were with him, he did about him a girdle full of golden peeces of coine,[59] and fled into the Porters lodge, having first tied a ban-dog at the doore and set against it the bedsteed and bedding thereto.

By this time had the Avant curriers of the maine armie broken into the Palace: and meeting noe bodie searched as the manner is, everie blind comer. By them was hee plucked out of his lurking hole: and when they asked who he was (for they knewe him not), and where upon his knowledge Vitellius was, he shifted them of with a lie: after this, beeing once knowen, hee intreated hard (as if he had somewhat to deliver concerning the life and safetie of Vespasian) to be kept sure in the mean season, though it were in some prison: and desisted not untill such time as having his hands pinnioned fast at his backe, an halter cast about his necke, and his apparell tome from his bodie, he was haled halfe naked into the Forum.

Among many skomefull indignities offered unto him both in deede and word throughout the spatious street sacra via from one end to the other, whiles they drew his head backward by the bush of his haire (as condemned malefactours are wont to be served) and set a swordes point under his chinne, and all to the end he might shew his face and not holde it down: whiles some pelted him with dung and durtie mire, others called him with open mouth Incendiarie[60] and Patinarium:[61] and some of the common sort twitted him also with faults and deformities of his bodie (for, of stature he was beyond measure tall: a red face he had, occasioned for the most part by swilling in wine, and a grand fat paunch besides: hee limped somewhat also by reason that one of his thighes was enfeebled withe the rush of a chariot against it what time he served Caius[62] as his henxman

---

59. "15 shilling peeces and better."
60. "Or firebrand, because he burnt the Capitoll."
61. "Or Platter Knight, for his gormandize and huge platter aforesaid." See chapter 2, §2.
62. Caligula.

at a Chariot running): and at the last upon the staires Gemoniae with many a small stroke all to mangled he was and killed in the end: and so from thence drawne with a drag into the River Tiberis.

One saying only by him, as he was led along amid mockery and torment, and that indeed worthy of a man, was recorded, when to a *tribune* who stood insulting him he answered, "Yet once I was your emperor." And presently, on the very spot where two days before the body of the murdered Sabinus had lain, Vitellius, too, lay dead.

Rome was taken on the 21st of December A.D. 69. Within a very short while the Vitellian Army in Campania laid down its arms, and Lucius Vitellius was put to the sword. The ten months' fighting was ended. It remained for the wise and thrifty Vespasian to heal the wounds which that bitter civil strife had cut so deep into the body of the Roman State.

NOTES

F.—Valens' March to the North

Tacitus' account of this is very perplexing. According to it, Valens receives the news of the mutiny of the Ravenna fleet "while on the march," *i,e.* from Rome. He was, of course, marching by the Via Flaminia. This road runs through Southern Etruria for a few miles after leaving Rome, enters Umbria near Ocriculum, and continues in this district up to and beyond Ariminum, which town is in Umbria. From Ariminum there is a choice of roads. The coast road runs north to Ravenna, crossing the Rubicon a few miles from Ariminum. This river formed the northern boundary of Umbria. The main road, however, strikes away northwest from Ariminum, leaves Umbria near the town of Cesena, and continues *via* Faventia to Bononia, whence a road runs north to Hostilia, while the highway continues in a straight line to Placentia.

The puzzle is to discover where Valens was when he heard of the mutiny of the fleet Tacitus' account is that, when the news came, if Valens had hastened he might have reached Caecina while the latter was still wavering, or have reached the legions before the critical battle. There were actually some who advised him "*ut per occultos tramites vitata Ravenna Hostiliam Cremonamve pergeret.*" But he halts where he is, and sends to Rome for reinforcements. When these arrive in small numbers, *viz.* three *cohorts* and one *ala*, he is unable "to force his way through the enemy" (*vadere per hostes*). He is fearful, too, of their scanty loyalty. "*Eo metu cohortes Ariminum praemittit, alam tueri terga iubet: ipse . . . flexit in Umbriam atque inde Etruriam.*" In Etruria he hears of the battle at Cremona, and makes his way to the sea at Pisa.

From this account, studied in connection with the geography, I conclude that Valens must have been already on the road between Ariminum and Ravenna when the news of the fleet's mutiny came. Had he still been south of Ariminum the following difficulties present themselves:—

(a) There was not the slightest need for him to march "*per occultos tramites*" if he desired to get to Hostilia as quickly as possible while avoiding Ravenna. The quickest route for him, if still south of Ariminum, was by the main road *via* Bononia. But if he were already north of Ariminum and near Ravenna, then the cross-roads recommended to him, *e,g.*, from Cesenatico to Cesena, would save time.

(b) When his reinforcements have arrived he will not march *via* Ravenna, as they are too weak. He therefore "sends the infantry before him to Ariminum, and bids the cavalry guard his rear." Now, if he is marching in a hurry north to Ariminum, these dispositions are too ludicrous for words. The danger is all in his front: he therefore puts his cavalry to guard his rear; the need for speed is urgent: he therefore places his infantry at head of the column! But if he is *retiring* on Ariminum from the north the arrangement is clear. The cavalry are properly placed to guard the rear of the retreat He himself, however, does not accompany the column, as he has given up the plan of getting to the Po at all.

(c) He himself "turns aside first to Umbria, next to Etruria." But if he is south of Ariminum he is already in Umbria. For he cannot have been still within a few miles of Rome. (Why should the cavalry guard his rear, above all, in this case?) If he has already crossed the Rubicon, he *may* have recrossed it into Umbria before leaving that district again for Etruria and the west. But even this would give him but a mile or two in Umbria, as he clearly did not accompany his troops to Ariminum, which is hard by the boundary of the province. The words "*flexit in Umbriam*" are, indeed, almost unmeaning. Valens' obvious route, if (for reasons (a) and (b)) we believe him to have been north of Ariminum, was to proceed *via* Cesena to Faventia (Faenza), thence cross the mountains by the well-known road to Florence and the valley of the Arno, and so to Pisa at the mouth of this river.

This ridge of the Apennines is *not* easily crossed even by a small company, as those who have roamed about the Prato Magno chain or crossed from the Casentino and La Verna to Badia Prataglia and Urbino can tell. Even the road over the Consuma Pass has only just been opened. The mountains are truly magnificent, and I saw no snow on Falterona in September. But the going is hard. I doubt if Valens and his small faithful band disturbed the autumn leaves in Vallombrosa. North of the Metaurus and the Furlo Pass (whence the Arno valley can be reached by Urbania and Borgo San Sepolcro, or by Gubbio farther south) the first good track to the Arno valley is the route now followed by the railway from Faenza *via* Brisighella and Borgo San Lorenzo to Florence. If Valens was in the neighbourhood of Rimini and wished to get speedily to Pisa, this was his natural road.

If, then, Valens had crossed the Rubicon travelling north, his near approach may account for the sudden mutiny by night at Ravenna, which seems to have surprised Caecina before he was ready also to play the traitor. For Tacitus says that Valens could still have reached him by rapid movement before he, too, went over.

But if there were, as Tacitus suggests, a secret agreement between Caecina and Bassus, Valens must have been near at hand indeed if he could have arrived in time to dissuade Caecina from following his fellow-traitor's example.

The whole discussion may at least serve to illustrate Tacitus' inexcusable vagueness in his military history. His interest in geography is evidently of the most casual description. One other example of this blemish in the history may here be appropriately mentioned. Valens is presently captured by the Flavians at the Iles d'Hyères, near Toulon. When Tacitus next mentions him it is to remark casually that he is in prison at Urbinum. Why at this little mountain city in Umbria, of all places in Italy? Why, when, and how did the Flavians take him *there*? Doubtless his head was useful to the enemy marching for Rome, and it must have been forwarded to them for use at Carsulae, eighty miles to the south. After all, Hasdrubal's head travelled a longer journey down the same road. But why the unlucky Valens should have been escorted for execution to Urbino, which lies up in the hills ten miles from Fossombrone and away from the main road south, is a problem to which I can give no answer, and Tacitus vouchsafes no explanation. If Valens had been a Garibaldi fleeing through these mountains for dear life, Urbino might have been his San Marino, and the problem would be easier. But Valens was a prisoner.

CHAPTER 3

The Rebellion on the Rhine

Strong heart with triple amour bound.
Beat strongly, for thy life-blood runs,
Age after Age, the Empire round—
In us thy Sons,
Who, distant from the Seven Hills,
Loving and serving much, require
Thee,—thee to guard 'gainst home-born ills,
The Imperial Fire!

Rudyard Kipling.

§1 THE TRIBES OF THE "LOW COUNTRIES"

The Rhine is the only great river of Europe which, although not absorbed into a larger stream, yet fails to keep its name as far as the sea for at least the greater bulk of its waters, and thus all but loses, as it were, its own identity. After a course of some five hundred miles from the Lake of Constance, of which more than four hundred, from Basle northwards, have lain entirely in German territory, the river a mile or two below Emmerich crosses the Dutch frontier and, almost immediately dividing into two channels, surrenders its name. The northern channel, called the Lek, flows by Arnhem to Rotterdam; the southern channel, called the Waal, by Nymwegen, (in Dutch "*Nijmegen*"), to Dordrecht. Fifteen miles above Dordrecht the River Maas enters the Waal from the south, and the combined stream is called the Merwede as far as that town.

Here at Dordrecht the southern stream is again divided. A broad northerly channel, the De Noord, flows to join the Lek a few miles above Rotterdam, and this channel from that point to the German Ocean takes the name of the Maas again. The southerly stream from

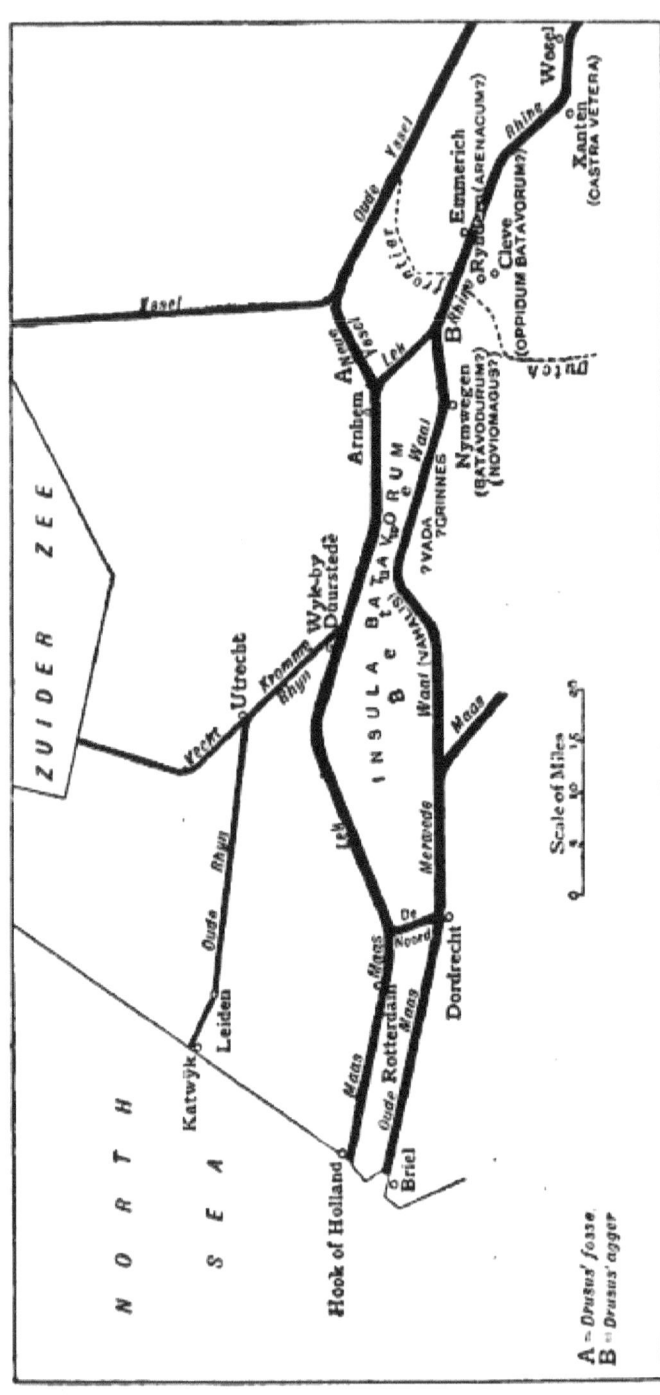

Dordrecht to the sea by Briel is called the Oude Maas. The actual name of the Rhine clings only to a small channel leaving the Lek by Wyk, and called the "Crooked Rhine"—*Kromme Rhyn*. This at Utrecht again divides: one branch, now called the Vecht, flowing north to the Zuider Zee; the other, under the name of the "Old Rhine"—*Oude Rhyn*—passing by Leiden to the North Sea at Katwyk. A sketch plan may serve to illustrate these divisions of the stream for the last hundred miles of its course from Emmerich to the sea.[1]

The land enclosed by the two arms of the Rhine, the Lek on the north and the Waal on the south, measuring some sixty miles in length and about twelve at its greatest breadth, was known to the Romans as the "Island of the Batavians"—*Insula Batavorum*. These folk were a German tribe who originally counted as part of the larger tribe of the Chatti, who dwelt chiefly north of the Taunus mountains by the upper waters of the Lahn, (now Hessen-Nassau). But quarrels at home had driven the "Batavians" to take up their goods and chattels and wander off to the north-west, until they settled in the "Island" and westwards of it as far as the sea. There they were when Julius Caesar heard of them, and there they have remained ever since, still as in Tacitus' day "famous for valour." The Dutch name "*Betuwe*" for the land in the eastern part of the "Island" preserves their name, as their descendants continue to preserve their independence of their neighbours and remote kinsmen, the Germans.

Side by side with them in their "Island," probably in the western part of it, there dwelt another tribe of close kinship with them, speaking the same language, and not inferior to them in courage, though fewer in numbers. These, by name the Cannenefates,[2] seem to have spread also northwards along the narrow strip of land between the Zuider Zee and the ocean, from Amsterdam to Helder in "North Holland," if the Dutch name for the coast here, *viz*. Kennemerland, keeps their memory. North-east of the Zuider Zee and along the marshes, dunes, and islands of the coast dwelt the Frisii, a hardy race of cattle-breeders and fisherfolk, as are their descendants, the men of Friesland, today. In Germany and Gaul tribe after tribe have wandered over the country, and the history of these lands is a veritable kaleidoscope of races.

---

1. No attempt is made to show the actual course of the streams, whose windings are innumerable, but distances are roughly to scale.
2. In inscriptions the name is spelt in at least five different ways, but Cannenefates seems the most common.

But the great gift of the German rivers to their children in the Low Countries has been so great a security from enemies, owing to the difficulty of attack and the poverty in earlier days of the plunder to be won, that their sturdy valour, already famous in Roman days, has known how to maintain them in unconquerable possession of their still quiet land of slow-moving streams. And the Romans, perhaps better than any race since their day, knew how to make of these peoples faithful and useful allies rather than ever bitter foes.

The Batavians were not called upon to pay tribute, but supplied as many as one thousand cavalry and nine thousand infantry to the Roman Army. The eight *cohorts* of Batavians attached to the Fourteenth legion were stalwart if quarrelsome troops, proud of their nation and of indomitable courage. The Imperial bodyguard itself, which protected the person of the emperor at Rome, was formed of men of this tribe. They were commanded by their own nobles and not by Roman officers, and by virtue of this privilege also the Batavian regiments ranked high among the auxiliary troops of the Roman Army. Their kinsmen, the Cannenefates, in like manner paid no money to the Roman treasury but gave men to the army.

The Frisii sent hides yearly by way of tribute, and men as well. These also had been faithful allies of Drusus and Germanicus in their wars over the Rhine under the Emperors Augustus and Tiberius. But they were farther away from the Roman influence, and rose in revolt in the year A.D. 28. Since that time they had given no small trouble to the Romans; and though, later, Corbulo, the first general of his time, had punished them severely, the greater part at least of the Frisii remained independent of Rome after the Emperor Claudius had withdrawn all Roman troops to the west bank of the Rhine.

Their neighbours to the east, the Chauci, a tribe of very great size, resident between the Ems and the Elbe, mariners and fishermen, owned no allegiance to Rome. But at least the "Island" counted as being within the frontiers of the Roman Empire. For Drusus' great engineering works, made in 9 B.C., had done much to secure this. Under his direction the Roman Army of the Lower Rhine had in that year constructed both a Fosse and a Mole. The mole or "*Agger*" was thrown out into the Rhine from the left bank just above the parting of the channels below Emmerich, not far from Cleve.[3] By this the greater bulk of the river's water was directed into the northern arm, the Lek, and thus the "Island" was easily reached from the Roman shore, while it was separated from the tribes over the Lek by a great mass of water.

The use of this Agger was great, and it was strengthened again by Pompeius Paulinus in *A.D.* 55. The fosse was dug from the Lek, a mile or two above Arnhem, to the River Yssel, upon the course of the "New" or "*Guelders*" Yssel, and thus gave the Roman flotilla upon the Rhine access to the Zuider Zee. This was equally useful for the purpose of any hostile operations against the Frisii, and for interrupting in case of need the communications of the Batavians and Cannenefates with the Frisii and Chauci. By such means, and by requiring of them service in the Imperial army, the Romans for long years kept a grip over the two tribes of the Island. And their Gallic neighbours on the south, chief of whom were the Nervii in modern Belgium, had for long years past been fully subject to Rome.

Yet once, in the years *A.D.* 69-70, a great storm of mutiny of the native troops in the army, and of rebellion among the tribes in these the Roman "Low Countries," broke upon the Roman dominion and all but overthrew it. It was truly the "Indian Mutiny" of Roman history.

§2. THE CAUSE OF THE REBELLION

The cause of this rising was the natural love of independence and of liberty which was felt by the German tribes who came, however remotely, under Roman influence. In its beginnings, indeed, the real meaning of the war was hidden under the disguise of a movement in favour of Vespasian against the Emperor Vitellius, and the rising was not only encouraged, but even directly promoted, by the Flavian leaders. None the less this opportunity so recklessly given to the tribes was from the first but the mere pretext or occasion of their fighting. From the beginning of the revolt among the Batavians to their final proud submission, the war was an armed plea for liberty. The use made of this liberty, had the tribes won it, would doubtless have been ferocious and barbaric. Circumstances made of the war "one of the most singular and most dreadful in all ages," (Mommsen).

The motives of the leaders of the revolt were in large measure those of private revenge and selfish ambition. To the annals of the Roman army the war contributed little but a record of lamentable cowardice and dishonour. And yet, in spite of all these undoubted facts, the cause of the war succeeds in ennobling its history beyond that of the other

---

3. Cleve, probably the "*Oppidum Batavorum*" of *Hist,*, was then on the Rhine bank; it is now some distance away.

fighting of these two wild years of strife. Apart from the audacity or calmness of a few, the splendid courage of the Roman troops engaged upon both sides, or the misdirected loyalty of soldiers to their generals, there is no sunshine to light up the thick gloom which enwraps the civil wars of Otho and Vitellius, Vitellius and Vespasian. There was no great principle at stake in either war, and only such can justify the appeal to arms. The tribes were fighting for a principle. They fought savagely, ignorantly, treacherously. They were happy even in their ultimate defeat. Yet the cause of their rising did them honour.

That this was the cause of the rebellion is shown alike in the peoples and in the leaders who shared in the enterprise.

A. The Peoples of the Revolt.—The peoples rose for liberty. No other battle-cry would have gathered to the Batavians' standards the other tribes of the Rhine, some already subject to Rome, some threatened by her in past years, and eager for revenge as well as plunder. The obvious weakness of the Roman army on the German frontier, when Vitellius had drained it of all its best troops for his march to Italy, and the fierce internecine struggle raging in Italy itself, seemed to give the restless German tribes a unique opportunity for rebellion and defiance. Thus the Batavians and Cannenefates were not left long alone in their endeavour. They presently found allies in the Marsaci at the mouth of the Scheldt. The Frisii joined them at once. The tribes beyond the Rhine seized the chance offered them.

The Tencteri opposite Cologne, the Bructeri on the Ems, shared in the first attack on Castra Vetera.[4] Higher up the river, the Chatti from the north of Taunus, the Mattiaci from its southern slopes, the Usipi from the lands opposite Coblenz, made an early onslaught on the great Roman fort at Mainz.[5] The Chauci, the tribe lying to the east of the Frisians, sent the insurgent leader aid not only at the height of the struggle, but even again when he seemed in his last most desperate straits. Of all the famous German tribes beyond the Rhine known at this time to the Romans, not one gave the latter any help, and two only took no interest in the war. The Cimbri were but a shadow of their former selves; the Cherusci allowed their native indolence free play.

On the Roman side of the Rhine the Cugerni to the west of Castra Vetera joined the insurgents at once, and remained true to them

---

4. See below, §4.
5. See below, §5.

to the end. Their neighbours the Ubii, inhabiting Cologne and the surrounding district, had for some years past been a centre of Roman influence among the wilder tribes over the river, and were hated and distrusted by these in consequence. But the tide of German successes swept even these into the movement at last, though their motive was always self-preservation rather than any active dislike of Rome, and they returned to their early allegiance at the earliest possible moment.

Finally, there dwelt in Gaul a German tribe, the Tungri, far removed from the fatherland. These had expelled the Gauls from the district round the present town of Liège, in Belgium, in the valley of the Meuse (the Maas of Holland); and the city of Tongres, fifteen miles to the north of Liege, preserves their name. This folk supplied at least two auxiliary *cohorts* to the Roman army, and these had fought for the Vitellians against Otho. But the German rising excited at once their national feeling. One of the *cohorts* went over to the enemy in the first engagement; the other quickly followed suit; and the whole tribe threw in their lot with the rebels. Practically all "Germany" on both banks of the Rhine was at one time in arms against the Romans in this war. Only a truly "national war" could have produced such a unity among so many widely scattered tribes

The call to liberty found then an instant answer in the German's heart. The struggle between Roman and Teuton never ceased. "*Tam diu Germania vincitur.*" And this most dangerous plague of "nationalism" spread even to Gaul, though here the tribes, accustomed for a century to the Roman rule, resisted the infection longer, and many suffered no taint of it at all. But the Gallic districts on the north and north-east, which came into close contact with the Germans, could not but be affected by the movement.

The Belgae, chief of whom were the Nervii, famous foes of Julius Caesar in old days, were neighbours of the Batavians and Tungri. The small tribe of the Baetasii dwelt between the Nervii and Tungri in Brabant, where the village of Betz, near Brussels, recalls their name. The Moselle valley gave easy access from the Rhine at Coblenz to the spread of the disorder to its tribes, the Treveri, whose name is kept in that of the capital city of the valley, Trèves, and, higher up the river, the Mediomatrici, in whose territory Metz lies. The news of the rising penetrated the Ardennes, travelling up the long valley of the Maas, and reached the Lingones at the source of the river. From this tribe it could be carried over the watershed to the valleys of the Saône and

Rhone, and be told to the powerful tribe of the Sequani, who lay between these rivers and the Jura. And a little to the west of the middle course of the Maas, separated from the Treveri by this river, the Remi, "the leading canton in Belgica,"(Mommsen), quickly received tidings of the rebellion on the Rhine.

But from the days of Julius Caesar the tribes of Gaul had ever been jealous of one another, and, when even the national hero Vercingetorix failed to unite them all in his magnificent struggle against the Roman invader, no lesser man coming after him, when the Romans held the land in their masterful grip, could achieve even the like amount of success. Gallic nationalism was an ever-present peril to the Romans for more than a century after the death of its greatest champion. There was no single emperor from Augustus to Vespasian who was not made aware of its existence. Yet the attempt to win liberty was always spasmodic, and a tribe which took up arms for this cause at one time would be found a few years later resisting the similar efforts of a neighbouring canton. When Julius Vindex in the last year of Nero's *principate* gathered round his standard a hundred thousand Gauls to fight for Gallic independence,[6] the Sequani were among those who took up arms for him; but the Treveri and Lingones not only held aloof from his cause, but gleefully assisted the Roman Army of Germany under Verginius Rufus to crush the rising. The two tribes steeped their hands in the blood of the twenty thousand slain at Vesontio, (Besançon), capital city of their Gallic kinsmen, the Sequani.

Yet the Treveri had fought for Florus and Sacrovir when these rose against the Romans in the *principate* of Tiberius. And little more than a year had passed since the death of Vindex, when the policy of these three tribes was to be completely, almost ludicrously, reversed; when the Treveri and Lingones were to be found among the foes, the Sequani among the friends, of Rome. The German leader had every reason to declare with emphasis that "Gaul had fallen by its own strength," ("*Gallias suismet viribus concidisse*,"— Tac.). But all his urging of this home-truth was unable to get the mastery of this ineradicable tendency of the Celt. The great German historian of our own day, Mommsen, cannot refrain from gibing at this characteristic weakness of the Gauls; for when the attempt was made by them in the year 70 to follow the example of their German allies and to erect an *Imperium*

---

6. Tac.; Plutarch, *Galba*; see my *Life of Nero*.

Galliarum independent of Rome, he labels it "a tragedy and at the same time a farce."

When, therefore, the Gallic tribes, their neighbours, were invited by the rebel Germans to take part in their enterprise, their answer was far from unanimous. At first indeed they gave ready, even strenuous, aid to the small Roman Army which sought to make headway against the rebels. The Treveri stood stoutly on the defence against the Germans, even running a palisade and trench along the whole line of their threatened frontier, and contending vigorously with the assailants. A hundred years before, the Remi had been Caesar's most faithful allies, and now no Roman disaster shook their loyalty. The Sequani also refused always to join the enemies of Rome. But the early triumphs won by the insurgents, and especially the siege of Castra Vetera, the Roman stronghold of the Lower Rhine, made the loyalty of some others grow cold. They remembered the money which they gave each year to the Treasury, the men whom they were compelled to supply to the armies, of Rome. The Treveri, Lingones, Baetasii, and Nervii, joined the insurgents. The "hope of liberty" beguiled them.

And when once the iron hand of the conqueror was removed, the old struggling for primacy among the tribes could be renewed, and more than one folk dreamt of glory to be gained at the expense of their kinsmen, (*Mox valescentibus Germanis pleraeque civitates [Gallorum] adversam nos arma sumpsere spe libertatis et, si exuissent servitium, cupidine imperitandi*—Tac.). Surely Rome's end seemed hard at hand. Once more, as in Caesar's day, the Druids preached rebellion, proclaiming that the burning of the Capitol was a sign from Heaven that the Empire was departed forever from Rome. And the people were but too ready to be credulous when the priest preached a holy war. Not for a moment was any appeal made to any Flavian sympathies which perhaps some Gauls might have.

But they were bidden think of the ills endured for so many weary years, of the "hapless servitude which falsely they called peace." First war, then liberty, then Empire, but an *Imperium Galliarum*, not an Empire of Rome—such was the bait which ensnared them. The miserable pretext of Vespasian's name was quickly flung aside. The secret meeting of conspirators held in the private house at Cologne agreed gaily enough together: Liberty must first be firmly rooted in the land; then the tribes need but "discuss" together the question of the limit they might choose to set to their exercise of power, ("*Coalita libertate disceptaturas Gallias quem virium suanim tenninum velint*,"—Tac.).

These rebels had not even the wretched mockery of a senile emperor for whom to fight, as had our own *sepoys* in times past. "Far be it from us," cried Civilis to the Tungri, "to seek rule over others. It is not for this that we have taken up arms, that Batavians and Treveri may govern the nations. Far be such arrogance from us." When the company of urchins set out to rob the pastry cook of his richest cake, they fared out together in all amity; it was afterwards that they fell to quarrelling about the largest slice.

B. The Leaders of the Revolt.—This cause, the desire to be freed for ever from the Romans, was professed by the leaders of the revolt, at first secretly, but later on with open frankness. Their names seem those of Romans; their military experience had been gained in Roman armies and Roman camps; but they were no more Roman in sympathy than they were in race. Long since, the history of Arminius, somewhat grotesquely celebrated as the " liberator of Germany," had shown that a Roman education was not the slightest guarantee for loyalty, but rather an inducement and encouragement to disaffection and secret treason. Other instances since had confirmed this gloomy fact. The native chiefs would come to Italy for education, would learn Roman manners and the Roman language, and return home to kindle rebellion against Rome. As early as the first century of our era education bred sedition. *Omne ignotum pro magnifico*. It had been better if the ruling nation had been less well known to the princes of Germany. It was easy for them to see signs of her weakness and vacillation. It was hard for them to realise the grim strength of courage and determination which was still, even after many years of Empire, the bedrock of her people and even of some among her rulers.

So both Rome and the Germans paid dearly for their common mistake. But while the common folk who rose against Rome may win men's admiration, little of this can be reserved for those who of selfish ambition played upon their people's ignorance, turned the arts which they had learnt from Rome, the skill which they had there acquired, to the hurt of their teachers, and therefore inevitably added ingratitude and treachery to the more venial charge of self-seeking which can be brought against them.

The three chief leaders of the Gauls in the revolt were Julius Classicus and Julius Tutor of the Treveri, and Julius Sabinus of the Lingones. The one great German leader was Julius Civilis.

Classicus was prefect of the *ala* Treverorum, which served as an auxiliary squadron in the Roman Army. Tutor had been appointed by Vitellius "*prefect* of the bank of the Rhine."[7] Sabinus boasted that he was great-grandson of Julius Caesar himself. Yet there was little Roman about these men save the name Julius, and this was the commonest of names for the chieftains of Gaul.[8] Classicus was the noblest by birth as well as the wealthiest in his tribe. He was a descendant of its early line of kings, and his royal ancestors had ever been the adversaries rather than the allies of Rome. Tutor fought the Romans to the last. Sabinus used his supposed descent only to bid his followers call him

Caesar. Julius Civilis,[9] above all, was all the more a barbarian at heart for the Roman veneer upon him.

This man was of Royal Batavian stock. He had served twenty-five years in the Roman Army, and was, according to his own story, an early friend of Vespasian himself. He was brave, eloquent, and a ready speaker. Twice he had run no small risk his life: once under Nero, when the then Governor of Lower Germany, Fonteius Agrippa, sent him in chains to Rome to answer a charge of planning rebellion; once, still more recently, when in January A.D. 69 the Army of the Rhine declared for Vitellius. From the former peril Galba's clemency had released him; from the latter his own influence with his tribe. For the Vitellian leaders feared lest his punishment should anger the Batavian *cohorts* who were at that time quartered among the Lingones.

Civilis, however, was not a man to forgive such insults. With the craft of a savage he hid his resentment for a time, but waited his opportunity. This came when Antonius Primus, the Flavian leader, just before his invasion of Italy, wrote to him inciting him to cause the Batavians to revolt, wishing to hinder thereby the sending of any reinforcements to Vitellius from Germany. Hordeonius Flaccus, the Governor of Upper Germany, himself specially appointed by Vitellius to guard the bank of the Rhine, urged the same upon him in a private interview.

---

7. *I.e.* to guard the strip between the Nava and Moselle (Heraeus). The general "*cura ripae*" belonged to Hordeonius Flaccus, Governor of Upper Germany (Tac.).
8. Cf. Julius Florus of the Treveri; Julius Sacrovir of the Aedui (Tacitus); Julius Vindex, the Aquitanian noble, Julius Valentinus of the Treveri; Julius Auspex of the Remi (*Hist.*); Julius Briganticus, the Batavian (*Hist.*); Julius Calenus of the Aedui (*Hist.*); *etc.* Claudius was also a common *praenomen*.
9. According to the Medicean MS. of *Hist*, iv. "*Julius Paulus et Claudius Civilis.*" But we have Julius Civilis, *ap. Hist*, i, and Frontinus, *Strateg*, iv. 3. 14. Hence the MS. reading in iv. is altered to read "*Julius Paulus et Julius Civilis*" (Halm), or "*Julius Civilis et Claudius Paulus*" (Heraeus).

Encouraged by these two Romans, Civilis declared for Vespasian, even as Vindex in the preceding year had risen nominally on Galba's behalf. But just as Vindex had harboured other thoughts in his heart when he revolted, so Civilis nourished a "deeper plan."[10] When in November Antonius, now that the Battle of Cremona had been won, sent again bidding him cease from further warfare, Civilis threw off the mask. By refusing to obey, he changed the outward aspect of the Batavians' revolt from participation in the civil war to that of flat rebellion against Rome. He had never intended anything else from the beginning. His very personal deformity—for he had lost the sight of one eye—he was wont to quote as sign of his enmity against the Romans, comparing himself in this also to Hannibal and Sertorius, the foes of Rome.[11] But neither Sertorius nor Hannibal was guilty of the cruel tricks which delighted the German savage. The massacre of the heroic little garrison of Castra Vetera, when they surrendered at last on promise of their lives and, disarmed and marched out five miles along the road, were there butchered in cold blood, Civilis professed to deplore.

Even the Nana at Cawnpore was saved from this hypocrisy by drunkenness. It was after this deed that, to celebrate the work of destruction which was, he gleefully thought, now fully accomplished, the German barbarian fulfilled the vow which he had made when he took up arms, and for the first time cropped short the hair which, stained red with dye, flowed about his shoulders. And others also should have joy of his gallantry and triumph. To rejoice the heart of the fierce maiden prophetess Veleda, who dwelt amid the black forest on the River Lippe's banks, one Roman *legionary legate* was reserved as booty from the butchery. Happily his escort murdered him while yet upon the journey towards her. And for his little son's delight, so ran the tale, this Civilis, this eloquent Roman soldier of twenty-five years' service, set up captives tied to stakes, to be the mark for the child's darts and javelins. This was the leader who plunged his tribesmen into desperate war, and above all others shook the structure of Roman dominion on the Rhine to its lowest foundations.

§3. The Roman Army on the Rhine

The usual garrison of Germany, or "Army of the Rhine," consisted

---

10. The "*altius consilium*" to which he "*studium partium praetendit*" (Tac.).
11. Heraeus' note is comic enough to deserve repetition: *Er war einäugig, wie Hannibal und Sertorius (gleichfalls Todfeinde Roms), Ziska und Nelson; vgl. die Bemerkung* Plutarch's *Sert.* I."

of eight legions and a corresponding number of auxiliaries. Of the legions four were in Upper, and four in Lower, Germany, these two provincial districts meeting at a point about halfway between Bonn and Coblenz, near the village of Brohl.[12] The troops of each district were under the command of a *legate* of at least *praetorian* rank,[13] although the civil administration in them remained in the hands of the Governor of Gallia Belgica until the *principate* of Domitian,[14] and the collection of taxes was controlled by the procurator of that same province until at least the middle of the second century of our era.[15] The Rhine was now the limit of Roman military occupation and administration. The Emperor Claudius had withdrawn all Roman troops to the left bank of the river in the lower province after Corbulo's campaign in *A.D.* 47, and Dubius Avitus, after a punitive expedition against the Frisii ten years later, had again retired behind the river.

In the upper province since the days of Augustus there had twice been trouble with the tribe of the Chatti in the valley of the Main, which enters the Rhine at Mainz, and two Roman armies had penetrated up the valley of the tributary to punish the natives—the first in *A.D.* 41 under Galba, who later became Emperor of Rome; the second, nine years later, under the poet Publius Pomponius Secundus. But though the small tribe of the Mattiaci under the Taunus hills remained under Roman control, and Romans enjoyed the hot springs of Wiesbaden and worked the silver mines in the neighbourhood, (Pliny), no Roman troops seem to have been quartered in the Main valley or on the right bank of the Rhine, except that the bridge-head opposite Mainz was occupied by a *castellum*, and is therefore still called Castel today. It was not until the annexation of the Neckar valley by Vespasian in *A.D.* 74-75 that the Romans began to push their military frontier forward beyond the Rhine in the upper province, and the chapter opens concerning the great defensive works, walls, forts, ramparts, and palisades which were made to link the Rhine and Danube together.[16]

---

12. Cf. Mommsen, *Provinces*.
13. *I.e.* who had at least been *praetor* at Rome.
14. The first known "*legatus Germaniae*," as distinct from the "legate of the army in Germany," is Javolenus Priscus, the jurist, in *A. D.* 90.
15. Procurator of Belgica and of both Germanics.
16. By far the best succinct account of the Roman "Limes" here, and of its history from Vespasian to Marcus Aurelius, has been given us recently in the last published work of our Master in Roman History, Professor Pelham, in his paper, "A Chapter in Roman Frontier History" (*Transactions of the Royal Historical Society*, N.S. vol. xx. 1906).

Claudius' invasion of Britain had caused a considerable displacement of troops on the Rhine frontier, since in the first century A.D. the "German Army" was the most conveniently placed of all the legionary forces in Europe for the purpose of invading the island and strengthening the army of occupation when it had landed and gained its first victories. Hence in A.D. 68 only seven legions lay on Rhine.[17] And the civil wars, above all the Vitellian invasion of Italy in the spring of the next year, had very greatly drained away the strength of the Rhine Army to the south. By the summer of A.D. 69 nearly one hundred thousand men of all arms must have been withdrawn by Vitellius from the German provinces. To a certain small extent new levies had partially replenished the legions, or the portions of the legions, which had been left behind. But the new recruits hastily enlisted on the spot were drawn largely, if not entirely, from the local *auxilia*, and were Roman in nothing but in name and in the citizenship which their enrolment in the legions gave to them. There was therefore a great deterioration of the troops, not only in numbers, but also in quality, discipline, fidelity, as the event was but too quickly to prove.

In the autumn of A.D. 69 the Batavian chief Civilis declared for Vespasian. At that moment the troops on the Rhine seem to have been distributed as follows:—

(1) The *Legionaries.*—The *legionaries* nearest the sea were those in camp at Castra Vetera,[18] nearly one hundred and fifteen miles from the coast, and twenty-five from the parting of the channels at the east end of the "Island of the Batavians." This place, situated at Birten by Xanten, on the left bank of the Rhine just below Wesel, was then the chief fortress of Lower Germany, and was garrisoned always, until the days of Domitian,[19] by two legions encamped together. The two legions in A.D. 69 were the Fifth Alaudae and the Fifteenth Primigenia, the latter under Munius Lupercus as *legate*. But the main bulk of the Fifth with its eagle had marched for Italy, and only a detachment (*vexillum*) was left in camp. The Fifteenth, on the other hand, had sent only a detachment to the south, and its eagle stayed behind with the greater part of the regiment. But, taken together, the men of the two legions at Vetera mustered scarcely five thousand men, and did not amount to the strength of a single legion when this was fully up to strength.

Thirty-five miles up stream from Vetera lay Novaesium, the mod-

---

17. See chapter 1, §2.
18. This I call "Vetera" simply henceforward, following Tacitus.
19. See chapter 3, §1.

ern town of Neuss on the left bank, twenty-two miles downstream from Cologne, and nearly opposite Düsseldorf.[20] This was the camp of the Sixteenth legion, the most "stay-at-home" of all the legions on the Rhine, and its eagle had never left Germany, though up to A.D. 40 it had been quartered at Mainz. Its *legate* was probably Numisius Rufus, but he was at this time for some unexplained reason, not with his legion, but at Vetera. This legion had sent a *vexillum* to the war in Italy. Its strength in camp therefore at Novaesium cannot be put above four thousand men at most.

No legionary troops were at this time stationed at Cologne. But twenty miles upstream from Cologne, at Bonn, there lay the First legion under its legate Herennius Gallus. Most of the men of this, the "premier regiment" in the Roman Army, had been summoned to Italy. In spite of new levies it could place only some three thousand men in the field.

In Upper Germany, the only *legionary* troops at this time on the Rhine were those in camp at Moguntiacum, the modern Mainz, then as always the chief Roman fortress on the upper course of the river, and about a hundred miles south-east of Bonn. This also was a "double camp," and contained the two legions, Fourth Macedonica and Twenty-Second Primigenia. The latter was under the command of the *legate* Dillius Vocula, who was the only general of the smallest merit upon the whole course of the river when the revolt broke out. The Fourth had sent a detachment to Italy, and its eagle stayed behind. It therefore may have numbered some four thousand men at most. Its regimental reputation was a poor one, and it was not to increase this in the coming war. The bulk of the Twenty-Second legion had marched south with the Vitellians. The whole *legionary* garrison of Mainz can scarcely have numbered more than six thousand men.

Finally, at Vindonissa, the modern Windisch, near Basle, one hundred and seventy-five miles south of Mainz, there should have been encamped the Twenty-first legion Rapax, a regiment notorious for savage courage marred by a tendency to insubordination. But the entire legion had by this time vanished with Caecina over the Alps, there to do desperate deeds.

The entire legionary Army of the Rhine, therefore, at this time numbered barely some 18,000 men, distributed as follows:—

---

20. Neuss is now a mile and a half from the Rhine. The actual site of the camp is said to have been at Grimlinghausen, a mile away from the modern Neuss upstream. Neuss itself was on the river as late as A.D. 1310.

At Vetera: Leg. V. and XV.	= 5000 men
,, Novaesium: Leg. XVI.	= ?4000 ,,
,, Bonn: Leg. I.	= 3000 ,,
,, Mainz: Leg. IV. and XXII.	= ?6000 ,,
Total	18,000 men

(2) The Auxiliaries.—It is quite impossible to form any estimate at all of the total number of auxiliary troops at this time forming part of the garrison of the Rhine. A little is known of their nationality, their position, and their value; nothing at all of their numbers.

In nationality the auxiliary *cohorts* found upon the Rhine before the year *A.D.* 70 were mostly natives of Germany, Gaul, or the Upper Danube. Thus the *cohorts* of Batavians, Cannenefates, Tungri, and Ubii were Germans; those of Belgae, Nervii, and Nemetes[21] were Gauls; those of Raeti and Vindelici were natives of the districts on the Upper Danube. *Cohorts* of other races also served on this frontier, such as those of the Asturians and Vascones from Northern Spain, the Breuci from Pannonia, and Silaunenses perhaps from the east. But it seems certain that the majority of the auxiliary *cohorts* was composed of native troops levied near the frontier itself. Cavalry squadrons were in like manner furnished by the Cannenefates, Batavians, and Treveri.

The places of encampment for some of these are known. Nearest the sea of all troops of the Roman Army upon this frontier were two *cohorts* of Gauls who occupied some petty Roman forts in the Island of the Batavians, and probably other corps besides of Nervii and Tungri very recently enlisted. In garrison with the *legionaries* at Vetera there were Ubii, cavalry of the Treveri, and one squadron of Batavian horse under Claudius Labeo. Labeo was himself kinsman to the insurgent leader Julius Civilis, but hated him so intensely that his loyalty to the Romans was unshaken alike by imprisonment and constant pursuit which he endured at the hands of the rebels. He was throughout a constant thorn in their side. Higher up the river there was one squadron of horse at Asciburgium (Asberg by Mors[22]); at Novaesium there were some auxiliaries; at Bonn *cohorts* of the Belgae, with the Italian *ala* Picentina; and at Mainz were the *cohorts* of the

---

21. The Nemetes dwelt upon the eastern slopes of the Vosges on the left bank of the Rhine by Speier, the Roman Noviomagus, and south of Speier towards Selz.
22. On the road between Vetera and Novaesium, twenty miles from the former (Tac.).

Batavians and Cannenefates.

The best troops among these auxiliary forces were certainly the eight *cohorts* of Batavians who had been attached to the Fourteenth legion. They had seen much service in Britain, and more recently during the Vitellian invasion of Italy. But their temper gave great ground for distrust. They had quarrelled fiercely with their comrades of the legion during Valens' march for Italy, and broken out into open mutiny, which it had been difficult to quell. They had repeated the offence later in the year while quartered at Turin with the legion, and the emperor had been compelled to separate them once and for all from the *legionaries*. They had therefore been sent back to the Rhine, and were, at the moment when Civilis raised the standard of revolt, in the lines at Mainz, together with their kinsmen the Cannenefates. Before news of Civilis' rising reached them, however, Vitellius, alarmed at last at the threatened invasion of Italy by the Flavian troops, sent recalling the *cohorts* of both tribes to Rome. They had started on the march when a messenger reached them from Civilis imploring their help. They hesitated not a moment, but abruptly turned and marched for the north.

The hatred of Rome thus displayed by these *cohorts* was commonly shared by all the German and Gallic auxiliaries at this time on the Rhine. The sudden flood of the mutiny swept the whole native army away, so that no single regiment could be trusted. Old and new grievances, the remembrance of ancient liberties, suspicion and long-nurtured ill-will felt towards the alien, jealousy of the regular army, dislike of the officers, all combined to excite the native troops against the Romans on the Rhine as they roused the *sepoys* against us in India fifty years ago. Their own native officers for the most part stimulated or acquiesced in their mutiny. Julius Classicus, the insurgent leader himself, was *prefect* of a squadron of horse of the Treveri. When an officer like Claudius Labeo was found to lead his men against the rebel army, they deserted him and went over to their brethren, and he was happy indeed to escape with his life.

It was, in fact, now for the first time that the Roman Army system in its method of recruiting native auxiliaries was seriously tested, and it broke down hopelessly. Recruiting, of course, was far more easy when the natives were enlisted to serve in clan-corps in or near to their own homeland. But that such a saving of trouble was very dearly purchased was a lesson first taught the Roman military authorities by the mutiny of the native army on the Rhine. That Vespasian had duly learnt this lesson will be shown in this chapter, §8.

In the autumn of the year *A.D.* 69 the Roman Army of the Rhine was therefore weak in numbers, and weaker still in discipline and loyalty. It was strewn in widely separated fragments along three hundred miles of frontier from Mainz to the German Ocean. Its commander-in-chief, the governor Hordeonius Flaccus, had but recently been appointed. He was old, slothful, timorous, a martyr to gout, secretly treacherous to the Emperor Vitellius, distrusted and despised by the troops. The army had lost its ablest leaders and many of its best troops. It was soaked through and through with disaffection, mistrust, inefficiency. It was ever more and more bewildered and distracted by the doubtful issue of the struggle for Empire raging furiously in Italy, and, when at last Vespasian's cause won the day, it was hostile to that new and unknown emperor. It saw the strength of the Roman Army and Roman State rent, as it seemed, in pieces before its eyes. It was upon this army, in a state so sorrowful and hazardous, that there suddenly burst the tempest of a great national insurrection, with the objects of which a great part of that army sympathised heartily. That disaster followed disaster, that this Army of the Rhine ceased to exist, that the flame of revolt ran along the entire length of the frontier like fire along a gunpowder train,—these were but natural results. Never had Rome known or endured the like. Her army had played her false. Yet in such an army how could she have confidence?

> In the course of a few months soldiers successively of Nero, of the Senate, of Galba, of Vitellius, and of Vespasian; the only support to the dominion of Italy over the two mighty nations of the Gauls and the Germans, while the soldiers of the auxiliaries were taken almost entirely, and those of the legions in great part, from those very nations; deprived of their best men; mostly without pay; often starving; and beyond all measure wretchedly led—they were certainly expected to perform feats inwardly and outwardly superhuman. They ill sustained the severe trial.—Mommsen, *Provinces*, vol. i.

But though her army on the Rhine disappeared, though her forts and frontier defences were shattered, though mutiny seemed victorious and treachery triumphant, Rome was still invincible.

§4. The War, up to the Relief of Vetera

A. The Clearing of the "Island."—Julius Civilis, the Batavian chief-

Coin of Galba.

Coins of Otho.

Coin of Vitellius.   Coin of Vespasian.

tain, had been encouraged to raise a revolt on the Lower Rhine in the interests of Vespasian, that he might keep Vitellius' troops on that river busily employed. In his heart he cherished the deeper design of striking for the liberty of his native land. The opportunity for action was quickly given him. The Emperor Vitellius, on news of the Flavian invasion of Italy, sent commands for a general conscription through the Batavian lands. The officers whom the governor appointed to carry out the orders acted harshly at least, and perhaps the graver charges of injustice and lust brought against them were not entirely lacking in truth. Civilis called his tribesmen into the secret recesses of one of their sacred groves and made to them a fiery speech.[23] They at once decided to rebel, refused to obey the Roman demand for men, and sent messengers to the Cannenefates their neighbours, and to the *cohorts* of their people stationed at Mainz, urging them to join.

The first blow was struck by the Cannenefates, who joyfully lent their aid. There was one of their tribe, Brinno by name, whose father had defied and fought the Romans in the *principate* of Caligula, and the son loved them no better. Placed upon one of the large German shields, and raised on high above the crowd by his eager followers, he was elected leader after the fashion of his tribe, and forthwith called them to arms. He sent also to the Frisii, calling them to the field, and with his tribesmen fell suddenly upon two Gallic *cohorts* of auxiliaries, quartered in the "Island." These fled, and, after burning some small Roman forts in the neighbourhood, fell back to the upper end of the island where with the rest of the Roman auxiliaries in the district they stood at bay.

Then Civilis himself took the field, at the head of a mixed company of Batavians, Cannenefates, and Frisii. Near Nymwegen or Arnhem,[24] he and his army attacked the auxiliaries. These now had the Roman Rhine flotilla on their flank to help them. But treachery quickly got the better of both army and fleet. A Tungrian *cohort* in the former, and the Batavian oarsmen employed upon the latter, played them false, and the Romans were speedily defeated and expelled one and all from the "Island," while the whole fleet of twenty-four vessels was either captured or destroyed.

It was time for the Roman *legionary* to come to the rescue. Hordeonius Flaccus sent ordering the garrison of Vetera to advance at once

---

23. Tacitus was not in the grove. Whether someone there later told him the speech, or he invented it, cannot be shown; the latter is the more probable.
24. Tacitus' geographical knowledge is vague and incredibly unsatisfactory.

against the rebels, under command of Munius Lupercus, *legate* of the Fifteenth legion. He marched the twenty-five miles downstream to the "Island," and threw his force into it over the Waal. His army was composed of the *legionaries* of the Fifth and Fifteenth legions, cavalry of the Treveri and Batavians, and also auxiliaries of the Ubii. He found Civilis quite ready to fight him, probably again in the neighbourhood of Arnhem. In the battle the native regiments with one consent betrayed him. The Batavians promptly went over to the foe: the Ubii and Treveri ran. His *legionaries* indeed stood firm, and, when the battle was lost, drew off in good order to Vetera again. But the outlook was ominous enough. A mere handful of *legionaries* could do little to withstand or suppress a national rising. And soon the rebels received reinforcements more valuable than any which Civilis had as yet gathered to his cause.

This befell when the *cohorts* of Batavians and Cannenefates from Mainz marched into Civilis' camp, proud and exultant after forcing their way through the Roman *legionary* line itself The men of the First legion had sallied out from their camp at Bonn to bar the way north to the rebel *cohorts*. They had trusted that the governor Flaccus was hard upon the rebels' heels with the garrison of Mainz, and they had hoped therefore to catch the *cohorts* between two fires. Their own legate, Herennius Gallus, had been reluctant to run the risk. His hesitation showed prudence if scanty pluck. For no Flaccus ever appeared pursuing after the enemy. The *cohorts*, experienced and bold veterans, feared not a whit the *legionaries* and their auxiliary allies whom they saw thrown across their road outside the gates of Bonn. They formed square and thrust hard at the Romans, whose auxiliaries fled as usual, and the angry *legionaries* found their line pierced, themselves flung aside, and the *cohorts* disappearing gaily down the road towards Cologne. Pursuit was out of the question, and the legion was left to digest its disgrace as best it could, while the *cohorts* marched calmly north, leaving Cologne untouched, past the ramparts of Vetera, and reached Civilis with their new honours thick upon them. The bitter recrimination which now occupied the leisure of the *legionaries* at Bonn did not greatly avail to sweeten the cup of a very notable defeat.

Civilis was justly encouraged. He was now leader of a very respectable force, ("*Justi exercitus ductor*,"—Tac.) and could carry the war outside the limits of the "Island" on his own account. Having made his entire army take the oath of fidelity to Vespasian, he sent a message to the garrison at Vetera, twenty-five miles away, bidding this do the like.

It defiantly refused. Thereupon with his entire available force marching by both banks of the Rhine and with his fleet moving up-stream in company, Civilis led the rebel force to the siege of Vetera. This stronghold of the Romans on the Lower Rhine must be taken.

B. The Siege of Vetera.—"The tide of warfare," it has been said, "ebbs and flows on an ocean which is studded with strategical objectives." But this tide of the German mutiny rolled fast in a narrow bed, pushing its surging flood steadily up the valley of the Rhine, and presently casting a secondary wave along the course of the lateral valley of its tributary the Moselle, while the main flood went steadily sweeping up the greater river to the south. Then in due course it receded heavily back down both the streams, and its last murmurs died away in the peaceful slow-moving waters of the Northern Sea. In its rising it lapped greedily round the walls of many a Roman fortress; in its ebb it left behind it white staring ruins, and rotting heaps of slain. Nowhere did it beat more furiously in its onset than upon the ramparts behind which the scanty little garrison of Vetera stood staunchly on the defensive. Hurled back ever and again, it still foamed up upon the defiant barricades, or worked stealthily to undermine the foundations of them. So in the end the cruel flood worked its will, and Vetera fell. But before this came to pass many weeks went by, of siege and relief, of hope and despair, of famine and surprise. The siege of Vetera is the one heroic episode in the first chapter of this war.

As was the case with the Residency of Lucknow and its small company of defenders, so Vetera and its garrison were but ill-prepared to stand a siege. Its troops, like our own, had sallied out to find the foe, and been beaten back to find shelter in its walls. They, like our own, felt the pinch of hunger as the days went by, and the assailants pressed them close, now by fierce onslaught, now by sullen blockade. They, like our own, had scarcely men enough to defend the walls, "only 5000 men to defend a camp built to hold two legions." They, like our own, were hampered and embarrassed by a crowd of civilians, traders, women, children, who took refuge behind the walls defended by the troops. For in the long years of peace upon the Lower Rhine many buildings had grown up round about outside the military camp "in manner of a township,"[25] where the Roman merchants and traders had their dwellings and stored their goods, and where the women and

---

25. "*In modum municipii*": an excellent example of the growth of towns as due to the system of permanent cantonments.

the children of these and of the troops had their homes.

All these buildings had for purposes of the defence to be destroyed, and the non-combatants given shelter behind the fortifications. This made the demand upon the stock of provisions all the heavier, and these, largely through the garrison's own fault, were already too scanty. The very defences themselves had been built in the days of Augustus rather to serve as a good base of operations directed against the German tribes over the river, and as a post from which to observe their movements, than to protect Roman *legionaries* against attack. The greatest and most prudent of all the emperors had not foreseen so desperate a reversal of fortune. Hence the very fortifications were inadequate. If the Roman did not entirely accept the modern maxim that the history of entrenched camps is almost always the history of capitulations, yet at least he too relied on arms in the field rather than on stone walls for victory and for safety.

Yet for all this there was never a moment's thought of capitulation, of even parleying with the rebels. They sent answer to Civilis:

> They would not listen to a traitor's advice nor to that of enemies. Vitellius was their emperor: they would keep their faith to him and their weapons until their last breath. Let not a runaway Batavian think to control the destinies of Romans. Let him rather expect the due penalty of his desertion.

In the old spirit of the Romans in Gaul a century earlier, they provoked the enemy to wrath and bade him do his worst. Walls and entrenchments were hastily strengthened, and the garrison waited for the coming of the rebels.

They had not long to wait. Furious with wrath at the answer given to his challenge, Civilis passionately hurled his motley army upon the fort. Here veteran troops advanced under the worn colours of the Roman army, and plied all Roman arts of siege-craft. There wild barbarians rushed to swarm over the defences, brandishing on high the rudely carved images of wild beasts, which signified each its special tribe and nation, and had been brought from the gloomy recesses of sacred forests to urge their savages forward to the work of plunder and of butchery. With rocks and stones hurled by the catapults mounted on the walls, and with fiery spears, the garrison, grimly fighting, drove back all assaults, and when night fell the fort was still inviolate. Civilis' first attempt had failed.

The insurgent leader knew that but a few days' provisions were all that remained to the besieged. He ceased from further direct attack, and his army was spread round the walls, waiting for hunger or for treachery to do the work where force had failed, like some crafty beast of prey couching long before the final spring. Now, if ever, the Romans higher up the river must march to relieve the garrison and raise the blockade.

C. The Advance of the Relieving Army.—Even the old infirm governor, Hordeonius Flaccus himself, saw that Vetera must if possible be saved. Not only did he issue orders at Mainz for the instant sending of a relieving army from that camp, but he himself accompanied it. Fearful, however, of the toils of a march, he journeyed by water downstream, which failed to increase the small respect in which his troops already held him. The officer appointed to lead the force by land was Dillius Vocula, *legate* of the Twenty-Second legion. His army consisted of picked soldiers from the two legions encamped at Mainz, the Fourth and Twenty-Second, and was constantly increasing in numbers during the march to the north by the addition of Gallic auxiliaries who, at Flaccus' orders, came to join the army.

The distance from Mainz to Vetera was one hundred and seventy-five miles. For the first hundred miles, as far as Bonn, Vocula met with no opposition, and advanced by forced marches. At Bonn the men of the First legion were added to the relieving column. And at Cologne, twenty miles on, Hordeonius Flaccus, finding himself hopelessly unpopular with the troops, finally handed over the entire control of all the operations to the legionary *legate*. Vocula had put down disaffection and lack of discipline with a firm hand, and the soldiers admired him the more they feared him.

But from Cologne onwards the difficulties of the relieving army multiplied. Vocula was hampered not only by lack of supplies and an inefficient commissariat staff, but also by an exceptionally low Rhine. The state of the river not only made all navigation very difficult, and delayed the corn ships, but it also made it necessary to post patrols at intervals all along the left bank to prevent parties of Germans crossing and falling upon the flank or rear of the Roman column as it advanced. Progress was, therefore, very slow, the more so as the men were dispirited, and troops in this state of mind march very badly. "The old defences of the Empire," they said, "were deserting them: the gods were angry." At Novaesium, however, twenty-two miles below Cologne, fresh reinforcements were picked up in the men of the

Sixteenth legion; and the *legate* of that legion, Herennius Gallus, now shared with Vocula the responsibilities of command.

But here part of the army was left in camp with Flaccus, the governor. The foe were now close at hand, and a fortified base camp was necessary. The rest of the column then marched slowly forwards as far as Gelduba, where a small fort on rising ground overlooked the Rhine, (Pliny *Nat. Hist.*). This is now the village of Gellep, between Kaiserwerth and Ürdingen. Here the two generals, Vocula and Gallus, halted their men. Vetera was only twenty-five miles away, but the country was swarming with foes in front and on both flanks. The fort was holding out stubbornly, and the generals of the relieving army would take no risks with their own force. The position at Gelduba was strongly entrenched, and some time actually was spent in drilling and exercising the army.

More valuable training, however, was afforded by an expedition of part of the force under Vocula against a hostile tribe, which threatened the left flank of any farther advance. These, the Cugerni, were Germans, and possibly the remnants of the ancient Sugambri, whom Tiberius sixty years before had settled on the left bank of the Rhine. They now dwelt in the district round the modern small town of Goch, thirteen miles west of Xanten (Vetera). They had joined Civilis, and a raid upon their territory, it was hoped, would teach them to keep quiet for the present. During Vocula's absence a stranded corn ship led to a fight between the Romans left in camp at Gelduba and the marauding Germans, who came down upon the vessel to plunder her. In this the Romans got the worse, and lost the ship. The troops, as usual, were furious with their general Gallus, and only Vocula's timely return and stern treatment of the ringleaders stopped another incipient mutiny.

The patrols on the river bank had proved quite unable to prevent German roving bands from crossing the stream. Vocula, therefore, found the enemy active behind him, threatening his supply trains, and ravaging the lands of his still faithful allies, the Ubii round Cologne. Even Marcodurum, the present Düren on the Roer, twenty-four miles west-south-west of Cologne, garrisoned carelessly by a cohort of this loyal tribe, who trusted for safety rather to their distance from the Rhine than to vigilance, was surprised and sacked by the enemy, contemptuous alike of the Roman camps at Novaesium and Gelduba. That the relieving army was itself in a state of semi-blockade at Gelduba is shown by its long-continued inactivity.

Meanwhile the Germans grew weary of the blockade of Vetera. The garrison might be starving, but it gave no signs of any thought of surrender. The approach of the relieving army also seemed to call for greater efforts by the besiegers, and while Vocula and his men were miserably wasting time at Gelduba instead of pushing right through to the beleaguered fortress, a fierce assault by the enemy again tested the endurance and valour of its garrison to the utmost. All messages to them from the relieving column, all news of its despatch or approach, had been carefully intercepted by Civilis. For all they knew they were left to their fate, to starve or to perish fighting, unless they would betray their honour. And now a still greater mass of German savages from over the Rhine flung themselves upon the entrenchments. The night did but add to the perils and horrors of the day. Huge fires were seen blazing in the enemy's lines, just outside their ramparts, and the figures of the barbarians were lit up by the flames as they sat drinking and carousing. Then, hot with wine, the savages swarmed again to the assault. But the light of the fires made their bodies an easy mark for the steady, deliberate, and unerring aim of the *legionaries*.

Many of their bravest chiefs had been picked off, while the walls of the camp, dark and frowning, defied the blind shooting of the enemy, before Civilis noticed the error of his men. Then the fires were stamped out, and the blackness of night covered the movements of besiegers and besieged alike. But the *legionaries* fought grimly on by ear, now that sight failed them. Heavy stakes and stones were hurled down into the darkness where the noise was loudest The sound of scaling ladders planted against the walls called them instantly to the spot. They thrust the stormers back with their shields, and followed their flight with a rain of javelins. Yet many of the foe made good their footing on the ramparts, there to meet death from the short stabbing sword of the *legionary*.

The grey dawn brought new methods, but no relaxation of attack. The Batavians wheeled a great two-storied tower crammed with men up to the Praetorian gate, where the level ground gave them easy access. It was battered to pieces by the Romans with poles and beams, and a sudden sally drove the enemy off. If one more rash than his comrades approached within reach of the walls, he was suddenly gripped by the iron hand of a crane, whirled up into the air before his fellows' very eyes, and flung a mangled body over the rampart wall into the heart of the camp. Once more the garrison had repelled this most savage of onslaughts. The discomfited Germans drew off, and sate down sullenly again to beleaguer the fort which no courage of theirs could take.

D. The Relief of Vetera.—At this point there arrived in the Roman camp at Gelduba the news of the battle of Cremona. It made no difference to the military operations. The tidings, it is true, were at once sent to Civilis. He was informed that the Roman Army on the Rhine had renounced its allegiance to Vitellius and declared for Vespasian. His object, therefore, had been won, and it was time for him to cease from all further hostilities. Civilis took no notice, but with still greater energy urged on the war. Thereby he at last threw aside the mask, and the struggle, which up to this point could have been in theory viewed merely as a chapter in the history of the Civil War, henceforward took on its true colours of a national rising of the Germans against Rome. Politically and historically this was most significant. But its only influence upon the course of the war was that it lent all the greater reason for hate, if not the greater hatred, to the combatants on both sides.

The relieving army was not left undisturbed in camp at Gelduba. Civilis, keeping enough men to carry on the blockade of Vetera, sent the rest to rush the Roman camp. Sacking a small fort on the way at Asciburgium, near Mors, twenty miles south of Vetera, the Germans completely surprised the Roman Army, and, forcing their way into the lines, began a ready massacre in the midst of the general panic. The German and Gallic auxiliaries of Vocula were utterly terrified, and their cowardice all but led to a complete disaster. From this the Roman general was saved only by the timely arrival of some *cohorts* of Spanish auxiliaries, the Vascones. These, who had recently been levied by Galba, none the less understood the primary duty of the soldier, and, hearing the noise of the fighting when they were still some distance from the camp, marched straight to the sound. They came unexpectedly upon the enemy in the rear, and the consternation which they caused gave time to the *legionaries* to rally from their first shock of surprise, and drive the Germans with heavy loss from the camp. But Vocula or his sentries had done little to earn the esteem of the army by this engagement.

Neither did he follow up at once the success which, somewhat in his own despite, he had gained. Had he done this, in the opinion of the Roman historian, the German Army would have melted away, and Vetera would have been relieved without further trouble. But still Vocula tarried at Gelduba, and thereby gave Civilis the chance to play one last card. Direct assault had twice failed. Hunger had been defied. The attack upon the relieving army had been repulsed. Perhaps stratagem would give him the prize which seemed so nearly in his grasp. The garrison had heard nothing of the approach of a relieving force, until one morning they saw paraded outside the ramparts the captive standards of a Roman Army and a string of Roman prisoners. They were colours and men taken in the attack on Gelduba, and were contemptuously displayed as sole survivors of the one army which could have come to save the fort. But Civilis' trick recoiled on his own head.

One of the prisoners—and history would have done well to record his name—shouted to the besieged a few words, enough to tell them the truth, that the Army of the Rhine was not destroyed, but was even then hard at hand. His captors struck him dead to earth, but his heroism had saved the garrison from despair. And soon, as they strained their eyes over the illimitable expanse of plain towards the south, they saw smoke rising upon the horizon. Vocula and his army had struck camp at last, and the burning houses, which on their advance they put to the flames, gave the signal of their approach. The whole German beleaguering force drew out to meet the coming foe. The anxious garrison saw their comrades rapidly advance, and halt.

Next came a moment's pause, when it seemed as if they would entrench themselves against the German onslaught. But then the whole weary army, animated as by one wild longing for battle, in little order but with fierce shouts, dashed upon the waiting Germans. Every gate of Vetera was at once flung open, and the besieged garrison sallied out to join in the last desperate onset on the enemy. The fighting was bitter. But presently down went the rebel leader's horse, and the rumour spread fast that Civilis was slain. The Germans fled in wild panic, and the Romans at last marched into the camp which had been so stoutly defended.

§5. Flood Tide: The Success of the Mutiny

A. The Retention of Vetera.—Vetera was successfully relieved. There then followed on Vocula's part an action which remains the one military puzzle of this war. The general strengthened the defences of the camp, sent away all non-combatants under escort upstream to Novaesium, took one thousand of the best men from the old garrison and added them to his own force, and with this small addition to his strength retired again up the river to Gelduba. In actual fact, against his orders more than one thousand followed the return march, and when these were commanded to return to Vetera they refused, saying that they had endured the hardships of a siege long enough already. There was, therefore, a Roman garrison still left behind in the fortress, of numbers smaller by more than a fifth than before. It is true that a certain amount of provisions had been supplied to them; they were relieved from the presence of a hungry unwarlike crowd of civilians, and their defences had been improved.

None the less they sent after Vocula, complaining bitterly that he had abandoned them to their fate, and imploring him to return. Certainly they were left to themselves in the middle of a savagely hostile country, and at any minute the fate from which Vocula had marched to save them might seem to threaten them again. Had they been once relieved only to endure again the agony of suspense, the perils of assault, the miseries of blockade? The Germans had vanished; but when the Roman army withdrew southwards, how could it be but that they would reappear in greater numbers and lively exultation? Then, would Vocula again come to save them? Who knew but that the uncertainties of war would compel his presence elsewhere? If this were the case they, a weakened garrison, must endure the extremest penalties at the savages' hands.

When once the relief of Vetera had been accomplished at the cost of such toil and fighting, one of two courses might have seemed open to the Roman general. He might have held the fort with his whole force and made it the base of operations for an advance upon the foe whom he had just heavily defeated. Or, if he judged this too rash, he might, now that the primary object of his march, the rescue of the garrison, had been gained, have evacuated and destroyed Vetera, falling back with the whole army as far towards Mainz as he thought it expedient, taking the rescued with him.

A very few days proved clearly that the first of these plans was beyond his strength, owing to the difficulty of supplies. The enemy were by now complete masters of the river. All supplies, therefore, had to come by road from Novaesium. A first convoy got through safely, while Civilis was recovering from his recent defeat. But a second attempt met with woeful results.

Vocula had again despatched the corn collectors with a strong escort and waggons north to Novaesium. The escort was guilty of scandalous carelessness. They never gave a thought to the possible appearance of the enemy, but stowed their heavy weapons gaily in the empty waggons, and strolled blithely along the road beside them or wandered over the countryside. Presently the convoy halted. There was an obstacle on the narrow road in front. Up from ambush sprang the Germans and fell upon them. Sheer desperate fighting, lasting all the day, did at the end carry the Romans through to Gelduba, where they found protection at the camp there. But to escort a laden convoy thence back along the road to Vetera seemed beyond their powers.[26] It was clear that Vocula, if he stayed at Vetera, had not men enough to guard his line of communications and to carry on offensive operations as well.

The Roman historian himself at this point passes judgment upon Vocula in a manner which does little credit to the general's military intelligence, and none at all to his own. It is a veritable masterpiece of improbability, almost of folly. Tacitus states his belief that, after his victory over Civilis outside Vetera, Vocula ought again immediately to have pursued the flying enemy. If, instead of this, he busied himself in strengthening the fortifications, "as if another siege were threatening," "he had misused victory so often that he was rightly suspected of preferring war, " ("*Sed Vocula, omissis fugientiam tergis, vallum turrisque castrorum augebat, tamquam rursus obsidium immineret, corrupta totiens victoria non falso suspectus bellum malle.*"—Tac.). This preference, it is to be supposed, was for war rather than peace, and not for war rather than victory. Presumably the general felt that his talents were best displayed in war, and therefore desired this to continue! He therefore fortified Vetera instead of pursuing the enemy.

It is hard to speak calmly of such a judgment, of him who passed it, of those who seem to accept it.[27] Vocula had already had every reason to distrust the temper of his own troops, to appreciate the greatness of the danger threatened by the Germans' bravery and cunning. He had just extricated a beleaguered garrison with very serious difficulty. He was involved in a country swarming with savage foes. His own life was every moment at stake—not only imperilled by the enemy, but

---

26. I do not know why Mommsen (*Provinces*, vol. i.) supposes the attack on the convoy to have been when it was proceeding "with provisions" in the reverse direction from Novaesinm to Gelduba. It is clear from that the waggons were empty, and that the "*quantum in regressu discriminis adeundum foret*" is a thought for the future, not an experience of the past.
27. As *e.g.* in Church and Brodribb: "The line of conduct which he actually pursued was so inexplicable as to suggest suspicions of treachery, which the historian himself seems to have thought justified by the facts" (*The History of Tacitus*). *Cui bono* the "treachery"? Vocula at least lost his life.

also by mutiny and treachery among his own troops. Only inflexible severity and success in war had kept his own regiments in hand. Had another immediate success been possible for him, as Tacitus supposes, not only military fame and honour, but self-preservation itself, must have compelled him to do his utmost to secure it.

If Vocula did not pursue the enemy, either at once or after some days had passed, the simple explanation is that he did not feel himself strong enough to do so. His object had been the rescue of the garrison. This was at last effected. But pursuit was a very different matter. Even after a battle fought and won for the sake of victory upon the field, immediate pursuit does not follow as a necessary consequence.

> The fear of a return blow provoked by premature pursuit and of losing the fruits of victory in the endeavour to make it more complete will always restrain him (the commander-in-chief). . Every battle entails extreme excitement and the utmost strain of all the intellectual and physical forces. A state of exhaustion accordingly follows as a natural consequence. After a victory, moreover, there is a feeling that further sacrifices are purposeless, or that they would not be sufficiently recompensed by the probable additional results.[28]

Certainly for immediate pursuit after a desperate battle, and with troops utterly worn out by marching and fighting, Vocula could have neither inclination nor the means. For an advance northwards against the Germans after allowing his men a few days' rest, the general had neither men nor, as has been seen, food enough. Truly it needed "the most unmilitary of historians" to suggest that the suspicion, product

---

28. Von der Goltz, *The Nation in Arms*. Of course this writer insists that this reluctance to pursue is due chiefly to modern conditions of wax: "This immediate pursuit," he goes so far as to say, "has not only nearly always not taken place in late wars, but it lies in the nature of the modern battle that it will, as a rule, be absent." The Russo-Japanese War confirms his statement. Cf. too the very striking sentence of our own British general: "It is perhaps necessary to have been a responsible commander during an attack to realise the immense reaction of relief when success is attained, a reaction coincident with an intense longing to tempt fate no further. 'You have won the battle,' a voice seems to whisper in your ear: 'the enemy are going: for God's sake let them go; what right have you to order still more men to lose their lives this day?'" (Sir Ian Hamilton, *A Staff-Officer's Scrap-Book*, vol. i.). Part of this feeling would hardly be applicable to Vocula, or indeed to any other general in savage warfare. But the "reaction" felt after victory would be all the stronger when the fruits of victory were the very tangible ones of a rescued garrison, and these had been fully secured by it.

of ignorance and malignity combined, was true, that Vocula failed to pursue because he desired to protract the war. This, too, must be added to the large rubbish-heap of Tacitus' "military" judgments.

The Roman general was therefore unable either to advance against the Germans from Vetera or to remain there with his force. But—the real problem—why did he not then evacuate it altogether?[29]

It cannot be supposed with probability that Vocula deliberately intended to sacrifice to his own safety the remnants of the garrison whom he left behind; that to cover a dangerous retreat it was necessary to leave a force behind him in Vetera, although he knew that this force would, as a consequence, be destroyed. It is true that, if this situation had then actually existed, a Roman general might have been willing to demand this self-sacrifice of his rear-guard. This had actually happened but a short while before in Judaea, where at Bethoron a gallant little rear-guard of four hundred men had willingly laid down their lives in order to ensure the safe retreat of the main army.[30] When Havelock relieved Lucknow, he found himself unable to extricate the garrison and non-combatants.

He therefore, being also unable to keep open his line of communications, allowed himself and his force to be besieged anew until Colin Campbell's second army of relief advanced to save the whole. There were Roman commanders who would, under these conditions, have done their utmost to extricate the troops and have left the non-combatants their pitiable fate.[31] But, as a matter of fact, things were not yet so desperate with Vocula and his army. The non-combatants had been sent away to safety without difficulty. The whole force might have been withdrawn with still greater ease, since the Germans took

---

29. Mommsen supposes that when the convoy was cut up Vocula went temporarily to Gelduba to its support, but always intended to return to Vetera. His men, however, refused to return "and to take upon themselves the further sufferings of the siege in prospect; instead of this they marched to Novaesium, and Vocula, who knew that the remnant of the old garrison of Vetera was in some measure provisioned, had for good or evil to follow" (*Provinces* vol. i.). There is not a hint of anything of this in Tacitus, and, though we may criticise the motive ascribed him by the historian, yet in the fact as stated that he chose to do what he did we must needs believe. Surely Mommsen's view is based on a wrong interpretation of the words "*aliis redire in castra abnuentibus*"?

30. See my history of the *principate* of Nero.

31. *E.g.*, Suetonius Paulinus, on his retreat from London towards Chester in *A.D.* 60. Cf. my *Nero*. But it must be remembered in his excuse that his army was then the one and only hope of every man, woman, or child of the Romans at that time in the island of Britain.

some time to recover from their defeat.³²

That the Roman general had some stratetical object in view when he left a garrison in Vetera is certain. That in this he made a bad miscalculation events quickly proved. That he himself recognised this and made heroic, if unavailing, efforts to repair his mistake was also speedily to be shown. His intention was probably to keep the Germans in check by a fort threatening their rear if they advanced south, while he himself was busy collecting all available forces with which to return to Vetera and, using it as his base of operations, penetrate the enemy's country and finish the war. Now that the news of the battle of Cremona had come, he may have looked for the speedy arrival on the Rhine of reinforcements from over the Alps, and have marched south to meet them and move them forward.³³

That some weeks must pass before the struggle in Italy was ended Vocula perhaps did not foresee. And certainly he did not anticipate the series of disasters which immediately after his return up the Rhine befell the Roman arms on the river. In holding Vetera, even though this fort had now been strengthened beyond the fear of capture by assault, he committed an error of overconfidence, somewhat akin to that of which the Federal Government at Washington was guilty when, in defiance of the advice of its military commander, it ordered the garrison at Harpers Ferry to stay at its post in September 1862. In both cases the fort was meant to check the depredations of a vigorous foe. In both cases the fort was sacrificed and the garrison lost.³⁴ It is possible that Vocula had this reason as well for seeking to retain Vetera in Roman hands, that he saw that the Gallic tribes in the neighbourhood of the Lower Rhine were becoming restless and that conspiracy was hatching among them. This was a new and a terrible danger. If the Romans evacuated the one great Roman fortress on the lower river, this evacuation might well be the spark which exploded the mine.

B. The Death of Vocula.—No sooner had Vocula and his main

---

32. It was once suggested to me by an Undergraduate, in answer to an invitation to a class in lecture for suggestions, that Vocula only went to Vetera to get his thousand men, and did not care what happened to the rest. I fear this does not seem to me very probable. In view of the difficulties which the relieving column had to face, this would seem to be a case of plenty to do and little to get, without Sam Weller's comment. Neither would Vocula have strengthened the fortifications in this case. This suggestion, like Mommsen's, I therefore banish to a note.
33. As suggested to me by another Undergraduate on the same occasion.
34. See Note G, "Vetera and Harper's Ferry" at end of chapter.

army left Vetera and marched back to Novaesium, passing Gelduba on the way, than Civilis and his Germans appeared, following hard upon his heels. They took Gelduba, and their cavalry pressed forward to Novaesium, outside of which place they met and routed the Roman horse. Inside there raged mutiny and bloodshed. Flaccus, the governor, was dragged one night from his bed and murdered by a mob of soldiers. Vocula himself barely escaped the same fate by disguising himself in the garb of a slave.

But the approach of Civilis frightened the *legionaries* back to their obedience. Then, however, there came the news of peril on the Upper Rhine, even at Mainz itself, which was being threatened by a mixed force of Germans, belonging to the three tribes of the Chatti, Usipi, and Mattiaci. Vocula was compelled to hasten to its relief, lest he and his army should be cut off completely from his communications with Italy and the hope of reinforcements. The tribesmen were caught unawares and routed with loss. Mainz was saved for the time. But meanwhile the whole of the lower course of the Rhine was left to itself, and the rebellion spread unchecked.

Then indeed, at the beginning of the year *A.D.* 70, the Roman cause seemed at the lowest ebb, and the Gauls first wavered, then renounced their loyalty. The victories of their German neighbours excited them; the news of the burning of the Capitol became the text for the Druids' eloquence concerning the coming doom of Rome; and rumours also reached them of successes gained upon the Danube frontier by Dacian and Sarmatian tribes. It was surely time for them to show their national patriotism, when care for their own safety seemed to suggest this course. The three Gallic chieftains, Classicus, Tutor, and Sabinus,[35] met secretly in a private house at Cologne, and their council was attended also by representatives of the tribes of the Ubii, Tungri, Treveri, and Lingones. The conspirators decided to call the Gauls to arms, and to block the Alpine passes against the coming of fresh troops from Italy. The infection of mutiny had gripped them at last.

The hatching of the plot was at once betrayed to Vocula at Mainz. His troops were fractious and insubordinate. They still resented Vespasian's triumph, and grudged to own him as their emperor. The general was sorely straitened on every side. Yet he never hesitated or flinched. Certainly he had made mistakes, but he was a true Roman—the only one left upon the Rhine. He marched at once downstream for Cologne, and thence for Vetera. With so deadly a new danger threatening, the

---

35. For these leaders see §2 above.

garrison must at all costs be relieved and the fort evacuated. He had left them, as events now showed, in dire peril. He would not abandon them without an effort to save them. Already he was well-nigh within sight of the camp when his auxiliary leaders, Classicus and Tutor, deserted with their tribesmen to the Germans. The traitors had been waiting their best opportunity. They allowed the general to surround himself with foes and to see the object of his determination all but won. Then they played him false. There is little that is sweet about Gallic falseness.

Freedom is better won by sacrifice than by black treachery. Vocula had no choice left him but to retreat. He withdrew his *legionaries*, all that remained to him, back to Novaesium. He knew them to be desperate, and not for one moment to be trusted. Emissaries from the mutineers were almost openly busy in their ranks. There was no succour, no refuge for them nearer than Italy. The Germans were up in their front, the Gauls of the Moselle valley on their flank and rear; the savages across the Rhine were separated but by the river, on which was only a German fleet. Many of his men preferred a Civilis to a Vespasian. They were cowed and angry. To such a recreant band of men, once Roman soldiers, their general, Vocula, made at Novaesium his last appeal. The purport of it was long remembered in after years. The historian, however great a master of the sham rhetoric of the schools, could hardly have invented a speech which breathes so passionate a scorn—the scorn of a Roman whose troops threatened to join Germans and Gauls against the Imperial city. Their old comrades of the *auxilia* were urging them to murder their officers and come over to them.

Vocula knew the whole. Many implored him to escape secretly while yet there was time. But he despised safety if so be that he could save his honour and, if there should yet be shame in their hearts, the honour of his troops as well. He faced them, noisy and turbulent, with treachery and murder in their thoughts, boldly and alone. He told them:

> As to his own fate, he cared not a whit. But the honour of the Roman Army was at stake. What though fortune seemed to fail them, though their courage seemed for the moment shaken? Could they forget the examples of old days, those many times when Roman legions perished at their posts rather than yield ground to the foe? Such memorials did not fail them. Would they march humbly in the train of Germans and of Gauls against the walls of Rome? mount guard for a Trevir? ask a Batavian for the battle signal? For eight hundred and twenty years the army

of the Roman people had done homage to Jupiter, their great and glorious god, by offering the spoils of countless triumphs won. To Jupiter, and to Quirinus, parent of their city Rome, he turned to pray that they might never suffer a Tutor and a Classicus to defile the camp of a Roman Army.

He ended his appeal, and a confused clamour was heard in the ranks. But it was not the clamour of repentance and applause. The men of the last Roman Army on the Rhine had made their choice. Vocula had failed. So let death come to him when it willed. His very slaves baffled him when, like a Roman, he would have turned his sword against himself. It mattered very little. The murderer, a deserter, was sent by Classicus, and passed openly on his business through the ranks of the men to their general's tent. So Vocula found rest from soldiering at last

A fouler page of history was never written in the military annals of Rome.[36]

C. The Loss of Germany.—Vocula was dead; the other *legates* of the traitor legions were in chains. The men joined the rebels, part of whom under Tutor fell upon Cologne and Mainz, and took both without trouble; part under Classicus hurried to make an end at last of the heroic little garrison at Vetera, which Civilis still besieged in vain. Now all the tossing waves of mutiny surged round the last stronghold of the Romans on the Rhine. It stood alone, as a grim dark rock amid the foaming of the raging western sea. Still the scanty, hungry garrison held out desperately. There was no one now to shout the news of relief to come, nor any need for the barbarian to parade prisoners before their eyes. The rebel army, mutineers and Germans, lay passive round about the walls, waiting the end.

Every living animal within the camp was consumed for food. The besieged devoured roots and shrubs, the very grass in the streets and on the ramparts. Even then the rebels dared not storm the fort, but won the hungry men at last to surrender by the solemn promise of their lives.[37] Then all who were left of the Four Thousand laid down their arms and marched out defenceless through the gate, trusting to

---

36. Cf. Mommsen: "In Roman military history Cannae and Carrhae and the Teutoburg Forest are glorious pages compared with the doable disgrace of Novaesium."
37. And Tacitus calmly writes: "*Donec egregiam laadem fine turpi macularent.*" Whose is the cold "disgrace" if not his who cannot realise the sufferings and the heroism of these men? No doubt he felt, as he penned the lines, that he was the truest Roman of them all—he, a stilted pleader at a decadent Bar.

the word of a savage. They marched five miles along the road. Then the barbarians fell upon them. Those who escaped fled back towards Vetera. They found their fort in flames, and perished with it. So the Four Thousand of Vetera died, as did the garrison of Cawnpore.

The legionary *legate* Lupercus was saved from the massacre to be sent to the prophetess Veleda, (Valaeda?), of the Bructeri. As he was being taken up the River Lippe his escort slew him. A few of the under-officers were kept as prisoners. This was the end. The Roman legions on the Rhine were traitors or destroyed. Some of the former, men of the First and Sixteenth regiments, were ordered by the mutineers to Trèves, under command of a certain Claudius the Holy, a man, says the historian, with one eye lost, repulsive of appearance, and even more weak in intellect. He was a worthy leader of such troops. But one auxiliary squadron of Italian horse, the *ala* Picentina, could brook the misery and disgrace no longer. They defiantly left the line of march and rode bravely back to Mainz, there to wait for better days. On the road they met by chance with Vocula's assassin and slew him. His name is given to us; but why should the scroll of infamy be lengthened needlessly?

Only Claudius Labeo now was left, and he strove to hold out with his auxiliary corps of Baetasii, Nervii, and Tungri behind the line of the Maas. It was a vain hope. His native troops promptly joined the German rebels, and Labeo was happy to escape, a fugitive.[38]

The tide had reached its height. The Roman Army of the Rhine was no more. All Roman forts were burnt, save Mainz, and Vindonissa, a lonely fort far in the south, then without a garrison. Civilis and his Germans were triumphant. Germany was free. The "Empire of the Gauls," the *Imperium Galliarum*, had, as it seemed, dethroned Rome from her supremacy in northern lands. "The whole proud Army of the Rhine, the first army of the Empire, had surrendered to its own auxiliaries. Rome had surrendered to Gaul," (Mommsen).

§6. THE EBB: REDUCTION OF THE GALLIC REVOLT

A. The Gathering of the Romans.—Then at last Rome bestirred herself. It was now the spring of the new year *A.D.* 70, and the Civil War was ended. The Flavian cause had triumphed. Vespasian was on his way to Italy. Mucianus, until he came, was regent at Rome. In quick succession the latter despatched legions from Italy northwards to the scene of war. No longer were treacherous auxiliaries, half-hearted and

---

38. For Labeo see §3 above.

mutinous *legionaries*, captains inert, unskilled, or betrayed, to contend with Germans and Gauls, flushed with victory over so contemptible a foe. But a veritable Roman Army of eight veteran legions under brilliant and tried generals was now to strive with tribes who could gain freedom, but who used it in heart-breaking quarrels among themselves. Men who fight for freedom are not seldom apt to translate it in terms of mastery over others. For the woes of the uncivilised at least, liberty from Rome was not a *panacea*.

Five legions were sent from Italy to the Rhine. Three of these belonged to the victorious Flavian army. These were the Eighth Augusta, the Eleventh Claudia, and the Seventh Claudia.[39] Two others had been part of Vitellius' army, the Second Adjutrix [40] and the famous Twenty-First Rapax. But for war against the German these soldiers were of equal service. These five legions crossed the Alps by the three passes of the Great St. Bernard (Pennine Alps), Little St. Bernard (Graian Alps), and Mont Genèvre (Cottian Alps). Summons also were sent to Britain for the Fourteenth legion, the old and deadly foes of the Batavian *cohorts*,[41] and to Spain for two legions, the First Adjutrix[42] and Sixth

---

39. An MS. imperfection has led some editors to substitute XIII. Gemina for VII. Claudia, ap. Tac. *Hist*. Both Halm and Heraeus have omitted the Third legion altogether. Since E. Ritterling's paper (in the *Westdeutsche Zeitschrift für Geschichte und Kunst*, Jahrgang xii. (1893), Heft 2, "*Zur römischen Legionsgeschichte am Rhein*," i., VII. Claudia must be read.

40. For this legion see chapter 2 §7.

41. See chapter 1 §4.

42. There is no doubt of the MS. reading "*sexta ac prima ex Hispania accitae*," i.e. I. Adjutrix. Halm, however, substitutes "*decuma*" for "*prima*," i.e. Leg. X. Gemina, following a suggestion first made, so far as I know, by Sir Henry Savile, in his translation of the *Histories* three centuries ago. The reason for the change seems to be that X. Gemina, undoubtedly a Spanish legion, is found later engaged in this war upon the Rhine (*Hist*, V.), while the presence of I. Adjutrix is not elsewhere mentioned. Also, it is urged, the order VI. and X. is more natural than VI. and I. Ritterling, however (*op, cit.*), argues convincingly for the MS. reading and destroys the objections. That I. is not again mentioned is due to the fact that it belonged to the Upper army, the records of whose war are lost, thanks to the sudden break in the Tacitus MS. after Book v. c 26. The legion has, however, left records of itself in Germany, dating to the years *A.D.* 73 and following. Cf., too, Hardy, *Studies in Roman History*. The cause of the arrival of X. Gemina, not given in Tacitus, is well explained by Ritterling as follows:—In the summer of the year there was a great inroad of Sarmatians into Moesia, which resulted in the defeat and death of the governor, Fonteius Agrippa (Josephus, *Bell. Jud.* vii. 4 fin.). Vespasian, therefore, sent Rubrius Gallus as governor to Moesia, and ordered Annius Gallus to send Leg. VII. Claudia from Upper Germany to his help. In place of VII. Claudia he received Leg. XIV. from Cerialis in Lower Germany, and X. Gemina was called up from Spain, (continued next page),

Victrix. These speedily arrived.

The army was divided into two, and two commanders were appointed. Petilius Cerialis, the cavalry leader of the last part of the Flavian advance to Rome,[43] was selected to conduct the war on the Lower Rhine; Annius Gallus, Otho's old general,[44] was bidden clear the Upper Rhine of rebels, and bring the hostile tribes again to subjection. The larger part of the army, consisting of the Legions I. Adjutrix, VII. VIII. and XI., was given to Gallus. Cerialis had at first only the Twenty-first legion under his command. But it was not long before the remaining three legions, II. VI. and XIV., joined him. And, so far as the incomplete records of the war are concerned, the great brunt of the fighting fell on him. Practically nothing is known of Gallus' equally successful operations in the Upper German province.[45]

The Twenty-First legion, marching by the most direct route of the Great St. Bernard, arrived first at its old headquarters Vindonissa. There it was joined by the auxiliaries of Noricum under Sextilius Felix, who marched through Raetia over the Arlberg Pass, and so by Feldkirch to the Lake of Constance and the Rhine. A special picked squadron of cavalry of mixed nationality, called the *ala* Singularium, also joined the army here. Significantly enough, it was commanded by Civilis' own nephew, Julius Briganticus, whose hatred of his uncle was cordially felt in return by him. This army under Cerialis was to march at once downstream on Mainz and Lower Germany. Meanwhile the greater part of the troops, diverted over the other two passes to the valley of the Rhone, was to march up that river upon the hostile Gallic tribe of the Lingones. These subdued, this army under Callus could either threaten the Treveri on their rear and thus secure Cerialis from their attack, or, if Cerialis, operating from the Rhine, had already received their submission, could march by Besançon for the Upper Province to complete the work in that district which Cerialis, pressing ever northwards, had left unfinished. (See note following).

★★★★★★

Note:—This is the strategy, I think, to be deuced from the very fragmentary hints in Tacitus' narrative. It is clear that the Lingones had to be subdued, and, from Frontinus, *Strat*, iv. 3. 14, that

to be sent to Cerialis in place of Leg. XIV. In the autumn of *A.D.* 70, therefore, VII. Claudia is in Moesia, XIV. in Upper Germany, X. Gemina in Lower Germany, where it is found, *ap. Hist*, v. 19.

43. See above, chapter 2 §7.
44. See above chapter 1 §5.
45. Tacitus' unfinished MS. tells us nothing of this. See below §7.

they were actually so subdued. When, however, this happened is uncertain, but that it befell early, and at Gallus' hands in co-operation with Cerialis' advance north, seems to me probable. For the army destined for the Lower Rhine must hasten forward as speedily as possible, but must not have its advance endangered on its left rear. If Cerialis and not Gallus subdued the Treveri in the Moselle valley, this was due to the facts, probably, that the Lingones gave Gallus some trouble, that the Treveri were cut off from the Lingones by the Mediomatrici higher up the valley (cf. below), and turned their whole attention, therefore, to the Rhine, and that, therefore, Cerialis could not afford to advance upon the Germans leaving his rear endangered by them. It is a great pity that even the Tacitean account of Gallus' operations is not preserved to us.

At Mirebeau-sur-Bèze, thirteen miles north-east of Dijon, and so in the Lingones' land, were recently found building tiles stamped *Vexilla legionum*, with marks of the legions I. VIII. XI. XIV. XXI. Mommsen—ap. *Hermes*, xix.—regarded this as evidence of a reserve depot built by the detachments of these legions during their advance to the north in this year A.D. 70. But there are difficulties in the way of this view, *e.g.* the presence of *vexilla* of XIV. and XXI.—for XIV. as a whole has not yet arrived from Britain (cf. iv.), and XXI. is only heard of as being, apparently as a whole, at Vindonissa. Ritterling), followed by *Hardy*, therefore refers these *tegulae* to the muster of the Upper German Army for Domitian's war against the Chatti in A.D. 83, or against the rebel Antonius Saturninus five years later. Probably, therefore, they are not to be connected with the strategy of A.D. 70 or the reduction of the Lingones, though the idea is a tempting one.

★★★★★★

B. The Struggle with the Treveri.—While this Roman Army was gathering to reap the harvest of vengeance, all was confusion and dissension in the rebel ranks. The insurgents had not even to wait for the coming of the Romans to suffer their first reverse. The Lingones under Sabinus attacked their neighbours the Sequani and were rudely repulsed. This first blow to Gallic Unity, "*Sequanorum prospera acie belli impetus stetit*), added to the rumours of the approach of the new Roman Army, caused the feeling in Gaul to change. The new movement was speedily voiced in a great Gallic Council, which itself was called together by the Remi, the tribe inhabiting the region between the Rivers Marne and Aisne, a folk long since notorious for its loyalty to the Romans. The Council voted for submission and peace. Old intertribal animosities determined the vote. Only Treveri and Lingones refused compliance, and their warriors still remained in the field. But, even so, no concerted action was taken by the three chief rebel leaders—Civilis of the Germans, Classicus and Tutor of the Gauls. Their preparations to meet the coming attack were scanty and inadequate. To Tutor the task of blocking the Alpine passes does seem to have been entrusted; but he left them serenely alone, and the Romans had no difficulty in crossing any one of them. Civilis went gaily hunting after the slippery fugitive Labeo, who lightly baffled all his efforts to catch him. Classicus peacefully rested upon his uncertain laurels.

Such efforts at defence, however, as Tutor made succeeded in collecting a considerable army composed not only of the Treveri with infantry and cavalry of the sometime Roman Army, but also of new levies furnished by three small tribes—the Triboci in Lower Alsace, the Vangiones in the district of Worms, and the Caeracates.[46] With this force Tutor at first showed some activity. Sextilius Felix was in command of the advance guard of Cerialis' army, and sent forward one auxiliary *cohort* to reconnoitre on the march from Vindonissa. This *cohort* came into touch with Tutor's men and was destroyed. But on the advance of the Roman Army in strength, the Gaul's force melted away rapidly.

The former veterans of the Roman Army returned promptly to their old allegiance, and the native soldiers of the three tribes followed them over into the Roman camp. Tutor was left with none but the Treveri to obey him. He was therefore forced to fall rapidly back before the Roman advance, and, avoiding Mainz, now garrisoned by the *ala* Picentina which wished him no good,[47] he retreated to the northern bank of the River Nava, where he hoped to be able to make a stand. This small stream, the modern Nahe, flows into the Rhine between the townships today of Bingen on its right and Bingerbrück on its left bank. At the latter was the Roman town of Bingium, and the road from Mainz northwards crossed the Nahe by a bridge to the town. This bridge was destroyed by the Gauls who lined the farther

---

46. A tribe not elsewhere mentioned, but perhaps situated on the left bank of the Rhine behind Mainz.
47. See above, §5

bank to frustrate the Romans' passage of the stream.[48] But Felix, on arriving opposite the enemy's position, was not long baffled. A deserter showed him a ford, and Tutor's men were driven from their position. Tutor fled, and the tribesmen were scattered and sorely dismayed.

By this time Cerialis himself had arrived with the *legionary* army at Mainz. Evidently distrusting his Gallic auxiliaries, he dismissed them to their homes, saying to them briefly that a war undertaken by Roman troops needed no help from them, but was as good as ended already. The Gauls retired both thankfully and humbly—"*proniores ad officia quod spernebantur.*" Cerialis' action was not the result of disdainful self-confidence, but rather of great wisdom and insight into the native character. After the recent disasters which had befallen Roman troops on the Rhine, it was good policy for the new general to openly assure the Gauls, by word and deed, that even they were not indispensable. British officers have before now used similar methods with native troops, and with good results.

At Mainz, Cerialis quickly decided that his next step must be the reduction of the Treveri in the Moselle valley. Eager as he was to penetrate to the heart of the mutiny in Lower Germany, he could not advance beyond Coblenz, where the Moselle enters the Rhine, unless he had secured himself from attack on the rear by these most troublesome Gauls. Gallus was engaged to the south of them with their allies the Lingones. The Treveri could not at once be left to him. The time had come to make an end of their resistance. Already they were isolated from help. The traitor *legionaries* of the First and Sixteenth legions who had been sent to their capital city, now Trèves, had felt the prick of repentance as soon as the Roman Army had forced the passage of the Nahe. They solemnly administered to themselves the oath of loyalty to Vespasian, and, though at once the boy rebel-leader Valentinus hurried to the town, they remained defiant of him, and marched away upstream to the friendly folk of the Mediomatrici, centred round the modern Metz. Here they halted and waited cautiously on the development of events. To Valentinus and to Tutor, who, after his defeat, had found his way also to Trèves, was left only the melancholy pleasure of butchering in cold blood the two captive *legates* of the legions. So Freedom was justified of her barbarian children.

The Treveri now prepared for resistance to the last, being greatly encouraged by Valentinus' youthful energy and raging. The road to

---

48. This, as Heraeus says, must have contained more water in Roman days than it does today.

their capital city left the Rhine north of the inflow of the Nahe, and crossed undulating country to the Moselle below Neumagen. Thence it ran to Trèves, keeping on the right bank of the river. From Bingen to Trèves the distance is some seventy miles. Cerialis would doubtless advance by this road. His intention to attack them was soon discovered by the tribe. Valentinus, therefore, and his army moved out of the capital six miles downstream, where they took up and fortified a position at Rigodulum, the modern hamlet of Riol, on rising ground overlooking the Moselle. Encamped here, they covered the approach to their city. Here, therefore, Valentinus waited for Cerialis' coming.

The other rebel leaders, Civilis and Classicus, on hearing of Tutor's defeat at Bingium, had joined forces, and now sent to Trèves bidding Valentinus not to fight. It is possible that their plan was to evacuate the valley of the Moselle and to draw the soldiers of the Treveri north to join their own main army. If this was their intention, it failed,—partly owing to the natural reluctance of the tribesmen to surrender their homes to the enemy; partly, perhaps, because the boy leader scorned the counsel of the older men; partly by reason of Cerialis' rapidity of movement. This general having once decided upon a short campaign against the Treveri, wasted no time. In three days he marched his men sixty miles up the Moselle, and was upon the native army.

There was but little spirit left in the tribesmen, and they made but a feeble defence of the position at Riol. The hill had the Moselle on its left, and the brook of the Fellerbach circling round its rear. Its crest was lined by the defenders. The position may be sketched as follows:—

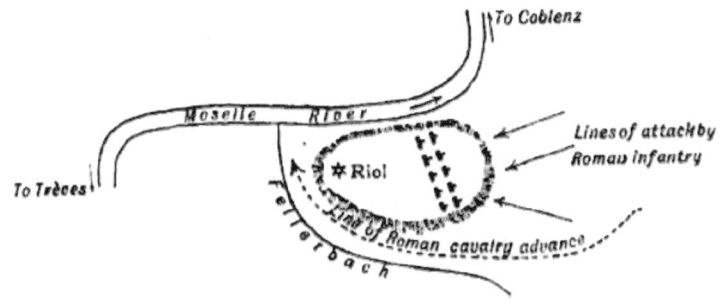

While the Roman cavalry were sent round the hill by the slopes between its crest and the brook, the infantry were launched in a frontal attack up hill against the foe. They stormed it with vigour and success, and Valentinus' army was hurled, a routed mass of fugitives, down the further slope upon the cavalry waiting to receive them and hew them down. They went down the hill, says the Roman historian, like a house falling, "*Ruinae modo.*" Valentinus himself was taken prisoner, but Tutor, if he ever took a part in the defence, escaped. Next day Cerialis entered Trèves unopposed. There he was presently met by the repentant *legionaries* from Metz. He had sent for these to co-operate with him in his attack on the Treveri by advancing upon the tribesmen's rear. They arrived, however, too late to take any part in the engagement at Riol. They were pardoned by the general, and received into his army. The Treveri also, and such of the Lingones as were with them,[49] made their formal submission, which was accepted, and no further penalty was imposed on them. The Roman general prepared to stay for some days in the town, until reinforcements should reach him and enable him to essay the last and most perilous part of the campaign by moving against the Germans. Meanwhile he busied himself in receiving the tribes' submission, and in speech-making. All seemed safe on the Moselle, but in fact was far from being so.

For while the Roman Army lay resting in the town by the river, on the hills to the north of it the tribesmen were gathering in great numbers. Civilis and Classicus themselves had hastened towards the town, and Tutor joined them. Lingones and Batavians, Ubii and Tencteri and Bructeri, all were massing together under shelter of the friendly hills. A great storm was preparing to sweep down upon the valley which reposed at last so peacefully beneath.

This news of the gathering of the tribes reached Cerialis in due course, and roused him from his sense of security. At once he issued orders that the *legionaries* should fortify their camp at Trèves. The general, says the Roman historian, was blamed by many for allowing the natives to collect together on the hills undisturbed. But only the sending out of flying columns could have hindered this, and this method not only demanded more men than Cerialis had as yet at his disposal, but it also was far too dangerous; for such columns might easily have

---

49. This and iv. are the only mentions of the Lingones in connection with the whole campaign against the Treveri. It does not seem at all probable that the whole tribe was engaged in the defence of their allies' capital. But again we cannot be certain of anything about them in the absence of information about Gallus' movements.

been entrapped and cut to pieces among the hills by the swift tribesmen. No blame attaches to the Roman on this account; but he can hardly escape censure for his serious failure to appreciate beforehand the suddenness and ferocity of that favourite Gallic device, a surprise.

The city of Trèves, Colonia Augusta Treverorum, was founded as a Roman town perhaps by Augustus, and owed its colonial status to the Emperor Claudius. It lay on the right bank of the Moselle. Its Roman remains, covered some of them with creepers and greenery, far surpass in beauty those of any other Roman town in Europe whose picturesqueness has been spoilt for ever by the excavator's spade. These, however, date to a later time than the first century of our era. But still to the spectator, standing on the vine-clad hills to the north-west of the city, and looking down on its towers and rose-red walls in the rich plain at his feet, where one busy bridge spans the rapid river, it is easy to see again the little slumbering settlement, the Roman bridge, the camp of the Roman Army on the left bank beyond the bridge, the drowsy sentinels, hardly aware that dawn is already breaking on the surrounding hills, and the wild onrush of the Gauls, striking their last blow in history for freedom from the Roman. The enemy rushed to the assault in triple column. The Batavians came swarming down from the heights which overhung the camp on north and west; Ubii and Lingones hastened up the road which led from the camp northwards down the river's left bank; Bructeri and Tencteri rushed through the gap left between road and river. A sketch may serve to illustrate the onslaught:—

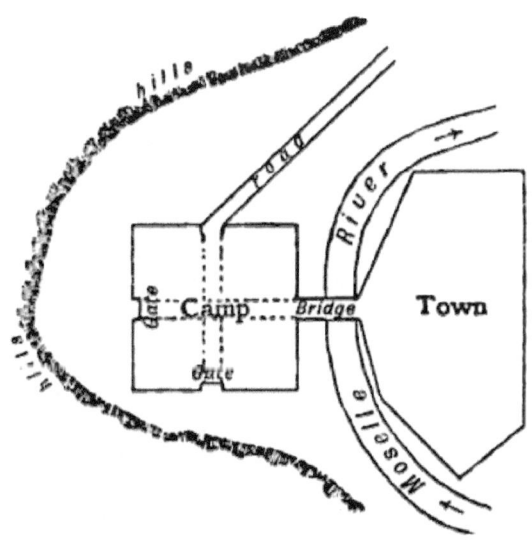

On the night of the attack Cerialis was sleeping, not, as was his duty, in the general's quarters in centre of the camp, but in the town. The sentries, probably on that account, were the more careless. The enemy were upon them and over the ramparts before any alarm was given. Then, as at the surprise of Gelduba, followed a scene of wild confusion, slaughter, and plunder. The *legionaries* fought desperately enough in little knots of men, and their officers sought to cheer them on to a stout resistance. But their exultant and agile foes rushed through the camp and seized the bridge, driving over it a mob of terrified fugitives. At the town end of the bridge their general met them. Hastily roused from sleep, Cerialis had hastened to the noise of the fighting, and now played verily the man. To rally some of the fleeing, and with them make a fierce attack on the bridge, was the work of a moment.

The bridge was retaken, and the general, at the head of such troops as he could muster, crossed it to the camp. His coming saved the day, by that time well-nigh lost. His entreaties and rebukes, his energy, as he hastened from post to post reckless of his life, restored discipline and courage to the *legionaries*. The steadiness of the Twenty-First legion shamed the wavering men of the two unlucky traitor legions, but newly restored to the rank of Roman soldiers. The Germans and Gauls, thinking that the victory was won, were already scattered far and wide through the camp, gleefully gathering up the spoil. But their chief spoil that day was the saving of their lives—by the few who at the last escaped back over the ramparts to the hills, leaving the camp strewn thick with the bodies of their slain. Trèves and the Roman Army were saved. That same day the enemy's camp on the heights was stormed, and the foe melted away to the north. Civilis, Tutor, and Classicus saved themselves by flight. A handful of the leading men of the Treveri[50] still followed their leaders' fortunes. But the resistance of this tribe was now finally at an end.

C. The Advance to Cologne.—But Cerialis could not tarry longer at Trèves. He and his army were needed urgently at Cologne, and it was now safe for him to continue his advance down the Rhine towards that city. Its inhabitants, the "Agrippinenses," easily the most cultured and Romanised of all the Germans on the river, had remained loyal to the Roman cause so long as they dared, and their city had hardly escaped destruction at the hands of the angry Germans across the Rhine in their hour of victory. A timely recognition by the Agrippinenses of

---

50. Tacitus is careful to give a most precise number, *viz.* 113!

facts and the humble answer which turns away wrath had saved their city. But now again the tide of German triumphs had turned and was sweeping fast out to sea. The citizens were eager to return to their old faith, and to propitiate the wrathful Romans by a sweet-smelling sacrifice. Twenty miles away to the south-west of Cologne, at Tolbiacum, the modern Zülpich,[51] Civilis had placed in garrison one of his most warlike and valued *cohorts*, of Chauci and Frisii combined. Now, fresh from the scene of his bitter defeat at Trèves, the German leader, sore and angry, was hurrying towards Cologne, where his own wife and sister, together with Classicus' daughter, had been left as pledges of the alliance. The anxious citizens resolved to carry out at once their desperate resolution.

The unsuspecting Germans, scattered through the houses in the city, were massacred. The famous *cohort* at Zülpich was invited to a banquet and there largely entertained, while wine flowed freely. As the guests lay buried in drunken slumber, their hosts stole from the hall of feasting, made fast the doors, and burnt the whole with fire to the ground. Then the Agrippinenses sent begging Cerialis to march instantly to their succour, and save them from the vengeance of Civilis.

By forced marches the Roman general outstripped the Germans and reached the town in time. Civilis, at the bitter news, turned aside, and retreated northwards, sorrowing for his lost *cohort*. But though Gaul was also lost to him, though his women-folk were prisoners in the Romans' hands, the courage of the rebel general never failed him. The Gauls must be let make their peace with the foe. The Treveri and Lingones had at last been quelled. The Nervii and their German neighbours, the Tungri, followed the example; for the Fourteenth legion, landing at Boulogne from Britain, marched through the territory of these tribes on its way to the Rhine, and scared them into submission.

Yet for all this Civilis was not moved. Still he had his Germans, Batavians, and Cannenefates left to him. With these he had begun the revolt. With these he had driven the Romans from the Rhine. With these he would yet maintain his cause. A couple of small reverses soon "spoilt the fame of the victory" at Trèves, and showed to Cerialis that the Germans were yet to be subdued. A small Roman flotilla, known as the Classis Britannica, which kept guard in the North Sea and Channel, was attacked on the German coast by the Cannenefates and

---

51. Famous later for the defeat here in *A.D.* 496 of the Alemanni by the Franks, and Clovis' consequent conversion to Christianity.

dispersed.[52] And one of Cerialis' advance squadrons of cavalry was cut to pieces by Civilis at Novaesium. The Gallic bid for Empire had failed; but the German army mustered north of Vetera still dauntless. There were mutineers yet in arms, and Cerialis' hardest task lay before him, (Tacitus' narrative).

§7. THE SUBMISSION OF THE GERMANS, (TACITUS' NARRATIVE).

Cerialis found no difficulty in advancing from Cologne down the Rhine until he came again to the neighbourhood of Vetera, where Civilis had collected together his largest possible army, intending to make a resolute stand at this place. Both the Roman and the German general had received reinforcements since they had met in their first encounter at Trèves. Cerialis' strength had been more than doubled by the arrival of three new legions—the Fourteenth from Britain, and the Second Adjutrix with the Sixth Victrix from Spain. Numerous auxiliary troops, both horse and foot, were now added to the *legionaries*. Civilis had persuaded men of the Cugerni and Transrhenane tribes to join his banner. Germany was in the field against Rome.

It was by this time autumn. The great river, which in the preceding year had caused such trouble to Vocula and the other Roman commanders by its scanty stream and shallows,[53] at this time rolled a full flood to the sea, and the low ground round Vetera was a great morass of mud and swamp. In such ground for battle the lightly-armed Germans delighted. Used to swimming from their childhood up, stronglimbed and tall in stature, the natives of the Lower Rhine had no fear of sudden plunges into treacherous pools, of quaking ground, or hurrying stream. But the short, sturdy *legionary* of Rome, encumbered with heavy armour, and easily lured in his ignorance on to treacherous ground, fought but badly, because with little confidence, on any but firm soil. Certainly the German river was striving to help its children.

The spot first selected by Civilis in the neighbourhood of Vetera on which to offer battle was carefully chosen and prepared. Swampy by nature, a dam cleverly thrown into the Rhine from the bank had impeded the flow of the stream, and added thereby to the depth of water on the ground. The river was on one side of it—a refuge for swimmers if they were driven off the field. And the memory of tri-

---

52. Probably it had, as Mommsen suggests, just conveyed the Fourteenth legion from Britain to Gaul.
53. See §4 above.

umphs already won at Vetera spurred the Germans on to emulate their former deeds. The conflict, skilfully provoked by the German and rashly accepted by the Roman, ended in a bad reverse for the latter. The swamp was like that road of historic fame in Virginia on which the Federal officer, sent to reconnoitre it, reported that the road was there, but "he guessed the bottom had fallen out."

Water and mud successfully worsted Cerialis' struggling men, and for the moment ill-fortune seemed again to haunt the Romans on the Rhine. But the check was only for a day. Next morning Cerialis renewed the battle; and, after a stubborn contest, a deserter showed the cavalry a path by which they could skirt the morass on firm ground and fall upon the Germans' flank. This decided the battle, and the enemy fled. But the Roman fleet, which Cerialis had expected to appear to cut off the German flight across the Rhine, did not come. The cavalry pursuit was checked by heavy rain and nightfall. And the Germans, therefore, made good their retreat without serious loss.[54]

Civilis by this defeat was compelled to cross the Waal into his last refuge, the "Island of the Batavians."[55] He therefore evacuated the *Oppidum Batavorum* (which was built probably on the site of Lohengrin's town, Cleve, some seven miles south-east of the parting of the channels), carried off all that he could from it, and burnt it to the ground. To add to the security of his position in the island, he destroyed Drusus' mole, and thus diverted the greater bulk of the waters of the Rhine from its northern arm, the Lek, into its southern, the Waal.[56] The Romans, he judged, had not enough vessels to bridge the greatly swollen waters of the latter channel, and his own communications over the shallow northern branch with his friends beyond were made both safe and easy. Once in the Island, though driven back like a hunted beast to its lair, he turned savagely and stood at bay. Now, too, the Chauci sent him men besides to help him in the defence of his "Island" home.

Cerialis and his army[57] pushing northwards found themselves stopped by the Waal. There was no help for it. The river must be bridged

---

54. This part of Tacitus' narrative is made both dull and unreal by a number of invented speeches. Their pretty rhetorical tropes do but hinder the military narrative, and I omit them all.

55. For the whole of the following narrative, the plan of the "Island" §2 must be consulted.

56. See §1 and §2 above.

57. Leg. X. Gemina from Spain now takes the place of Leg. XIV. sent to Upper Germany. See §6 footnote 42.

before they could get to grips with the foe. And the year was growing old; the river, swollen by autumnal rains, was rising ever higher. There seemed little promise of a speedy finish. Cerialis distributed his army along the southern bank of the river; sent emphatic messages bidding the tardy fleet come at once to his help; and ordered the winter quarters for the troops to be rebuilt at Novaesium and Bonn.[58] His main army was divided between four camps on the Waal. The two eastern camps were allotted to the *legionaries*. These were Arenacum, given to the Tenth legion, which perhaps was situated at Ryndern by Cleve; and Batavodurum, the camp of the Second legion, almost certainly at Nymwegen. Here, too, the soldiers began to attempt the building of a bridge.[59] The auxiliaries' camps were at Grinnes and Vada, but these places cannot now be identified.

The river, however embarrassing it might be to the Romans, was small obstacle to the movements of Batavians. The fourfold distribution of the Roman Army seemed to give to Civilis a notable opportunity of a simultaneous attack upon all four camps. The Germans sallied out over the Waal, and fell at one and the same time upon them all but not with equal vigour. The *legionaries* had little trouble in driving off the assailants. But Grinnes and Vada were attacked with great determination, and it was not until the Roman commander-in-chief himself came to his hard-pressed auxiliaries' help at the head of a picked troop of horse that the Germans were forced here also to fall back again over the river. By evening the enemy had all again crossed the Waal, swimming or by boats, and the attempted surprise had this time failed.

But the Romans could do very little without their fleet. Cerialis, therefore, left the army, and journeyed up-stream to look for it and to superintend the building of the camps at Novaesium and Bonn. The Roman historian gives a number of reasons to explain the fleet's delay. The sailors were afraid; they were employed elsewhere; they had not been given time enough in which to arrive. One of these three explanations would have been enough. The effect of the three combined is somewhat ludicrous. But Cerialis did manage to discover his navy,

---

58. Destroyed, after their victory over Vocula, by the Germans in the previous year.
59. It is abundantly clear at least that all four camps were south of the Waal. The proposed identifications, therefore, of Arenacum with Arnhem, and Batavodurum with Wyk-by-Dürstede are quite impossible, as both Arnhem and Wyk are on the Lek. At Nymwegen there are today a railway bridge and also a swing-bridge. I have not found on the map another bridge over the Waal between it and Bommel, thirty odd miles to the west. If, however, Noviomagus is identified, as is usually the case, with Nymwegen, Batavodurum must be sought elsewhere.

and brought it back with him rejoicing. His was a short-lived joy. It happened on a night black with clouds that Cerialis and his escort were encamped beside the river on the return journey. The ships, the object of his toils, lay moored in the stream beside the camp. The sentries gazed sleepily out into the night. The general was not on the admiral's galley, where his ensign flew, but dallying, so scandal said, on shore with a native woman.

A band of Germans silently crossed the river a short way above the camp, and stole down beneath the ramparts. The sentries noticed nothing, and the foe clambered quietly over the defences. In a moment the sleeping troops found their tents falling upon their heads. The Germans had cut the ropes. Then hideous and ferocious cries rent the stillness of the night, as the natives fell with joy to slaughtering the Romans, recumbent and struggling beneath the fallen canvas, or emerging bewildered and half-naked into the open. Others of the foe, coming in boats downstream, hurled grappling-hooks aboard the ships and towed them away.

Their chief triumph was the capture of the general's ship and ensign. The squall had been a sharp one, and had broken with fury over the hapless Romans. Then it passed away. The Germans vanished. The Romans were left to straighter their disordered camp and peg their tents again. But when morning broke, the angry and mortified *legionaries*, gazing disconsolately out over the river, saw their own ships, crowded with the laughing foe, moving over to the opposite bank. Only the flagship was not there: it was being towed up the Lippe River,[60] yet another offering to Veleda, the maiden prophetess. But to the Germans' grief they had found no Cerialis asleep on board the ship.

Autumn was passing into winter, and no progress had of late been made. The Waal still rolled between. Civilis, exulting in his new-won ships thought the time come for a naval display. In the broad channel of the Maas, hard by the modern Rotterdam,[61] he gathered together all his motley crowd of vessels, gay with every kind of bunting and parti-coloured sails. A favouring breeze sent them merrily upstream, until they hove in view of Cerialis and his astonished men. The Ro-

---

60. The Lippe flows into the Rhine at Wesel, a few miles above Xanten.
61. The review is held in a "*spatinm velut aequoris electum, quo Mosae fluminis os amnem Rhenum Oceano adfundit.*" The broadest part of the Maas would be that where the De Noord channel enters the Lek above Rotterdam. From this point to the sea the Lek takes the name of the Maas.

man was not to be outdone. He had collected other craft and still had the remnants of his former fleet which had escaped the grappling-hooks. His pilots, too, were now experienced men. The Roman fleet therefore put out from the shore, and drifted slowly, with sails furled, down the stream to meet the advancing foe. Each gallant fleet passed the other, moving in column of line ahead. As they sailed by a few missiles flew between. And there ended the last great naval engagement of the war.

Heavy rain had fallen, and the campaigning season in those inclement barbarian northern wilds was fast drawing to a close. Even Civilis must have found his position in the Island uncomfortably damp. For he quietly evacuated it, and drew all his men with him over the Rhine, (*i.e.* the Lek), to the northern bank. Then at last Cerialis and his men struggled over the Waal without resistance, and the Island, so long the object of their patient striving, lay at their mercy. Plunder was pleasant, but of a truth the land was very damp. The entire Roman camp bid fair to be washed for good and all away. And now once more their errant fleet had lost itself. Behind them the swollen waters of the Waal rolled heavily seawards. Their position was uncomfortable.

So uncomfortable in fact was it that, in Tacitus' opinion, a third onslaught by the Germans must now have put an end once and for all time to Cerialis and his men, in which case the Yorkshire Wolds might have preserved their independence of Rome a few years longer.[62] But now, for his part, Civilis had had enough of war. For some eighteen months he had led an enjoyably exciting life, pursuing and pursued, defeated and victorious, triumphant and fugitive, faring now up, now down, the valleys of the Moselle and the Rhine. He had won fame, and, at least for a brief time, liberty from Rome for himself and his tribe. But by this time his own people showed signs of restiveness. The Germans, too, across the Rhine were grumbling, not liking the thought of having to support the rebel army through the winter months. Messages reached him from Cerialis offering life on submission, but full of threats if he refused compliance.

Even among Batavians there were traitors. Civilis judged it more profitable to surrender than to be surrendered to the Romans. His faithful Batavians were quite capable of making a scapegoat of their general. Civilis therefore sent word to Cerialis, and a meeting was arranged between the two commanders, to take place on the River

---

62. Cerialis was Governor of Britain under Vespasian's *principate* from A.D. 71-73.

Nabalia.⁶³ A bridge over the river was broken in the middle, and at the two ends of the pieces left in place the two opponents stood to exchange speeches and arrange terms over the gap. But what thereafter took place remains unknown to us. For Civilis has hardly made a fair beginning of what was doubtless to be, at least in Tacitus, a long exculpatory harangue, than the text of the historian is, like the bridge, abruptly broken off. And, with this, Julius Civilis, the Batavian prince and rebel, vanishes for ever from our ken. History speaks of him no more.

But the war in Lower Germany was certainly at an end. Of that in Upper Germany, with which Annius Gallus was entrusted, no record remains. Gallus had four legions under his command, and besides the reduction of the Lingones, of which a Roman military writer makes one passing mention, the German tribes in the lower Main valley, who had raided up to the walls of Mainz, merited chastisement. If they did receive this it had no very lasting effect, for the Emperor Domitian thirteen years later found it necessary to conduct a serious campaign against the most redoubtable of these very offenders, the Chatti. But of any military operations on the Upper Rhine in *A.D.* 70, after the coming of Gallus, there exists no story.

Rome treated the rebels, both Gauls and Germans, with politic mercy. Only submission was demanded of them, and a return to their old condition of subjection. The Batavians and Cannenefates still paid no tribute. No Roman tax-gatherer was to plague their soil. They must continue to furnish troops to the Roman army as had been their duty, before the mutiny. And so the German "honour" suffered no infringement, (*"Manet honos et antiquae societatis insigne,"*—Tacitus). Rome had no desire for vengeance on the common folk, in spite of the losses which she had suffered at their hands. Veleda, the fierce prophetess maiden, was indeed captured later and brought a prisoner to Rome. But it is unlikely that she endured any worse fate than to become a subject for mediocre poets' verse, (Statius, *Silvae*).⁶⁴

But Rome's attitude to some at least of the tribal chieftains was sterner: for it was always the ambition of such men, both in Gaul and Germany, which was dangerous to the peace of those lands and

---

63. This river is nowhere else mentioned, and Tacitus, of course, gives no clue which leads to any certain identification. It may have been the Lek, or the Kromme Rhyn, or the New (or Guelders) Yssel. The last is the favourite choice. See the plan §1 above.
64. See Note H, end of chapter.

to her own supremacy. Cerealis explained very clearly to the Treveri the reason of Rome's presence on the Rhine. The Roman historian makes him declare:

> We have not planted ourselves upon the Rhine to guard Italy, but for fear lest some second Ariovistus should make himself lord of the kingdom of the Gallic lands. Men talk of liberty, and use other such specious words. There was never a man, if he sought for power and dominion for himself at cost of others' slavery, who did not use such language. Should we Romans ever be expelled, which may Heaven, avert! what remains for all the world save a never-ending war of nation against nation?—Tacitus

It was true, every word of it. The right of Rome to control Gaul and "Germany" was to this extent precisely the same as our right to govern India and its many peoples. The *Pax Romana* had to be preserved upon the Rhine lest bloody war should in due course, after long years of savage horror, beget one chief as Tyrant. This reason had made Julius Caesar in old days march his trembling army against King Ariovistus the German. Chieftain after chieftain in Gaul in the Caesarian period between 59 B.C. and 50 B.C. had dreamt this dream of lordship for himself. Vercingetorix had all but made of the dream a waking vision. Peril of disturbance from such ambition in Gaul or Germany had haunted Tiberius, Caligula, Claudius, Nero. In their last sore straits Civilis and Classicus had even sent proffering Cerialis the "*Imperium Galliarum*";[65] so strong and deep-rooted has been the notion of kingship on the Rhine.

Therefore, her honour at last splendidly vindicated, and the mutiny finally quelled, Rome showed mercy to the peoples; but some at least of the leaders of the revolt felt the power of her wrath. Civilis almost certainly bargained for his life. Classicus and Tutor are never heard of more. It is idle to speculate upon their fate. But the boy leader Valentinus, who had revived a dying cause, was sent to Vespasian, and by him executed. And most significant of all was the fate of Julius Sabinus of the Lingones. After his defeat by the Sequani [66] he disappeared entirely from the Roman sight. The house to which he had fled was shortly

---

65 Unless, indeed, this offer was but a ruse to lull Cerialis into security at Trèves while the foe were gathering in the hills for their night attack on the camp. Cerialis, of course, sent no answer to the offer (Tac.)

66. See §6 above.

afterwards burnt to the ground, and men commonly thought that he had sought death for himself in the flames. But for nine long years, so runs the romantic tale which impressed the imagination of Greek and Roman writers, Sabinus lay hid with his faithful wife Epponina in a secret cave. There she gave birth to two boys, and the little lads grew up with father and mother in their dark and gloomy cavern. For nine years they were hidden. After nine years they appealed to Vespasian for pardon. After nine years the emperor ordered their execution in cold blood, though he spared the boys. So should we English have treated the villain Nana, could we but have caught him. Sabinus' deeds were no atrocities of a Nana, nor even of a Civilis. But he had dared to call himself Caesar, and for him there remained no mercy.[67]

§ 8. The Lessons of the Mutiny

Gauls, Germans, and Romans, all had learnt lessons taught them by the great mutiny.

A. The Results in Gaul and Germany.—The cause of the rebellion had been the natural aspiration for freedom felt by all men worthy of the name. This aspiration had been fed, in case of the Gauls, by a century of striving for liberty, by memories both new and old of risings and struggles on its behalf; in case of the Germans subject to Rome, by more recent recollections of independence, by the lively example of their kinsmen over the Rhine who, once like themselves in servitude to the Roman, had boldly struck for freedom, won it, and retained it; and by the harsh, careless, and unjust treatment which they had endured at the hands of the military agents of the Roman Government. Moreover, there was not a race or people, save the effeminate and worthless subjects of the old Syrian monarchy, who, conquered by Rome, had not at least once risen against their masters in desperate rebellion before they had learnt to receive and to enjoy the yet prouder and more ennobling position of citizens of the Roman Empire. To the Batavians their broad streams flowing to the boundless unknown ocean, and their pathless wastes, by themselves spoke of wide unfettered liberty. They were not men tamely to bow their necks beneath the yoke of alien domination, if so be that they could break it and cast it off.

---

67. Tac.; Dio, lxvi.; Plutarch, Amat. Tacitus promises to give the whole story when he comes to the year in question (*i.e. A.D.* 79): but this part of his work, if it was ever written, is of course lost to us. Plutarch stays that he was personally acquainted with one of the boys.

And never had so fair an opportunity been given to both Gauls and Germans to strike a blow for freedom as during these terrible months of Civil War following on the death of Galba, when the Empire, which subdued them and, as they said, oppressed them, seemed rent utterly in pieces by the fury of contending selfish factions. The malcontents indeed had not been men had they let their chance pass unheeded.

But the great effort miserably failed. And no like opportunity occurred again. Moreover, the course of mutiny had shown the tribes their weakness, while Rome at the end was wisely merciful, and trampled neither on their lives nor on their honour. The Imperial State remembered her duty to her subjects, lessons learnt by her long since in Italy and Spain and Macedonia, and now taught to her again on the Rhine. The meanest Roman henceforth who did outrage, were it but to a child of the conquered peoples, was a greater and more despicable traitor to his country than he who risked his life in mutiny against her.

The war had proved that neither Gauls nor Germans could for long combine in a national war against the Roman. It was easy to preach eloquently on nationalism; it was impossible for the nationalists to overcome for any length of time the local jealousies which proved the ruin of the movement to the end. Civilis, who openly disclaimed with patriotic indignation any desire on part of Batavians or Treveri to rule any other tribe, is found contemplating a war for this object with calm confidence in the prospect of a German victory. Civilis' own nephew fought fiercely to the death against him, (Julius Briganticus). Tencteri hated Ubii; Ubii massacred Chauci and Frisii; Sequani fought Lingones. The Gallic tribes rose in the "hope of liberty." But the desire for rule over their neighbours was a more powerful, if more secret, motive with them. There was to be "One Gallic Empire."

This, doubtless, was excellent. But whose district should be chosen as the seat for that Empire? Indeed this was an apple of discord cast in upon the banquet of the victors by Mischief smiling. And most Gauls thought that Rome's impartial if alien rule was better after all. And therefore the mutiny of the years *A.D.* 69 and 70 was the last rising on behalf of independence which affected Gaul or the German tribes on the Roman side of the Lower Rhine. The page on which is written the record of Gallic rebellion against the Roman conqueror contains the history of a hundred and twenty years. But now at last the leaf was turned, and no story of Gallic self-sacrifice or treason on behalf of liberty embellishes or sullies the chapter any more.

> This was the last blood shed for the cause of ancient Gaul, the last act of devotion to a social order, a government, a religion, the return of which was neither possible nor desirable.—Thierry, *History of the Romans under the Empire*.

Whether a mutiny in the "native army" is caused by "outward and accidental causes" or by the "inner necessity of things" is a question likely to be always debated. Some would still maintain that there existed no such inner necessity for the *sepoy* mutiny in India, and would perhaps still point confidently to the "apparently complete quiet" which has prevailed in the Indian Army since the Mutiny as proof of their contention. In like manner the German historian ascribes the Batavian mutiny to "outward and accidental causes," and cites the peace prevailing after it upon the Rhine as the evidence for his contention. Yet surely it was no mock plea for liberty which called so many German tribes and peoples round Civilis' standard, and made them faithful to their leader well-nigh to the very last. We honour the barbarian and the mutineer too greatly if we ascribe to him the pure feeling of passionate devotion to an ideal such as sent thousands of Italy's sons joyfully to the dungeon, to the gibbet, and to death on the field, sixty years ago.

Liberty to the ancient German may have spelt little save revelling in lust, in plunder, and in butchery. Therefore civilised man applauds the victory of Rome, of peace, order, government, and law. The barbarians' temper was wild and passionate; their deeds were treacherous and foul; their cruelty was savage. Yet the seed which, when planted in so rude a soil, sprang up a rank and poisonous growth, in kinder and more congenial climes has borne the noblest fruit which ever glorifies Man and marks him apart from the brute. Not liberty, but the use men make of it, is its sole justification. But the fierce Batavian mutineer, the veriest German savage, who dreamt perhaps vague dreams of freedom, deserved indeed no victory, yet his merited failure was not utterly barren of honour. In the history of races as well as of individuals the child is father of the man.

But the German children had learnt their lesson. They were quick at least to see that petulance brought punishment, and their manhood was not yet. Though we may venture to think their rising due to other causes besides those of the recruiting officer and the happiest of opportunities, yet for its issue it is enough to cite the same historian's words:

> The Roman Germans were merged in the Empire no less completely than the Roman Gauls; of attempts at insurrection on the part of the former there is no further mention. At the close of the third century the Franks, invading Gaul by way of the Lower Rhine, included in their seizure the Batavian territory. Yet the Batavians maintained themselves in their old, though diminished, settlements, as did likewise the Frisians, even during the confusions of the great migrations of peoples, and so far as we know, preserved allegiance even to the decaying Empire as a whole.—Mommsen.

B. The Results in the Roman Army.—The Roman Government showed that it too had learnt lessons from the mutiny in its treatment of both the legions and the auxiliary forces on the Rhine.

(1) The Legions.—The outbreak of the mutiny had revealed serious defects in the prevailing system of "clan-regiments," taken from the native tribes to serve as auxiliaries in the Roman Army, when at least these were stationed in the country of their birth. The rapidity of the spread of the movement, the feeble resistance to it offered by, and even the mutinous tendencies shown in, the regular *legionary* regiments along the whole course of the river, made manifest that some defect of organisation existed also in this, the more important, branch of the Roman Imperial military system.

It seemed evident that the legions on the Rhine in *A.D.* 69 were tainted with native German sympathies. This pointed to the fact that the recruiting system was to blame. The Emperor Augustus had sought to establish the general practice that recruits for legions serving in the western part of the Empire should be drawn from the eastern provinces, and that legions on duty in the latter should be recruited from the west. The principle was the same as that in the modern Kingdom of Italy, where Lombard and Tuscan regiments tend to be quartered in the south, Sicilian and Calabrese in the north of the peninsula. By such means the army itself becomes a means of promoting unity and unification.

Moreover, in the event of a disturbance, the troops on the spot are more likely to be utterly true to their military discipline because they do not share in, or perhaps even realise, local feelings and aspirations. But to combine this sound principle of recruiting with the equally wise system of permanent military camps upon the frontiers of the

Empire was proving a very hard task for the government.

These camps, again devised by the extraordinary foresight of Augustus, were invaluable to the peace of the Empire, the popularity of the army, the prosperity of the provinces, and the Romanisation of the outlying districts of the Empire and the tribes beyond its limits. But as time went on, and the children of the legions grew to manhood, the regiment, stationed for years together at the same frontier camp, could not but gather its recruits from the sons of its soldiers, many of whom married the women of the district, and from the native auxiliaries serving side by side with them.

The result was that Augustus' principle of recruiting was not to be reconciled with, and had to yield to, his system of permanent cantonments. And hence a legion and a locality became identified so closely that the interests and hopes of the latter became those of the former. To the Roman Empire the introduction of the territorial system into the army had grave disadvantages.

The six legions engaged at first in the German rising of *A.D.* 69 were the First, Fourth, Sixteenth, and Twenty-Second, whose men proved mutinous and treacherous, the Fifth Alaudae and Fifteenth Primigenia, some of whose men at least fought most gallantly and died for Rome. Of these six legions it appears that the First had been in Lower Germany, the Sixteenth in Upper Germany, since the days of Augustus; the Fourth and Twenty-Second since *A.D.* 43. Thus the leaven of local sympathy had had time to work with these men. It is true that the Fifth legion Alaudae had also been in Lower Germany since Augustus' time, save for a passing excursion to Britain under Claudius. But this regiment had great traditions of bitter fighting with the Germans, in former days under Lollius, and recently under Corbulo.

The small heroic *vexillum* left behind at Vetera when the bulk of the legion marched for the Vitellian cause to Italy was, therefore, proud to preserve its regimental tradition. Its comrades of the Fifteenth legion were probably swayed by the example of the men of the Fifth who were in garrison with them. It is possible, too, that the Fifteenth legion was but newly raised, and had been but a few years in Germany, so that its loyalty in this case would be a striking illustration (from opposites) of the thesis advanced above that the mutinous tendencies might be produced by a long stay in Germany. If, however, this legion also had been in the country since *A.D.* 43, as some suppose, the loyalty of their comrades must be held responsible for the bravery of its own soldiers.[68]

When the revolt was ended, and the new emperor, Vespasian, dealt with the question of the garrison of the Rhine, he made sweeping changes in its composition. So shrewd a soldier as was this sagacious prince might approve the pardon granted by his general to the mutineers who repented, but their regiments had stained their reputation beyond forgiveness. Vespasian promptly struck three of the "traitor legions" from the roll of the army. The First, the Fourth Macedonica, and Sixteenth Gallica ceased henceforth to exist. The place of the last two in the army list was taken by two new legions, the Fourth Flavia firma, and the Sixteenth Flavia felix. In the year *A.D.* 82 a third new legion was also added, the First Flavia Minervia *pia fidelis,* and was encamped at Bonn, where it still lay as late as the year *A.D.* 295. Only the Twenty-Second legion of the four disgraced regiments was spared, and kept still in the country in camp at Vetera from *A.D.* 71 to *A.D.* 90.[69] Vespasian's reasons for such a difference of treatment between this regiment and its three partners in dishonour are not preserved to us.

Some uncertainty attaches to the fate of the two loyal legions, the Fifth and the Fifteenth. It is quite possible that these were also both disbanded, (Mommsen's view). If so, Vespasian had evidently determined to make an almost entirely clean sweep of the regiments of the former garrison of the Rhine. It is, however, a greater pleasure to suppose that the proud and valiant Fifth did continue to exist, and sealed its long services to the Empire on the dire field of battle in Moesia against the Sarmatians about *A.D.* 92, perishing there to the last man.[70]

---

68. Legio XV. Primigenia seems to make its first appearance in Tacitus, *Histories,* i. *A.D.* 69. Pfitzner thinks it was created in *A.D.* 62; Grotefend, that both XV. Primigenia and XXII. Primigenia were created as separate from the two legions, XV. Apollinaris and XXII. Deiotariana, on the occasion of the invasion of Britain in *A.D.* 43. The name Primigenia implies "first existing"; *i.e*, when a legion was duplicated, the part which retained the old eagle was Primigenia; the other legion of the same number received a new eagle and retained the old distinctive title. But there are other explanations of the title, for which see Pfitzner, *Geschichte der röm. Kaiser-legionen.*

69. Tiles and tombstones of the legionaries of XXII. are found at Xanten and Nymwegen, without the addition of pia fidelis to the name of the legion which it subsequently gained.

70. The legion destroyed by the Sarmatians (cf. Suetonius, *Domitian*) has been supposed to be either V. Alaudae or XXI. Rapax. So Riese in the *Diz. Epigrafico*, believes it to have been the latter. Ritterling (*W,-D, Zeitschrift,*) believes that V. Alaudae did continue to exist, but was destroyed under Domitian by the Dacians, while XXI. endured this fate at the hands of the Sarmatians a few years later.

One fact at least is certain—that the garrison of the Rhine after A.D. 71 was, with the two exceptions of the Twenty-First and Twenty-Second legions, composed of entirely different regiments from those which had hitherto been encamped on the river.[71] In both Lower and Upper Germany there were again four legions. In the former district Legio X. Gemina was stationed at Noviomagus (possibly Nymwegen[72]); XXII. Primigenia at Vetera (by Xanten); VI. Victrix at Novaesium, till about A.D. 105, when it was moved to Vetera to take the place of the Twenty-Second; and XXI. Rapax at Bonn up to A.D. 82, when it was moved to Mainz, and its place at Bonn was taken by the new legion, I. Flavia Minervia.

This allotment of the legions shows that Vespasian thought it desirable to keep one legion in immediate touch with the Batavian land (at Nymwegen?), whereas hitherto there had been no *legionary* camp on the river lower down than Vetera. In Upper Germany, Legions I. Adjutrix and XIV. Gemina were encamped together at Mainz, the defences there being strengthened; XI. Claudia was stationed at Vindonissa; and, in between the two places, VIII. Augusta was stationed at Strassburg (Argentoratum), a camp which had not been occupied since its legion, the Second Augusta, had been sent to Britain in, or perhaps before, A.D. 43.[73]

In the system of recruiting for the legions Vespasian is not known to have made any change. No change, in fact, seemed possible. Neither were the legions shifted at short intervals from camp to camp, or summoned away save when urgent wars elsewhere made demands on the Rhine Army. For the loyalty of that army Vespasian must have relied on the change of regiments for the immediate present, and, for the future, on the absence of such local discontent as had excited the sympathy of the former Vitellian Army. He was not disappointed in his trust, and the legions on the Rhine gave him no cause of concern. Thus, after all, Augustus' system of permanent camps was justified.

(2) The Auxilia.—The practice of using clan-regiments of auxiliaries in their native country had proved disastrous during the mutiny. Doubtless it had had the effect of popularising this branch of the service and of making recruits easy to obtain. In the case also of war

---

71. But Legio XXI., usually in garrison at Vindonissa, had been absent at the time of the mutiny.
72. See footnote 59 above.
73. One recently found tile of Legio II at Strassburg is said to be earlier than A.D. 43 (*Westd, Zeit.* 1905).

in the adjoining districts such regiments might be expected to be well acquainted with the enemy's methods of fighting and the ground, and could obtain information and supplies far more easily from the country than could auxiliaries who were aliens and strange to the land.

As the Roman Army relied upon its auxiliaries for the all-important duties of reconnaissance and scouting, the advantages of using clan-regiments in their own country were indeed very great, quite apart from the great saving of expense of transport and maintenance which this system secured, and which counted not a little in the careful financial organisation of the wiser and more thrifty of the early emperors. There was, therefore, every reason for the choice of this system by Augustus and his immediate successors. But the mutiny had opened the eyes of the Roman Government to its risks. By the Flavian Emperors its many advantages were counted as nothing compared to its dangers, at least upon the Rhine. No attempt was made to abolish clan-regiments. This indeed would have been far too sweeping a measure, and might have destroyed the auxiliary system completely. But, with very few exceptions, such regiments, both infantry and cavalry, are found serving in countries other than those of their origin.

Thus the indigenous *cohorts* and *alae*, which before A.D. 70 had served on the Rhine, after that date were either disbanded or sent far afield to Britain, Raetia, Pannonia, Dacia, Moesia, even Mauretania.[74] In Lower Germany neither Germans nor Gauls seem to have been employed as troops under the Flavians. In Upper Germany there is still found under Vespasian and Domitian a squadron of Cannenefates, significantly removed from their own district at the mouth of the Rhine, and solitary *cohorts* of "Gauls," "Germans," and Bituriges. But the great majority of auxiliary troops in both provinces come from other countries. Cavalry squadrons of men from Africa, Ituraea, Moesia, Noricum, Thrace, serve in the Lower province. *Cohorts*, either infantry or mixed infantry and cavalry, of Dalmatians, Spaniards, Lusitanians, Vindelicians, are found in the Lower province; and in the Upper, of Aquitanians, Asturians, Dalmatians (at Wiesbaden and Bingen), Ituraeans and Damascenes from the East, Raeti (at Wiesbaden and Vindonissa), Pannonians (at Bingen), men of Cyrene (at Neuenheim), Thracians, and Vindelicians.

---

74. *E.g.*, in Britain are found Baetasii, Batavi, Cugerni, Frisii, Lingones, Menapii, Morini, Suebi, Tungri, Vangiones; in Pannonia, Batavi, Cannenefates, Helvetii; in Raetia (from *A.D.* 103) and Dacia, Batavi; in Moesia, Mattiaci, Ubii, Tungri; in Mauretania, Sugambri. (List from Riese see footnote 77.)

The mere list shows how complete was Vespasian's reversal of the former practice, how utterly different was the army, as well of auxiliaries as of *legionaries*, which garrisoned the Rhine in his own and his sons' days from that which was submerged by the great flood of the mutiny or helped to swell its volume.[75] Auxiliaries as well as *legionaries* are henceforward loyal to the Empire.

Vespasian was a soldier of sagacity and experience; it is probably in good part a merit of his if we meet with no later example of revolt of the *auxilia* against their legions.[76]

The garrison of the Rhine of men of all arms in Flavian times has been reckoned at some sixty-nine thousand men, of whom thirty-four thousand belonged to the Upper, thirty-five thousand to the Lower, German province. But as time went by, and men's memories of the mutiny grew dim, the Lower province, the scene once of its greatest fury and carnage, was found so peaceful that part of its troops, urgently needed by wars elsewhere, could with safety be withdrawn. Vespasian's annexation of the district of the Agri Decumates and the valley of the Neckar in A.D. 73-74, Domitian's warring with the Chatti some ten years later, employed the troops, without disturbing the peace, of the Upper province. And soon the storm-clouds came rolling up black and threatening ruin to the Roman Empire upon the Danube frontier.

Under Marcus Aurelius two legions only were left in garrison upon the Lower Rhine. The tide of war had swept steadily eastwards, carrying with it the line of Roman fortifications on the Upper Rhine

---

75. These details concerning the *auxilia* I take from Alex. Riese's valuable article "Germania" in the new *Dizionario Epigrafico* of Ruggiero, published last year. The whole subject of the auxiliary troops of the Imperial military system is as yet in a most dishevelled condition, and no good and complete treatment of it as a whole has yet, to my knowledge, been published. See Note H, "The Flavian Army of the Lower Rhine," at end of chapter.

76. Mommsen, *Provinces*, vol. i., who also comments on the disappearance from the *auxilia* after the date of native officers, such as Arminius, Civilis, Classicus. But the clan-regiments surely continued to exist, though Mommsen seems to doubt this. "The men serve, without distinction as to their descent, in the most various divisions." This, of course, is true of such corps as the First and Second *ala* Flavia Gemina, the ala Singularium, the numerous *cohortes voluntariorum civium Romanorum*, etc., found in Flavian times on the Rhine. And the "special" corps, *e.g., Cohors Sagittariorum*, continue to be raised. But the great majority of regiments in Riese's long list bear at least clan names, and presumably continued to be composed, at least largely (?entirely), of the natives of those tribes or countries whose names they bear.

and the military camps upon the Danube. The Teuton was yet to be at death-grips with the Roman. But the desperate struggle was to be waged upon both banks of the greater river and with new invading tribes. Few storms of war disturbed the calm surface of the Rhine after $A.D.$ 70, and those were of brief duration. And the German tribes upon the Roman bank joined with Rome's troops upon the river in accepting loyally and placidly her sway. The great mutiny left no heritage of ill-will behind it to any generation. Rome was always truly victor because she knew how to use victory well. Her citizens shirked no military duty for pleasure or for any folly of humanitarian sentiment which, if indulged in, defeats its own ends. In the strength as in the valour of her "National Army" she defied her enemies. Where she conquered she civilised.

To those whom she defeated she taught the use of arms on her own behalf, as well as order and law. Her very rebels and subject races learnt the patriotism of Romans, a patriotism of self-sacrifice and deeds, not of boasts and empty words. And therefore, still in the days of her emperors as in those earlier days when the citizen-soldier, trained from boyhood to the use of arms, crushed his Macedonian or Carthaginian enemy, and hurled the Asiatic back behind the barriers of Taurus and Euphrates, Rome was an Imperial State. Still her patriotism was no mock patriotism, loud-tongued, afraid of burdens. Still the rock of her strength, though fiercely assaulted by the jealous hatred of her enemies, stood firm, because it was not yet undermined by cowardice and pleasure-seeking on the part of her citizens.

NOTES

G.—Vetera and Harper's Ferry

The situation on the Potomac at the time of the Confederates' invasion of Maryland, following upon their brilliant victory of Second Manassas in September 1862, was so similar to that on the Rhine towards the end of $A.D.$ 69 that the former may, it seems to me, help to explain the latter so far as Vocula's decision not to evacuate Vetera is concerned. Of course no other comparison is intended, for never did the brilliant genius of the Southern commanders in civilised warfare more completely outshine the mediocre respectabilities on the Federal side than in this campaign, and the mere thought of a Stonewall Jackson and a Civilis together seems ludicrous. But a brief note may be desirable to explain the point of the comparison in the text.

A bare sketch may serve to illustrate the note: the Roman "equivalents" are printed in capitals. Points of the compass, of course, are of no matter in such a comparison, and the Potomac-Rhine may be taken as flowing in any direction:—

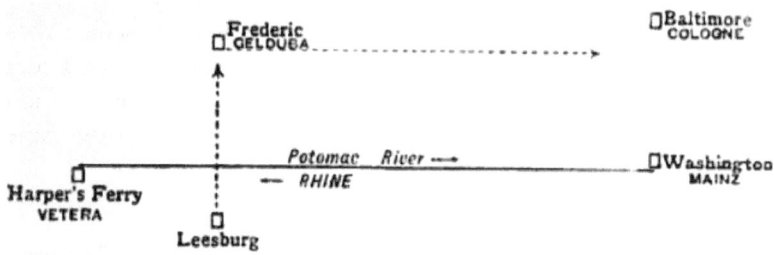

Dotted lines show the direction of attack (expected or actual) by the Confederates or Germans.

At Harper's Ferry there was a Federal garrison of twelve thousand men; at Washington, M'Clellan's main army of ninety thousand men. The Confederates, fifty thousand strong, invaded Maryland, from Leesburg to Frederic, and threatened an advance on Baltimore, if not on Washington itself. The question for the Federal authorities was whether, while there was still time, the garrison at Harper's Ferry should be recalled. M'Clellan desired this, but his political superiors overruled him. It was clear that so strongly garrisoned a fort must seriously threaten the line of communication of the Confederate invaders. Might it not be expected to stop their projected inroad entirely? And if from Frederic they turned on Harper's Ferry, surely they could be caught between two fires—the garrison and M'Clellan's army—and, outnumbered (as usual) by two to one, be annihilated. So the parallel works out thus:—

Can the $\begin{smallmatrix}\text{Federal}\\\text{Roman}\end{smallmatrix}$ garrison at $\begin{smallmatrix}\text{Harper's Ferry}\\\text{Vetera}\end{smallmatrix}$ hinder or frustrate the advance on $\begin{smallmatrix}\text{Baltimore}\\\text{Cologne}\end{smallmatrix}$ made by the $\begin{smallmatrix}\text{Confederates}\\\text{Germans}\end{smallmatrix}$ if these propose to neglect it and advance via $\begin{smallmatrix}\text{Frederic}\\\text{Gelduba}\end{smallmatrix}$, leaving the fort in their rear? And if not, can the foe not be driven back upon the hostile fort by the main $\begin{smallmatrix}\text{Federal}\\\text{Roman}\end{smallmatrix}$ army under $\begin{smallmatrix}\text{M'Clellan}\\\text{Vocula}\end{smallmatrix}$ advancing $\begin{smallmatrix}\text{up}\\\text{down}\end{smallmatrix}$ the river $\begin{smallmatrix}\text{Potomac}\\\text{Rhine}\end{smallmatrix}$ from $\begin{smallmatrix}\text{Washington}\\\text{Mainz}\end{smallmatrix}$?

In the result, the Federal Government risked it and ordered the garrison to remain. The Confederates thereupon dared to detach a force of twenty-five thousand men upon Harper's Ferry, despite the imminent peril from M'Clellan, and the garrison of the fort (somewhat ignominiously) surrendered after some show of resistance. Vocula similarly risked it, and also lost his fortress in consequence, under the circumstances detailed in the text. But I take it that the retention of both Harper's Ferry and Vetera was dictated by much the same military considerations.

H.—The Flavian Army of the Lower Rhine

A newly-found military diploma, of date April 15, *A.D.* 78, shows that there were then stationed on the Lower Rhine these six *alae*, *viz.*: *ala* Noricorum (placed by Ritterling at Burginatium by Calcar), *ala* Singularium (at Vada), *ala* Moesica (at Asciburgium), *ala* Afrorum veterana (at Vetera?), *ala* Siliana, and *ala* Sulpicia (? at Bonn, Noviomagus, or Neuss), and also the Cohors I. Flavia Hispanorum. To these must be added the *ala* Indiana (at Worringen). Ritterling supposes that all these troops made their first appearance on the Rhine under Vespasian. The actual recipient of the diploma, though belonging to the ala Moesica, is by nationality a Trevir. Otherwise this evidence is consistent with the view taken in §8.

Besides the above *cohort*, Ritterling gives the following *cohorts* to the Flavian Army of the Lower Rhine:—II. Asturum, II. Britt, I. and II. civ. Rom., III. Dalmatarum, VI. ingenuorum, II. Hispanorum, . . . Lucensium, III. Lusitanorum, I. Tracum (?), II. Varcianorum, I. Vindelicorum, and XV. voluntariorum. This is a completer list than Riese's, but the conclusions to be drawn from it are the same.

Also Legio VII. Gemina seems to have been employed on the Rhine by Rutilius Gallicus in *A.D.* 77-78 in his war with the Bructeri. It was probably in this war that the prophetess Veleda was captured (see §7).

Postscript

During the time of the writing of this book I chanced to have been reading again part of the story of the making of modern Italy, that great epic of the nineteenth century. The contrast between the two periods of war in Italy and struggle with the German enemy, that of my writing and that of my reading, could not fail to present itself vividly.

Ancient Rome won the unity of Italy, and then, in due course, her Empire, by the unflinching heroism and pure devotion to their country of her sons. Then it came to pass that greed and selfishness, ambition and passion, triumphed over patriotism, self sacrifice, simplicity. In this book we have seen rival Italian leaders contending in furious struggle for the personal mastery. And all the while Italy lay unheeded, sorely wounded. Her life-blood wets draining away; her sons slew one another remorselessly; while the danger from the northern barbarian gathered ever more gloomily upon her frontiers.

Now it is scarcely a generation since men have seen Italy won at last again to unity by the bravery and the endurance of her children. Mere boys and youths in the pride of their strength faced the cannon and the executioner with smiles on their lips; women endured all agony of pain and loss; men battled forward to victory in spite of peril, failure, and disaster. So unselfishness and patriotism won here their most renowned victory of modern times.

Hurtful indeed and well-nigh ruinous to Italy was the "year of the four emperors," when men fought for the sake of greed, or, more nobly, as in the case of our own Wars of the Roses, for personal devotion to some leader, but not for love of country. For any cause other than the highest a man, it might be thought, would not willingly die. Yet these men in Italy of olden days did face death cheerfully for causes lower, and many of them base enough. And this is a glory, albeit a lesser glory, of Roman manhood.

Salve, magna parens frugum, Saturnia tellus,
magna virum.

For there are diseases of the body politic which cost a nation the loss of strength and manhood, and these are more injurious than is Civil War. Such were in due course to inflict upon Italy yet greater miseries than did even the masterful strivings of the rivals for Empire, before the time of her redemption came at last. Greater perils to a land even than armed ambition and cruelty are that craven self-regarding sloth and that *verita* $\dot{a}\pi\acute{a}\tau\eta\ \tau o\hat{v}\ \pi\lambda o\acute{v}\tau o v$, deluding rich and poor alike by its enchantment, which, however fair-seeming may be the titles of peace and humanity under which they seek to disguise themselves—and what nobler names than these could ever be so misused?—would yet surrender the country indolent, poorly-armed, unready, to the sudden onslaught of a jealous and a vigorous foe.

Does the red stand for rose-leaves on our flag?

Galba—Otho
(Extract from *Tacitus*)

Whether the year 51 or 54 *A.D.* be accepted as the birth-year of Tacitus, he was old enough, in either case, to have been able to watch and to retain a lively recollection of the great convulsion of the empire which followed Nero's death. If born in the later of these years he was nearly sixteen, if in the earlier he was nearly eighteen: and with the sixteenth year commenced the manhood of a Roman; and at eighteen we have already seen that Pliny had put on a lawyer's gown. The *History* may accordingly be accounted the work of one having good opportunities for observation himself, and for making inquiry from others.

The *History*, when perfect, extended from the arrival of Galba in Rome, on the 1st of January, 69 *A.D.*, to the murder of Domitian in 96. If the books which are unfortunately lost bore any proportion to those extant, then we may fairly put down the number of them as thirty at the least. Unfortunately we possess only four books and the beginning of the fifth, and these comprise, and that not entirely, the events of those troubled years 69 and 70. The second chapter is a prologue to a tragic drama of the deepest dye, and prepares us for scenes of crime and calamity following one another in rapid succession.

Tacitus writes:

> I am entering on the history of a period rich in disasters, frightful in its wars, torn by civil strife, and even in peace full of horrors. Four emperors perished by the sword. There were three civil wars: there were more with foreign enemies: there were often wars that had both characters at once. Now, too, Italy was prostrated by disasters either entirely novel, or that recurred only after a long succession of ages. Cities in Campania's richest plains were swallowed up and overwhelmed—Rome wasted by conflagrations, its oldest temples consumed, and the Capitol

itself fired by the hands of citizens. Never, surely, did more terrible calamities of the Roman people, or evidence more conclusive, prove that the gods take no thought for our happiness, but only for our punishment.

In the election of a Caesar the senate might affect to confirm the choice of the soldiers; but it was the soldiers, or at least the terror of them, who really invested with the purple robe Servius Galba. He was chosen by the Spanish legions, to whom the example had been set by those of Gaul, who had put forward as Nero's successor Vindex and Virginius Rufus. The one perished in the attempt to become Caesar; the other, with courageous moderation, refused to be placed on that proud but perilous eminence. In their selection of Galba the soldiers to all appearance did wisely and well, for he had passed through many grades of both military and civil offices with much credit to himself. He reigned long enough and unfortunately enough to merit the description—it has become almost proverbial—that had he never been emperor no one would have doubted his capacity for empire.

He came to the throne under almost every possible disadvantage. He was old, he was ugly, bald-headed, and a gouty invalid. He kept his purse-strings tight: he spoke his mind indiscreetly: he was a slave to his freedmen and favourites: good in intention, he was infirm of purpose: a popular and humane provincial governor, he caused much blood to be spilt in Rome, not because he was cruel, but through weakness, indecision, or mere perplexity.

He came to a city peopled by his foes. The praetorians could not stomach a Caesar chosen by the legions: they could not conceal from themselves that the fatal secret was revealed, and indeed was pervading the provinces—that a "prince might be created elsewhere than at Rome." Highly had Nero favoured—nay, even flattered—his bodyguards. They were the props of his throne: their tribunes, and even their centurions, were admitted to his orgies: they stood beside him in the courts of justice: they accompanied him on his journeys: he enriched them, when his own coffers were empty, with the spoils of noble houses: he relaxed their discipline: he catered for their pleasures: they led the applause when he drove his chariot in the circus, or sang and spouted in the theatre. And now a Caesar was in their darling's place who knew not the *praetorians*—who had filled the capital with the ordinary *legionaries*, whom they had always affected to despise as the "Line." The treasury was known to be empty: the Caesar was said to be avaricious. "He loved no plays"; he was not musical; nothing was to be expected, much to be dreaded from, this septuagenarian and worn-out martinet.

The populace were not less hostile to Galba. Next to the praetorians, they were the late emperor's warmest supporters. He was ever giving them good dinners and shows and spectacles: he did not keep himself shut up in the recesses of the palace: his hand was heavy on the senators, and the senators they hated: but he was the king of the people; and, being so, what mattered it to them if he had put to death his adoptive brother Britannicus, or that termagant his mother Agrippina, even if she were a daughter of their once much-loved Germanicus?

Nero's freedmen, again, were among Galba's foes. They indeed had been making hay while the sun shone; they had "soaked up the Caesars countenance, his rewards, his authorities." Now evil days had come: inquiries were being made into the modes by which they had become rich—demands were being issued for restitution of their gains. Galba needed what they had gleaned; and it was "but squeezing them and, sponges, you will be dry again." The inquiries and demands were alike vain, for the sponges were already dry; they had squandered abroad all that they had nefariously gotten. If Galba had any friends, they were in his own army, or in the senate. But, by an indiscreet though honest declaration that he was wont to "choose his soldiers, not to buy them," he had also disappointed and estranged his own partisans. To rely on the senate was to lean on a broken reed. The senatorial chiefs were none of them men of bold aspirations or vigorous resolutions.

Ill luck dogged the heels of Galba even before he readied Italy. The *prefect* of the *praetorians*, Nymphidius Sabinus, who had taken an active part in Nero's overthrow, had met his successor at Narbonne (Narbo), and, with many compliments, tendered him allegiance, accompanied with a modest request to have one of the highest offices in the State conferred on himself. The ground, however, was preoccupied by Galba's adherents, who, not unnaturally, claimed place and priority in his favours. The prefect, deeply offended by such refusal, hurried back to Rome, and tried to persuade the body-guard to proclaim him, Caesar. This was too strong a measure even for the dissatisfied soldiery, and Nymphidius was slaughtered in the praetorian camp. But Galba, or his counsellors, pushed success too far by demanding the sacrifice of all Nymphidius's supporters who had not already destroyed themselves, and by putting to death a man of consular rank, Petronius Turpilianus, whom Nero had appointed to the command of his guards, and who was now condemned without even the formality of a trial. Such informal execution of "persons of quality" would have touched lightly an army or a populace already familiar with irregular sentences and short shrift. But Galba increased his evil repute as a man of blood when, on arriving at the Milvian Bridge in Rome, he ordered his soldiers to mow down Nero's marine battalions—they had troubled him with premature importunities—and over whose killed and wounded bodies he entered the capital.

Galba was not ambitious of empire. He had refused to accept the throne when offered him by the army on the death of Caligula; he had served Claudius faithfully as governor of Africa. The already aged veteran was prudently living in retirement, when Nero appointed him to be his legate in Spain, and for eight years he governed that province with great ability. But he was in the hands of evil ministers, and resigned himself entirely to them, and these ministers were at variance with one another: on one point alone did they agree—that at Galba's age some provision ought to be promptly made for a successor. But their harmony extended only to the general principle that Galba could not live much longer, and that there was already a formidable rival in the field.

We not unfrequently meet with persons in history whose characters it is scarcely possible to draw correctly—persons who disappoint cur hopes, and exceed our expectations of them. Of this class of men was Marcus Salvius Otho. Among the most profligate of Nero's companions, the Rochester of his court, he governed the province of Lusitania for several years with much credit to himself: the most luxurious and depraved of men while prosperous, his end was that of a hardy though unfortunate soldier. Nothing in his life became him like the leaving it—he died by his own hand, an Epicurean Cato: even as Rochester, if Bishop Burnet may be trusted, departed a good Christian. It is, however, to Galba's credit that he declined following the interested advice of his ministers in the appointment of a successor. "He was actuated," Tacitus thinks, "by concern for the State, and saw that the sovereign power was wrested out of Nero's hands in vain, if it were to be transferred to Otho—a duplicate of him."

In the choice of a colleague Galba appears for once to have judged for himself; and his selection, though it proved unfortunate, cannot justly be found fault with. Piso Licinianus came of an illustrious family on both sides. By the better sort in Rome he was respected, if not beloved; but his aspect and deportment savoured too much of the strictness of a primitive age. By the profligate and the frivolous he was called morose and sullen. This appointment necessarily crushed the hopes and aroused the wrath of Otho, who now began to intrigue in earnest against Galba.

All this time a storm was brewing in the north far more dangerous to the emperor, and far more disastrous to Rome and Italy, than Otho's plot. The very day on which Galba put on the consular robe—January 1, 69 *A.D.*—the legions of Upper Germany, when summoned to take the military oath to that emperor, tore down his images, demanded that the oath should run in the name of the senate and people, and that some other successor to Nero should be appointed. Aulus Vitellius had recently been sent by Galba as consular *legate* to Lower Germany, and on the very next day after this mutiny broke out, he was greeted in the camp at Cologne by the legions of Germany, or their delegates, as *imperator*.

The news of this movement in Germany hurried on the adoption. It was conferred with dignity by Galba, it was received with becoming modesty and reverence by Piso, and with plausible and perhaps sincere expressions of his desire to fulfil the important duties imposed on him. Galba conducted him to the praetorian camp, but as he did not promise a donative, his speech to the soldiers aggravated his former unpopularity. The way was now prepared for Otho. To the disappointed guards a notorious prodigal was far more welcome than a frugal emperor. On the morning of the 15th of January, Galba was present at a sacrifice, and Otho in attendance on him. The entrails of the victims betokened risk to the emperor—"in his own household there lurked a foe."

That foe, it had been prearranged, was summoned by a freedman to keep an appointment with a surveyor of works. With this excuse he quitted the emperor's presence and hurried to the place of tryst already agreed on—the Golden Milestone beneath the Capitol in front of the Eoman Forum. It may have been by chance, it may have been by design, to prevent premature alarm in the city, that only three-and-twenty common soldiers there saluted Otho as "emperor." Certainly he had expected more, since, dismayed at the thin attendance, he seems for a moment to have wavered in his purpose. But his partisans, better informed, drew their swords, thrust him into a litter, and bore him off to the *praetorian* camp.

Arrived at the camp, the commander on that day—one Julius Martialis, a *tribune*—it is uncertain whether he were an accomplice, or merely alarmed at so unlooked-for a visit—opened the gates, and admitted the pretender into the enclosure. There the other tribunes and centurions, regarding their own safety alone, and perhaps sharing in the delusion of Martialis—that this feeble body of traitors to Galba was but an advanced guard of numerous and powerful conspirators—forgot at once their duty and their military oath, and joined in, or at least connived at, an enterprise of whose aim they were still uncertain, and of the existence of which they had been ignorant a few minutes before. In fact, the privates alone seem to have been in the secret; but, as had often happened, and was often to happen again, they were too powerful for their officers.

The condensed phrase of the historian alone conveys the pith and marrow of the plot:

> Two common soldiers (*manipulares*) engaged to transfer the empire of the Roman people—and they *did* transfer it.

Otho meanwhile had bought the imperial guards. He attended at Galba's supper-table, gave handsome presents to the *cohort* on duty, and consoled the disappointed among the soldiers with gifts of land or money. The unconscious emperor, busy with his sacrifice, was really importuning the gods of an empire that was now another's. Piso harangued the troops: but the appeal of a stoical Caesar was addressed to deaf ears: the greater number of his hearers at once dispersed; the few who remained faithful to the two Caesars were feeble or wavering; the populace and the slaves clamoured with discordant shouts for Otho's death and the destruction of the conspirators. But what could a few domestic servants, a few frightened knights and senators, and an unarmed rabble, do against the praetorians, now advancing on the city? It was to little purpose that Galba's friends stood by him when he himself was undecided, when his ministers were wrangling with each other, and when every moment brought the conspirators nearer. The murder of Galba can only be described in the words of Tacitus—at least in those of his ablest English translators. (Church and Brodribb).

> Galba was hurried to and fro with every movement of the surging crowd; (the feeble old man, attended by only one half-armed *cohort*, had come down from the Palatine hill to the Forum); the halls and temples all around were thronged with spectators of this mournful sight. Not a voice was heard from the better class of people or even from the rabble. Everywhere were terror-stricken countenances, and ears turned to catch every sound. It was a scene neither of agitation nor of repose, but there reigned

the silence of profound alarm and profound indignation, Otho, however, was told that they were arming the mob. He ordered his men to hurry on at full speed and to anticipate the danger. Then did Roman soldiers rush forward like men who had to drive a Vologeses or Pacorus from the ancestral throne of the Arsacidae, not as though they were hastening to murder their aged and defenceless emperor. In all the terror of their arms, and at the full speed of their horses, they burst into the Forum, thrusting aside the crowd and trampling on the senate. Neither the sight of the Capitol, nor the sanctity of the overhanging temples, could deter them from committing a crime which any one succeeding to power must avenge.

When this armed array was seen to approach, the standard-bearer of the *cohort* that escorted Galba tore off and dashed upon the ground Galba's effigy. At this signal the feeling of all the troops declared itself plainly for Otho. The Forum was deserted by the flying populace. Weapons were pointed against all who hesitated. Near the lake of Curtius, Galba was thrown out of his litter and fell to the ground, through the alarm of his bearers. His last words have been variously reported, according as men hated or admired him. Some have said that he asked in a tone of entreaty what wrong he had done, and begged a few days for the payment of the donative. The more general account is, that he voluntarily offered his neck to the murderers, and bade them haste and strike, if it seemed to he for the good of the commonwealth. To those who slew him it mattered not what he said. About the actual murderer nothing is clearly known. The soldiers foully mutilated his arms and legs, for his breast was protected, and in their savage ferocity inflicted many wounds even on the headless trunk.

It will not be necessary to dwell long on the remainder of Otho's story, since he did little memorable during his short reign until the last moments of his life. "Uneasy lay the head that wore the crown." The last rites to Galba were scarcely paid; the acclamations that greeted Otho both in the senate and the camp were still ringing in all ears, when he found that he had reason to tremble.

Dean Merivale says:

> From the moment that he stepped through an emperor's blood into the palace of the Caesars, Otho was made aware that he

in his turn must fight if he would retain his newly acquired honours.

In swift succession, messengers followed one another, bringing him tidings of the progress of sedition in Gaul, and of the formidable attitude assumed by Vitellius at the head of the armies on the Rhine.

And who was this third candidate for the purple? Had it been worth while to murder Galba in order that Otho might succeed? Would it be worth the expense of more blood and treasure to despatch Otho, and replace him by a rival of whom no good report had ever reached the capital? Dear as Nero by his vices and cruelties had cost the senate and the people, and one or two of the provinces, yet at present the empire appeared to have lost rather than gained by his removal. It was bad for a score or two of statesmen and generals to perish yearly by the executioner's hands, or by suicide—that common refuge of despair; but it was worse for thousands to be mown down by the swords of infuriated soldiers, in a few weeks or even a few days. Aulus Vitellius, indeed, was not utterly evil. He was not wholly abandoned to the vices and pleasures of the city. He had gained for himself some reputation in letters and in eloquence; he had served with great credit for uprightness as proconsul and legate in Africa.

On his march from the Rhine he displayed some generosity in saving unpopular officers from the fury of the legions, among them Virginius Rufus; and some modesty in at first deferring to accept the title of Augustus, and positively refusing that of Caesar. His mother and his wife also helped to invest him with some vicarious merit. Both these matrons were examples of moderation in prosperity. Sextilia, like Cromwell's mother, looked with fear and distrust on her son's elevation, refused all public honours herself, and replied to the first letter he addressed to her under his new title of Germanicus, that *her* son was named Vitellius, and she knew of no other. This high-minded woman died shortly after his accession, seems to have been spared the spectacle of his gross and vulgar excesses, and certainly did not witness his shameful end. His wife Galeria bore herself as the spouse of a simple senator, and humanely protected the children of Flavius Sabinus, Vespasian's brother, from the daggers of the Vitellians. Like Galba, too, Vitellius committed no crime in aspiring to the throne; it was forced upon him by the *tribunes* and *centurions* at Cologne.

It is pleasant to encounter virtuous women in the annals of a period soiled by the names of a Poppaea, a Messalina, and an Agrippina;

we have therefore given a passing notice of the wife and mother of Vitellius. Of himself there is nothing more to be said on the score of virtue. "Tacitus," says Gibbon, "fairly calls him a hog," and in truth he was a most valiant trencherman. As soon as, perhaps even before, his arrangements were completed for despatching his legions from the Rhine to the Tiber, he appears to have thought that the highest privilege he had attained by his sudden promotion was that of keeping the most expensive table ever known in Roman annals. But Vitellius allowed not a day to pass unsignalised by the pomp and circumstance of his dinner. During his whole progress from Cologne to Italy—it was necessarily a slow one, since he needed many hours for refreshment and digestion—the lands through which he passed were ransacked, the rivers and the seas were swept, for delicacies for his table.

> The leading men of the various States were ruined by having to furnish his entertainments, and the States themselves reduced to beggary.

Such a commander could neither be respected nor enforce discipline. The Gauls suffered severely, but not so much as Italy, from the presence of the Vitellians. The evils of war are terrible, but not so terrible, says the historian, as was the march of the German legions. "The soldiers, dispersed through the municipal towns and colonies, were robbing and plundering and polluting every place with violence and lust. Everything, lawful or unlawful, they were ready to seize or to sell, sparing nothing, sacred or profane. Some persons under the soldiers' garb murdered their private enemies. The soldiers themselves, who knew the country well, marked out rich estates and wealthy owners for plunder, or for death in case of resistance; their commanders were in their power, and dared not check them."

Otho did not answer the expectations of his partisans in Rome. He was no longer the Otho of the Neronian time. He deferred his pleasures to a more convenient season: he moulded his new life to accord with the duties and dignity of his new position. Yet he got little credit by the change, for men not unnaturally thought that his virtues were a mask for the moment, and that, if he returned victorious, his vices would revive. Perhaps they w r ere wrong in their apprehensions. No indolence or riot disgraced Otho's march.

> He wore a *cuirass* of iron, and was to be seen in front of the standards, on foot, rough and negligent in dress, and utterly unlike what common report had pictured him.

In a few preliminary skirmishes the fortunes of the Othonian and Vitellian armies were pretty evenly balanced. But the emperor had hurried into the field with very insufficient forces; he seems, indeed, from the first to have despaired of the issue. His excesses in early life had enfeebled, not his courage, but his power of will. He had indecently exulted when the head of Piso was shown to him, but the spectre of Galba is said to have haunted him in the solitude of the night after the murder. Within twenty hours after his usurpation, he began to presage his own fall. In one thing he did not share the vices of Nero; he thirsted not for blood, for those whom he put to death were victims to the wrath of the *praetorians* or of the populace.

And so, indifferent to life and desponding of success, Otho went forth to do battle for his throne without awaiting the legions which had declared for him in Pannonia, Dalmatia, and Maesia. The *praetorian* guards were the kernel of his forces, but they were more than overmatched by the Vitellian legions trained in the German wars. The guards were indeed corrupted by the luxuries of Rome, and regardless of discipline. Like many French regiments in 1870, they elected their own officers, and obeyed or disobeyed them as they pleased. Spies, too, from the camp of the Vitellians, had found their way into Rome, and whispered to many who resented Galba's murder, that if his destroyer were slain or deposed, there would be another donative from his conqueror.

The battle which decided Otho's fate was fought at Bedriacum, a small town or hamlet situated between Verona and Cremona. At first fortune seemed to smile on the Othonians; a successful charge on their part broke the enemy's line, and one of his eagles was taken by them. But this, so far from discouraging, infuriated the Vitellians, and determined victory in their favour. Caecina and Valens, their commanders, proved themselves valiant and able officers, whereas Otho's generals early quitted the field. The slaughter was dreadful. Tacitus says:

> In civil wars no prisoners are reserved for sale.

The Vitellians were not merely better led and disciplined, but their reserves were large, and any chance of retrieving defeat by a second combat was made vain by the insubordination of the vanquished, who laid all the blame of discomfiture on their commanders, and threatened them with death.

Otho was not present in the action. His soldiers demanded, his two best officers advised, him to remain with the legions, or to defer a battle. They urged that fortune, the gods, and the genius (the guardian angel of pagan belief) of Otho must be crowned by victory. "The day" on which their counsel was accepted "first gave the death-blow to the Othonian cause."

Otho, now at Brocello (Brixellum), a few miles distant from Bedriacum, was awaiting without fear or drooping spirit—for his mind, in case of reverse, had long been made up—the report of the battle. Vague and discordant rumours at first reached his ear. But at last increasing troops of fugitives brought sure intelligence that all was lost. The soldiers who had accompanied him, without waiting to hear his opinion, exhorted him not to despair, but to try again "the fortune of the die." They themselves were ready to brave every danger; there were forces still in reserve: the Maesian and Pannonian legions would join them in a few days. Flattery, they said, had done its worst in urging him to leave the army, in hurrying on the unfortunate engagement. But it was not the voice of flatterers that now implored him to take heart, and to lead them against the enemy. The soldiers who were near him fell at his feet and clasped his knees: those at a distance stretched forth their hands in token of assent.

Plotius Firmus, who commanded a detachment of the bodyguard, joined his prayers to those of the legions, he said:

> The noble mind battles with adversity: it is the craven spirit that capitulates at once. Your soldiers, Caesar, have undergone much, yet do not despond: abandon not an army devoted to your cause; renounce not men as generous as they are brave.

They spoke to deaf ears. Otho had weighed all circumstances: the end was at hand: ambition in him was dead: he had been dazzled by the purple and its gold trappings: they had brought him only anxious days and sleepless nights: he had revelled with Nero: he had enjoyed some repose in his Lusitanian province: he had helped Galba to a throne; he had hurled him from it. He had shed blood enough already, he had tasted the extremes of luxury and "fierce civil strife," and all was vanity. He addressed to his faithful guards some words of gratitude, but he left none of his hearers in doubt as to his fixed purpose to have done with wars and with life—presently and for ever.

From the soldiers he turned to his weeping friends. Calm and untroubled himself, with a serene countenance, with a firm voice, he besought them to be calm and resigned. He advised all to quit the town without loss of time, and to make their terms with the conqueror. For all who were willing to depart he provided boats and carriages. From his papers and letters he selected all such as might, under a new Caesar, be injurious to the writers of them—all that expressed duty towards himself or ill-will to Vitellius—and committed them to the flames. He said:

> For the general good I am a willing victim. For myself, I have won ample renown, and I leave to my family an illustrious name.

Towards the close of day he called for cold water, and having quenched his thirst, ordered two daggers to be brought him. He tried the points of both, and laid one of them under his pillow. Once more assuring himself that all who wished had left the town, he passed the night in quiet. At the dawn of day, he stabbed himself through the heart. One wound sufficed, but his dying groans caught the ears of his freed men and slaves. They rushed into his chamber, and among them Plotius Firmus. In compliance with his earnest request, his body was burnt without delay. The ghastly spectacle of Galba's and Piso's heads fixed on lances and exhibited to a brutal soldiery and populace was doubtless present to his mind when ordering this speedy passage to the funeral pyre. His corpse was borne to it by the praetorians "with praises and tears, covering his wound and his hands with kisses."

Some killed themselves near the pyre—Tacitus says:

> Not moved by remorse or by fear, but by the desire to emulate his glory, and by love of their prince.

> Over his ashes was built a tomb, unpretending, and therefore likely to stand.

He ended his life in the thirty-seventh year of his age, and had reigned just three months. Rarely, if ever, does history present an example of swifter retribution for treachery and treason. The Vitellian generals moved in three divisions. Valens advanced through Gaul, and so by the Mont Genèvre into Italy; Caecina through the eastern cantons of Switzerland, and over the Great St Bernard; while Vitellius followed more leisurely in the rear of his *legates*. Every district through which they respectively passed was ravaged; villages, and sometimes large towns, were sacked or burnt; but the richer land south of the Alps was the principal sufferer. The soldiers of Otho, it was said, had exhausted Italy, but it was desolated by the Vitellians. The fierce warriors of the north, Romans only in name, fell without remorse on the borough-towns and colonies, and, as it were, rehearsed on their march the licence they hoped to indulge in at Borne. From Pavia Vitellius proceeded to Cremona, and thence diverged from his route to cross the plain of Bedriacum, in order to behold the scene of the recent victory. The aspect of the field of battle, and the brutality of the victor, are thus described by Tacitus:—

> It was a hideous and a horrible sight. Not forty days had passed since the battle, and there lay mangled corpses, severed limbs, the putrefying forms of men and horses. The soil was saturated with gore; and, what with levelled trees and crops, horrible was the desolation. Not less revolting was that portion of the road which the people of Cremona had strown with laurel-leaves and roses, and on which they had raised altars, and sacrificed victims, as if to greet some barbarous despot—festivities in which they delighted for the moment, but which were afterwards to work their ruin. Valens and Caecina were present, and pointed out the various localities of the field of battle, showing how from one point the columns of the legions had rushed to the attack; how from another the cavalry had charged; how from a third the auxiliary troops had turned the flank of the enemy. The *tribunes* and *prefects* extolled their individual achievements, and mixed together fictions, facts, and exaggerations. The common soldiers also turned aside from the line of march with joyful shouts, recognised the various scenes of conflict, and gazed with wonder on the piles of weapons and the heaps of slain. Some indeed there were whom all this moved to thoughts of the mutability of fortune, to pity and to tears. Vitellius did not turn away his eyes—did not shudder to behold the unburied corpses of so many thousands of his countrymen; nay, in his exultation, in his ignorance of the doom which was so close upon himself, he actually instituted a religious ceremony in honour of the tutelary gods of the place.

It was said that Vitellius expressed a brutal pleasure at the spectacle. He called for bowls of wine—he circulated them freely among his suite and soldiers—he declared that "the corpse of an enemy smells always well, particularly that of a fellow-citizen." We will now leave him in Rome, where he was of course greeted by the shouts of the populace, the flattery of the upper classes, and innumerable applications for places and favours. Well had Tiberius said of his Roman subjects, that they were "born to be slaves."

Vitellius
(Extract from *Tacitus*)

The legions in Syria and Egypt had taken the oath to Galba and Otho without a murmur, but when required for the third time within a few weeks to transfer their allegiance to an enemy of both those Caesars, they hesitated for a while and then obeyed with an ill grace. Between the armies of the northern and eastern provinces there had long been jealousies and rivalry, and the choice of Vitellius by the German, excited angry feelings in the Syrian camps. They were not less numerous, they were better disciplined and disposed, they had been very recently winning new laurels in the north of Palestine; why should they not put forward their claim to appoint a Caesar as well as the lazy and over-paid *praetorians*, or the mutinous legions of the Rhine? In one very important respect, indeed, they were better situated than either the bodyguards or the Rhenish divisions. Neither Otho nor Vitellius could be termed a happy choice, unless to be a notorious profligate or an unsurpassed glutton were a recommendation for empire. They, at least at Antioch and in Galilee, had two leaders of mark and likelihood, who had already proved their fitness to rule by their obedience and ability in lower stations.

The characters of these very capable leaders are thus drawn in a few strokes by Tacitus:—

> Syria and its four legions were under the command of Licinius Mucianus, a man whose good and bad fortune was equally famous. In his youth, he had cultivated with many intrigues the friendship of the great. His resources soon failed, and his position became precarious, and as he also suspected that Claudius had taken some offence, he withdrew into a retired part of Asia (Minor), and was as like an exile as he was afterwards like an emperor. He was a compound of dissipation and energy,

of arrogance and courtesy, of good and bad qualities. His self-indulgence was excessive when he had leisure, yet whenever he had served he had shown great qualities. In his public capacity he might be praised: his private life was in bad repute. Yet over subjects, friends, and colleagues, he exercised the influence of many fascinations. He was a man who would find it easier to transfer the imperial power to another than to hold it for himself. He was eminent for his magnificence, for his wealth, and for a greatness that transcended in all respects the condition of a subject. Beadier of speech than Vespasian, he thoroughly understood the arrangement and direction of civil business.— *Hist.*, i. 10; ii. 5.

Vespasian was an energetic soldier: he could march at the head of his army, choose the place for his camp, and bring by night and day his skill, or, if the occasion required, his personal courage, to oppose the foe. His food was such as chance offered: his dress and appearance hardly distinguished him from the common soldier; in short, but for his avarice, he was equal to the generals of old.

The Caesar "for whom fortune was now preparing, in a distant part of the world, the origin and rise of a new dynasty," had no illustrious images in the hall of his fathers. His family belonged to the Sabine *burgh* of Reatè, and had never risen to public honours, but he himself had seen much service. Nero's freedman and favourite, Narcissus, appointed him to the command of a legion in Britain, where he highly distinguished himself and earned triumphal ornaments. He was one of the consuls in the year 51 *A.D.* But those whom Narcissus promoted became the subject of the younger Agrippina's aversion, and not until after her fall did Vespasian obtain any further employment. In 52 he was proconsul of Africa, and, strange to tell, he left the province poorer than he came to it—a fact scarcely reconcilable with Tacitus's imputation of "avarice."

He was not only an unready speaker, but also an indifferent courtier, and got into disgrace with Nero for going to sleep while the Caesar was singing and playing before a delighted—or perchance a disgusted—audience of Corinthians, Olympians, or the fastidious men of Athens. Such behaviour was too much for Nero's patience, and the tasteless Vespasian was ordered to begone and take his impertinent naps in his own house. But when serious disturbances arose in Judaea, he was too good an officer to be overlooked, and was appointed to the government of Palestine, and to the command of the forces there, or to be sent thither, at the close of 66 A.D. At the time of this promotion he was in his sixty-first year.

Vespasian was proclaimed emperor by Tiberius Alexander, the *prefect* of Egypt, and it may be inferred without his own knowledge or consent at the moment. Long he pondered on the proposal even while surrounded by his own officers and men. It was, in fact, a very serious matter to be hailed "*Imperator.*" Within a few months three Caesars had perished—Nero by the hand of a slave, Galba by the swords of the *praetorians*, and Otho by his own dagger. The supplications of the army, and the urgency of Mucianus—they had been on bad terms, but were now reconciled—overcame his scruples, and he confirmed the choice of the prefect of Egypt by accepting the purple from the Syrian *legionaries*. An intensely practical man when not at a concert or a play, he instantly took measures for establishing his claim, but he did not hurry to Italy, although the eyes of all its better men had long been turned to Palestine.

The forces of the east were divided into three portions. Of these, one was deemed sufficient to encounter the Vitellians; a second, was retained in the east, to continue, under Titus, the Judaean war; to watch the Armenian and Parthian border was the task of the third. The revolt against Vitellius was making rapid strides: some provinces remained neutral; others, Britain and the Rhenish, could not afford to part with a cohort, and the emperor at Rome squandered in vulgar and brutal sensuality the money he needed for the payment of his troops.

The march of the Vespasians did not materially differ from that of the Vitellians. Again Italy north of the Po was ravaged, and once more on the field of Bedriacum an empire was lost and won. But among the leaders of the eastern army was one who by his energy and enterprise relieves the uniformity of the narrative. In Antonius Primus we find a Paladin; a Charles Mordaunt, Earl of Peterborough, the hero of the Succession War in Spain. At the head of three legions he seized the passes of the Julian Alps. Far inferior to the enemy in strength, his officers advised him to await the arrival of Mucianus. But delay suited not the eager spirit of Antonius, who, moreover, was resolved to win the victory alone. Twice he restored the fortune of the day at Bedriacum; and after a brave defence by the Vitellians, he broke through their camp before the walls of Cremona, and received the keys of that proverbially unfortunate city. From that moment the fate of Vitellius himself was decided.

The city had surrendered under a promise of protection, but Antonius did not, perhaps could not, keep his word. As yet he had not rewarded his soldiers with booty or licence. It is said that when taking a bath after the fatigues of the assault, he had complained of the water not being warm enough. "It soon shall be hotter," said an attendant; and his words were caught up by the soldiers as if they were a signal for burning the town. In a few hours one of the most beautiful of Cisalpine cities was reduced to ashes.

Vitellius, content with sending to the seat of war Caecina and Fabius Valens, abandoned himself to his wonted coarse indulgences; he neither attended to his soldiers nor showed himself to the people.

> Buried in the shades of his gardens, among the woods of La Riccia (Aricia), like those sluggish animals which, if you supply them with food, lie motionless and torpid, he had dismissed with the same forgetfulness the past, the present, and the future.

For cruelties, indeed, he found leisure occasionally. He was startled by tidings of revolt and disaffection. The fleet at Ravenna had gone over to the enemy. Caecina had made an attempt, an abortive one, to pass over to Vespasian. "In that dull soul joy was more powerful than apprehension." As soon as he learned that his own soldiers had put Caecina in irons, he returned exulting to Borne. Before a crowded assembly of the people he applauded the obedience of the legions, and sent to prison the *prefect* of the *praetorian* guard, who, as a friend of Caecina, might, he thought, follow his example.

Antonius had crossed the Apennines. In the valley of the Nar the two armies once more confronted one another; but deserted by their emperor, and without leaders, the Vitellians had no spirit for fighting. They were incorporated with the Vespasians. The slothful emperor, says Tacitus, "would have forgotten that he was, or rather had been one, had not his foes reminded him of his rank." Antonius offered him terms, which were confirmed by Mucianus. His life should be spared; a quiet retreat in Campania, the garden and the vineyard of Home, with a large income, was proposed to and accepted by him.

But Borne had yet to drink the cup of woe to the dregs. Once more, as in the civil wars of the commonwealth, the city was to be sacked and the temple of the Capitoline Jupiter to be burnt. Terms were being drawn up for a peaceful surrender of the capital and the abdication of the emperor. Flavius Sabinus, the elder brother of Vespasian, had remained during all these revolutions in Rome, and now represented him. In the temple of Apollo, on the Palatine, "the transfer of the empire was debated and settled."

But it was not accomplished so easily. Rome was filled with fugitives from the seat of war, and well aware that no mercy for them could be looked for if Antonius were once master of the city, they dinned in the ears of their sluggish chief, that for him the post of danger was a private station. Was Antonius a man to keep his word? Would legions who had shown themselves false, be true to promises or covenants? How long would he enjoy his Campanian retreat, or his ample revenues? He was compelled to return to his palace, not indeed to resume his functions, but to await his doom. For the last time he entered the Palatine house, hardly knowing whether he were still emperor or not.

The transfer which the soldiers refused to ratify was, however, considered valid by the senate, the knights, the magistrates and police of the city, and they urged Sabinus to arm against the German *cohorts*, to vindicate his brother's claim to the purple, and to defend Rome, the citizens, and himself from the fury of these ruffians. Sabinus complied; but his force was small; his measures were hurried and insufficient; he was attacked and routed by the Vitellians, and compelled to take refuge in the Capitol. Some communications took place between Sabinus and Vitellius, but they were idle, for the reply of the nominal emperor was merely an apology for the conduct of his supporters. He indeed "had not now the power either to command or to forbid. He was no longer emperor; he was merely the cause of war."

The following description has the appearance of being written by an eyewitness of the respective scenes:—

> The envoy of Sabinus had hardly returned to the Capitol, when the infuriated soldiery arrived, without any leader, every man acting on his own impulse. They hurried at quick march past the Forum and the temples which hang over it, and advanced their line up the opposite hill as far as the outer gates of the Capitol. There were formerly certain colonnades on the right side of the slope as one went up; the defenders, issuing forth on the roof of these buildings, showered tiles and stones on the Vitellians. The assailants were not armed with anything but swords, and it seemed too tedious to send for machines and

missiles. They threw lighted brands at a projecting colonnade, and following the track of the fire would have burst through the half-burnt gates of the Capitol, had not Sabinus, tearing down on all sides the statues, the glories of former generations, formed them into a barricade across the opening. They then assailed the opposite approaches to the Capitol, near the grove of the Asylum, and where the Tarpeian rock is mounted by a hundred steps. Both these attacks were unexpected: the closer and fiercer of the two threatened the Asylum.

The assailants could not be checked as they mounted the continuous line of buildings, which, as was natural in a time of profound peace, had grown up to such a height as to be on a level with the soil of the Capitol. A doubt arises at this point, whether it was the assailants who threw lighted brands on to the roofs, or whether, as the more general account has it, the besieged thought thus to repel the assailants, who were now making vigorous progress. From them the fire passed to the colonnades adjoining the temples: the eagles supporting the pediment, which were of old timber, caught the flames. And so the Capitol, with its gates shut, neither defended by friends nor spoiled by a foe, was burnt to the ground.

The historian proceeds to relate the final victory of the Vitellians. The besiegers "burst in, carrying everywhere the firebrand and the sword." Some of the Vespasian leaders were cut down at once: the younger of the Flavian princes, Domitian, unluckily for his own fame and the empire, escaped in the disguise of an *acolyte* of the temple, while Sabinus and the consul Quinctius Atticus were loaded with chains and brought before Vitellius. He received his captives "with anything but anger in his words and looks, amidst the murmurs of those who demanded the privilege of slaying them and their pay for the work they had done." He was preparing to intercede: he was compelled to yield; he was now a mere cipher; and the body of Sabinus, pierced and mutilated, and with the head severed from it, was dragged to the Gemoniae.

In a few days the Flavian legions were at the gates of Rome. Numerous engagements took place before the walls, and amid the beautiful gardens in the suburbs, generally ending in favour of the Flavians. The Vitellians were defeated at every point. But they rallied again within the city.

Tacitus says:

The populace stood by and watched the combatants, (as the people of Paris did when the Allies were, in 1814, fighting with the French for the possession of Montmartre;) and as though it had been a mimic combat—(of gladiators in the arena, or of the Red and Blue factions of charioteers in the Flaminian Circus)—encouraged first one party and then the other by their shouts and plaudits. Whenever either side gave way, they cried out that those who concealed themselves in the shops, or took refuge in any private house, should be dragged out and butchered, and they secured the larger share of the booty; for, while the soldiers were busy with bloodshed and massacre, the spoils fell to the crowd. It was a terrible and hideous sight that presented itself throughout the city. Here battle and death were raging: there the bath and the tavern were crowded. In one spot were pools of blood and heaps of corpses, and close by prostitutes and men of character as infamous. There were all the debaucheries of luxurious peace, all the horrors of a city most cruelly sacked, till one was ready to believe the country to be mad at once with rage and lust.

Amid this scene of carnage, it is some satisfaction to know that condign punishment fell on the German soldiers. They were driven to their last stronghold. The *praetorian* camp to which they had fled was desperately defended as well as strenuously assailed. The Flavians, expecting that Rome itself would stand a siege, had brought with them their artillery: with their catapults they cleared the battlements: they raised mounds or towers to the level of the ramparts: they applied fire to the gates. The gates were battered down; the walls were breached; quarter was denied; and, according to one account, fifty thousand men were slain.

Vitellius made a vain attempt to escape. His wife Galeria had a house on the Aventine, and thither he was conveyed in a litter, purposing to fly in the night-time to his brother's camp at Terracina. But, infirm of purpose, he returned to the palace, whence even the meanest slaves had fled, or where those who remained in it shunned his presence. He wandered through its long corridors and halls, shrinking from every sound: "he tried the closed doors, he shuddered in the empty chambers," he trembled at the echo of his own footfalls. In the morning he was discovered; "his hands were bound behind his back; he was led along with tattered robes; many reviled, no one pitied him." He was cut down by a German soldier, who may have owed him a grudge, or have wished to release him from insult. The soldiers pricked him on with their weapons when his pace slackened, or stopped him to witness his own statues hurled from their pedestals and broken by their fall. He was compelled to gaze on the spot where a few months before Galba had fallen. A sword placed beneath his chin kept his head erect, exposing to a brutal mob his haggard looks; his visage was besmeared with mud and filth; and, wounded as he already was, he was smitten on the cheek as he passed through the long files of his persecutors.

When he reached the Gemoniae, where the corpse of Flavius Sabinus had so recently lain, he fell under a shower of blows; Tacitus says (and he might probably have added senators and knights also);

And the mob reviled him when dead with the same heartlessness with which they had nattered him living. One speech, it was his last, showed a spirit not utterly degraded. To a *tribune* who insulted him he answered,—'Yet I was once your emperor.'

We must not pass over, though we can merely refer to, an episode in the *History* of Tacitus, that in which he treats of the revolt of the Germans. The destruction of three emperors, the disturbances in Judaea, the devastation of Italy, had severely strained the sinews of the empire. But its imminent danger at this period lay not south of the Alps, but on the borders of the Rhine and the Danube. The main interest of this episode consists not in sieges and battles, in the fidelity or faithlessness of States or individuals, in the lawless conduct of the armies, or the feeble and fluctuating measures of their generals. These were features common to every district visited by the civil, or more properly the imperial, wars of 69 and 70 *A.D*. The revolt of Germany was an insurrection against Roman rule itself, not against any one of the four competitors for the purple.

It was a widely spread, for a while an ably organised movement, and at more than one period it had the appearance of a successful one. It reveals to us how deeply that rule had been affected by the extravagance and cruelty of such Caesars as Caligula or Nero: to what extent by their indulgence they had demoralised the armies and degraded the majesty of the empire. Yet it also shows how strong and effective was its organisation: how unable to cope with it were the most valiant and disciplined of the rebels. Had the coalition of Germans and Gauls been sound and sincere, had the authors and leaders of it added to their enthusiasm the steady and sagacious temper of the warriors and statesmen who had made Rome the mistress of the world, it is difficult to see how the empire could have survived, bleeding and faint as it was at the time from a fierce civil conflict of about eighteen months.

The purpose of the confederates was to throw off then and for ever the yoke of Rome,—to effect on a far grander scale what the Italians had attempted more than a century and half before, when they set up a new capital, Italica, and threatened to destroy the den of the Roman wolves. It was a hostile empire that the Germans aimed at,—a far more formidable one than the Parthian had ever been, or than the great Mithridates had ever imagined. Independent Germany would not supply the legions with recruits: independent Gaul would not pay into the Roman treasury bars of silver, or sesterces. Both Gauls and Germans were well acquainted with Roman tactics; many thousands of both nations were enrolled in the legions or served as auxiliaries, and so were the better able to encounter them in the field.

On the other hand, the eastern provinces were ill fitted to recruit the armies of Rome, now in some measure thinned and exhausted by the civil war. By Italy itself, at least south of the Po, a very few *cohorts* only could be furnished. The brave and hardy Samnites and Marsians no longer existed in any number. They had been swept off in the Social and earlier Civil wars. Much of their land had become sheep-walks; and the place of hardy shepherds, ploughmen, and vine-dressers was filled up by slaves. The once populous Latium was divided among a few landholders, and towns like Gabii or Ulubrae now stood in huge parks, and when not quite deserted, were inhabited by a few peasants or tavern-keepers. The large farms, said Pliny the Naturalist, have been the ruin of Italy.

All these circumstances rendered the German revolt most grave and menacing. That it appeared so to Tacitus, is plain from several passages in his works. Could the Germans only be induced to destroy one another, Rome might sleep in comparative security, and thank her presiding deities for the feuds of her enemy. In his *Germany* he writes thus of a happy accident of the kind:

> The Chamavi and Angrivarii utterly exterminated the Bructeri, with the common help of the neighbouring tribes, either from hatred of their tyranny, or from the attractions of plunder,

or from heaven's favourable regard to us. It did not even grudge us the spectacle of the conflict. I pray that there may long last among the nations, if not a love for us, at least a hatred for each other; for, while the destinies of empire hurry us on, fortune can bestow no greater boon than discord among our foes.

In Antonius Primus we have at least the semblance of an adventurous and able leader of a division. He is a sort of Achilles or Joachim Murat; but in Claudius Civilis we have an able general and statesman combined. Tacitus evidently bestowed great pains on his portraiture. Civilis was of a noble Batavian family, and had served twenty-five years in the Roman armies. He must have been forty at least when he formed the project of revolt, since for a quarter of a century he had fought wherever the imperial eagles flew, or been stationed wherever there was a Roman camp. For some offence he had incurred the displeasure of a Caesar or his *legate*. He says:

> It is a noble reward that I have received for my toils: my brother murdered, myself imprisoned, my death demanded by the savage clamour of a legion; and for which wrongs I by the law of nations now demand vengeance.

Civilis perceiving, or surmising, that since Nero's death Rome was in no condition to war successfully with a distant ally, devoted himself thenceforth to what he justly considered a noble cause. The Batavian Wallace was no barbarian. Like the Cheruscan German hero Arminius, he had received a Roman education, and he had learned more than schoolmasters, lecturers, or books could teach him. He had seen the capital in perhaps its most low and degraded state; he had witnessed the public excesses and prodigality of Nero; he had perhaps heard, whispered with bated breath, of the orgies of the palace. The hour, it seemed to him, had come when he might deliver the Batavian island, if not Germany itself, from the tyranny and the vices of Rome.

As to the Germans of the Rhine, they had little dread from the garrisons or camps of the Caesar. Vitellius had withdrawn from many if not all of them their best troops when he despatched seven legions across the Alps; and in fact there was just then no Caesar. Galba had been murdered, Otho had destroyed himself, and Vitellius was daily exhibiting his unfitness for empire. Vespasian, whose character he knew, might give cause for some alarm to Civilis. They had once been companions in arms, and even friends; for the Flavian competitor for the throne was at one time, like Civilis himself, an obscure adventurer, and his chance of victory was still doubtful. The very attempt, however, of the Flavian was favourable to the designs of the Batavian, since he could and for a while did, pretend that he was recruiting and drilling soldiers for his former comrade; and he had even instructions from Antonius Primus to hinder any more German levies from being sent southward. Here, then, was an excellent mask for the first movements of the conspiracy of Gaul and Teuton against Rome.

By his eloquence, his skill in political combination, and by his knowledge of the character and condition at the time of the leading men of Rome and the empire, Civilis was enabled to effect a general confederation of all the Netherland tribes, both Celtic and German. He availed himself of the popular religion or superstition. The name of Veleda has already been mentioned. Tacitus says:

> She was regarded by many as a divinity.

The dwelling of this Deborah of the Bructeri was a lofty tower in the neighbourhood of the River Lippe (Luppia). Many were those who consulted, but none were permitted to see her. Mystery, she justly held—and her opinion has been held by many prophetic persons both before and since Veleda delivered oracles—"inspired the greater respect." The questions of her suppliants and the answers to them were conveyed by a relative of the prophetess. The first successes of the revolt greatly increased her reputation, for she had foretold victory to the Germans. With her Civilis was in constant communication—doubtless supplied her with the latest news from Gaul, Italy, and the Rhine; and thus her predictions, being not without foundation in facts, gained for the Batavian leader some allies, and induced many tribes of Germany to send him subsidies or supplies for his army.

The advantages possessed by the Batavians are thus set forth by their commander. Collecting his countrymen in one of the sacred groves, he thus harangued them:

> There is now no alliance, as once there was with Rome. We are treated as slaves. We are handed over to prefects and centurions, and when they are glutted with our spoils and our blood, then they are changed, and new receptacles for plunder, new terms for spoliation, are discovered. Now the conscription is at hand, tearing, we may say, forever children from parents, and brothers from brothers. Never has the power of Rome been more depressed. In the winter quarters of the legions there is nothing but property to plunder and a few old men. Only dare to look

up, and cease to tremble at the empty names of legions. For we have a vast force of horse and foot; we have the Germans our kinsmen; we have Gaul bent on the same objects.—*Hist.*

On another occasion, addressing the people of Trêves (Treveri) he says:—

> What reward do you and other enslaved creatures expect for the blood which you have shed so often? What but a hateful service, perpetual tribute, the rod, the axe, and the passions of a ruling race? See how I, the *prefect* of a single *cohort*, with the Batavians and the Canninefates, a mere fraction of Gaul, have destroyed their vast but useless camps, or am pressing them with the close blockade of famine and the sword. In a word, either freedom will follow on our efforts, or, if we are vanquished, we shall but be what we were before.—*Hist.*

The Roman view of the question Tacitus has given in the speech of Petilius Caerealis, the ablest officer engaged in the German war. He had shown in that the union of Gauls and Germans could not be depended on: that although trained in Roman barracks, the tribes of Rhineland and Batavia were unable, in the long-run, to mate and master the discipline, the swift and precise movements, of the regular legions. Gauls, he said, can have no real affinity with Germans. He proceeds:

> It was not to defend Italy that we (the Romans) occupied the borders of the Rhine, but to insure that no second Ariovistus should seize the empire of Gaul. Do you fancy yourselves to be dearer in the eyes of Civilis and the Batavians and the Transrhenane tribes than your fathers and grandfathers were to their ancestors? There have ever been the same causes to make the Germans cross over into Gaul—lust, avarice, and the longing for a new home, prompting them to leave their own marshes and deserts, and to possess themselves of this most fertile soil, and of you its inhabitants.
> Gaul has always had its petty kingdoms and intestine wars, till you submitted to our authority. We, though so often provoked, have used the right of conquest to burden you only with the cost of maintaining peace. For the tranquillity of nations cannot be preserved without armies; armies cannot exist without pay; pay cannot be furnished without tribute: all else is common be-

tween us. You often command our legions. You rule these and other provinces. There is no privilege, no exclusion. From worthy emperors you derive equal advantage, though you dwell so far away, while cruel rulers are most formidable to those near at hand. Endure the passions and rapacity of your masters, just as you bear barren seasons, and excessive rains, and other natural evils. There will be vices as long as there are men. But they are not perpetual, and they are compensated by the occurrence of better things.

Civilis was in the end unsuccessful. He was deserted, if not actually betrayed, by his allies; with the usual fickleness of barbarians, their zeal soon cooled down: some thought they did enough for him if they helped him to win a battle or two; some that they did enough for themselves when they had plundered a Roman colony or camp. Soldiers who went to their homes, or turned to common brigandage when they pleased, were not fitted to contend long with the severely disciplined Roman legions; and as soon as Vespasian was able to pour division after division into the seat of war, the Batavian commonwealth ceased to exist. Even Civilis perceived at last that he must come to terms with the legate, Petilius Cerialis. With the preparation for their interview the mutilated *History* closes abruptly; the fragment, however, is too interesting to be omitted.

The lower classes of the Batavians were murmuring at the length of the war; the nobles were still more impatient and spoke in fiercer language.

> We have been driven into war by the fury of Civilis. He sought to counterbalance his private wrongs by the destruction of his nation. We are at the last extremity. The Germans already are falling away from us; the Gauls have returned to their servitude; we must repent, 'and avow our repentance by punishing the guilty.'

These dispositions did not escape the notice of Civilis. He determined to anticipate them, moved not only by weariness of his sufferings, but also by the clinging to life which often breaks the noblest spirits. He asked for a conference. The bridge over the River Nabalia was cut down, and the two generals advanced to the broken extremities. Civilis thus opened the conference: 'If it were before a legate of Vitellius that I were defending myself, my acts would deserve no pardon, my words no credit. All the relations between us were those of hatred and hostility, first made so by him, and afterwards embittered by me. My respect for Vespasian is of long standing. While he was still a subject, we were called friends. This was known to Primus Antonius, whose letters urged me to take up arms, for he feared lest the legions of Germany and the youth of Gaul should cross the Alps. What Antonius advised by his letters, Herdeonius suggested by word of mouth. I fought the same battle in Germany as did Mucianus in Syria, Aponius in Maesia, Flavianus in Pannonia.'

The mutilation of ancient manuscripts is one of the curiosities, no less than of the calamities of literature. By an unaccountable coincidence—can it have been accident, or was it design?—the *Annals* also, as we have them, close with an interrupted speech of the dying Thrasea. In each instance so great is our loss that we may well apply to Tacitus the lines of Milton—

Oh sad Virgin, that thy power
Might raise Musaeus from his bower,
Or call up him that left half told
The story of Cambuscan bold.

ALSO FROM LEONAUR
AVAILABLE IN SOFTCOVER OR HARDCOVER WITH DUST JACKET

ZULU:1879 *by D.C.F. Moodie & the Leonaur Editors*—The Anglo-Zulu War of 1879 from contemporary sources: First Hand Accounts, Interviews, Dispatches, Official Documents & Newspaper Reports.

THE RED DRAGOON *by W.J. Adams*—With the 7th Dragoon Guards in the Cape of Good Hope against the Boers & the Kaffir tribes during the 'war of the axe' 1843-48'.

THE RECOLLECTIONS OF SKINNER OF SKINNER'S HORSE *by James Skinner*—James Skinner and his 'Yellow Boys' Irregular cavalry in the wars of India between the British, Mahratta, Rajput, Mogul, Sikh & Pindarree Forces.

A CAVALRY OFFICER DURING THE SEPOY REVOLT *by A. R. D. Mackenzie*—Experiences with the 3rd Bengal Light Cavalry, the Guides and Sikh Irregular Cavalry from the outbreak to Delhi and Lucknow.

A NORFOLK SOLDIER IN THE FIRST SIKH WAR *by J W Baldwin*—Experiences of a private of H.M. 9th Regiment of Foot in the battles for the Punjab, India 1845-6.

TOMMY ATKINS' WAR STORIES: 14 FIRST HAND ACCOUNTS—Fourteen first hand accounts from the ranks of the British Army during Queen Victoria's Empire.

THE WATERLOO LETTERS *by H. T. Siborne*—Accounts of the Battle by British Officers for its Foremost Historian.

NEY: GENERAL OF CAVALRY VOLUME 1—1769-1799 *by Antoine Bulos*—The Early Career of a Marshal of the First Empire.

NEY: MARSHAL OF FRANCE VOLUME 2—1799-1805 *by Antoine Bulos*—The Early Career of a Marshal of the First Empire.

AIDE-DE-CAMP TO NAPOLEON *by Philippe-Paul de Ségur*—For anyone interested in the Napoleonic Wars this book, written by one who was intimate with the strategies and machinations of the Emperor, will be essential reading.

TWILIGHT OF EMPIRE *by Sir Thomas Ussher & Sir George Cockburn*—Two accounts of Napoleon's Journeys in Exile to Elba and St. Helena: Narrative of Events by Sir Thomas Ussher & Napoleon's Last Voyage: Extract of a diary by Sir George Cockburn.

PRIVATE WHEELER *by William Wheeler*—The letters of a soldier of the 51st Light Infantry during the Peninsular War & at Waterloo.

AVAILABLE ONLINE AT **www.leonaur.com**
AND FROM ALL GOOD BOOK STORES

ALSO FROM LEONAUR
AVAILABLE IN SOFTCOVER OR HARDCOVER WITH DUST JACKET

THE ART OF WAR *by Antoine Henri Jomini*—Strategy & Tactics From the Age of Horse & Musket.

THE ART OF WAR *by Sun Tzu and Pierre G. T. Beauregard*—*The Art of War* by Sun Tzu and *Principles and Maxims of the Art of War* by Pierre G. T. Beauregard.

THE MILITARY RELIGIOUS ORDERS OF THE MIDDLE AGES *by F. C. Woodhouse*—The Knights Templar, Hospitaller and Others.

THE BENGAL NATIVE ARMY *by F. G. Cardew*—An Invaluable Reference Resource.

ARTILLERY THROUGH THE AGES—*by Albert Manucy*—A History of the DEvelopment and Use of Cannons, Mortars, Rockets & Projectiles from Earliest Times to the Nineteenth Century.

THE SWORD OF THE CROWN *by Eric W. Sheppard*—A History of the British Army to 1914.

THE 7TH (QUEEN'S OWN) HUSSARS: Volume 3—1818-1914 *by C. R. B. Barrett*—On Campaign During the Canadian Rebellion, the Indian Mutiny, the Sudan, Matabeleland, Mashonaland and the Boer War Volume 3: 1818-1914.

THE CAMPAIGN OF WATERLOO *by Antoine Henri Jomini*—A Political & Military History from the French perspective.

RIFLE & DRILL *by S. Bertram Browne*—The Enfield Rifle Musket, 1853 and the Drill of the British Soldier of the Mid-Victorian Period *A Companion to the New Rifle Musket* and *A Practical Guide to Squad and Setting-up Dtill.*

NAPOLEON'S MEN AND METHODS *by Alexander L. Kielland*—The Rise and Fall of the Emperor and His Men Who Fought by His Side.

THE WOMAN IN BATTLE *by Loreta Janeta Velazquez*—Soldier, Spy and Secret Service Agent for the Confederancy During the American Civil War.

THE BATTLE OF ORISKANY 1777 *by Ellis H. Roberts*—The Conflict for the Mowhawk Valley During the American War of Independenc.

PERSONAL RECOLLECTIONS OF JOAN OF ARC *by Mark Twain.*

CAESAR'S ARMY *by Harry Pratt Judson*—The Evolution, Composition, Tactics, Equipment & Battles of the Roman Army.

FREDERICK THE GREAT & THE SEVEN YEARS' WAR *by F. W. Longman.*

AVAILABLE ONLINE AT **www.leonaur.com**
AND FROM ALL GOOD BOOK STORES

ALSO FROM LEONAUR
AVAILABLE IN SOFTCOVER OR HARDCOVER WITH DUST JACKET

OFFICERS & GENTLEMEN *by Peter Hawker & William Graham*—Two Accounts of British Officers During the Peninsula War: Officer of Light Dragoons by Peter Hawker & Campaign in Portugal and Spain by William Graham.

THE WALCHEREN EXPEDITION *by Anonymous*—The Experiences of a British Officer of the 81st Regt. During the Campaign in the Low Countries of 1809.

LADIES OF WATERLOO *by Charlotte A. Eaton, Magdalene de Lancey & Juana Smith*—The Experiences of Three Women During the Campaign of 1815: Waterloo Days by Charlotte A. Eaton, A Week at Waterloo by Magdalene de Lancey & Juana's Story by Juana Smith.

JOURNAL OF AN OFFICER IN THE KING'S GERMAN LEGION *by John Frederick Hering*—Recollections of Campaigning During the Napoleonic Wars.

JOURNAL OF AN ARMY SURGEON IN THE PENINSULAR WAR *by Charles Boutflower*—The Recollections of a British Army Medical Man on Campaign During the Napoleonic Wars.

ON CAMPAIGN WITH MOORE AND WELLINGTON *by Anthony Hamilton*—The Experiences of a Soldier of the 43rd Regiment During the Peninsular War.

THE ROAD TO AUSTERLITZ *by R. G. Burton*—Napoleon's Campaign of 1805.

SOLDIERS OF NAPOLEON *by A. J. Doisy De Villargennes & Arthur Chuquet*—The Experiences of the Men of the French First Empire: Under the Eagles by A. J. Doisy De Villargennes & Voices of 1812 by Arthur Chuquet.

INVASION OF FRANCE, 1814 *by F. W. O. Maycock*—The Final Battles of the Napoleonic First Empire.

LEIPZIG—A CONFLICT OF TITANS *by Frederic Shoberl*—A Personal Experience of the 'Battle of the Nations' During the Napoleonic Wars, October 14th-19th, 1813.

SLASHERS *by Charles Cadell*—The Campaigns of the 28th Regiment of Foot During the Napoleonic Wars by a Serving Officer.

BATTLE IMPERIAL *by Charles William Vane*—The Campaigns in Germany & France for the Defeat of Napoleon 1813-1814.

SWIFT & BOLD *by Gibbes Rigaud*—The 60th Rifles During the Peninsula War.

AVAILABLE ONLINE AT **www.leonaur.com**
AND FROM ALL GOOD BOOK STORES

www.ingramcontent.com/pod-product-compliance
Lightning Source LLC
Chambersburg PA
CBHW022055160426
43198CB00008B/239